Baby Krishna, Infant Christ

Baby Krishna, Infant Christ

A COMPARATIVE THEOLOGY OF SALVATION

Kristin Johnston Largen

ORBIS BOOKS

Maryknoll, New York 10545

Founded in 1970, Orbis Books endeavors to publish works that enlighten the mind, nourish the spirit, and challenge the conscience. The publishing arm of the Maryknoll Fathers and Brothers, Orbis seeks to explore the global dimensions of the Christian faith and mission, to invite dialogue with diverse cultures and religious traditions, and to serve the cause of reconciliation and peace. The books published reflect the views of their authors and do not represent the official position of the Maryknoll Society. To learn more about Maryknoll and Orbis Books, please visit our website at www.maryknollsociety.org.

Library of Congress Cataloging-in-Publication Data

Largen, Kristin Johnston, 1968-
  Baby Krishna, infant Christ : a comparative theology of salvation / Kristin Johnston Largen.
    p. cm.
  Includes bibliographical references and index.
  ISBN 978-1-57075-932-1 (pbk.)
  1. Salvation. 2. Hinduism—Relations—Christianity. 3. Christianity and other religions—Hinduism. 4. Krishna (Hindu deity)—Childhood. 5. Jesus Christ—Childhood. I. Title.

BL476.L37 2011
202'.2—dc22

2011008823

To Duane Priebe and Winston Persaud,
my professors of systematic theology at Wartburg Theological Seminary,
for bequeathing to me a love of theology,
an openness to the religious other,
and the delight and excitement that come from thinking interreligiously,
outside the theological box.
I am deeply grateful to have had such mentors.

Contents

PART III
BEYOND INFANCY TO TODAY

Acknowledgments

The genesis for this book came some years ago during a Sanskrit course I was taking at the University of California, Berkeley, with Robert Goldman. I want to thank both Robert Goldman and Sally Sutherland Goldman for teaching me Sanskrit, introducing me to the *Bhagavata Purana,* and supporting my interreligious studies in general. They were wonderful teachers in every way.

I began work in earnest on this book thanks to a Wabash Grant that I received in the course of a workshop for pre-tenure theological school faculty in 2009. The workshop was enormously helpful in my overall scholarly development, and the grant freed up an entire summer to devote to this project. I am grateful for both the learning and the financial support I received.

Also during that summer, I began worshiping with a Hindu community in Columbia, South Carolina, at the Hindu Temple and Cultural Center of South Carolina. The entire community, especially Pandit Joshiji, was kind and welcoming to me, and I am thankful for their spirit of hospitality.

Several colleagues were very helpful in offering constructive criticism on various chapters of the text. I want to thank in particular Gerald Christianson, Rick Carlson, and Wayne Kannaday, all of whom read different parts of the book. The book is vastly improved because of their kind work, and any remaining errors are my responsibility alone. Here I want also to thank my faculty colleagues at Gettysburg Seminary, including the president and dean, for their ongoing support and encouragement.

Of course, I also want to thank the fine people at Orbis with whom I worked on this manuscript. First, Bill Burrows was the person with whom I had my first conversation about this project, and he was very supportive, referring me to Robert Ellsberg, who gave final approval of the project and also encouraged me in the writing process. Most important, I want to thank Susan Perry, senior editor, with whom I worked most closely.

Finally, my husband John not only read the manuscript but also was a critical dialogue partner for me throughout the whole writing process. I am grateful not only for his theological insights but also for his love and support.

As I put the finishing touches on this manuscript, the Christian church is celebrating the season of Advent, and baby Jesus is everywhere. In light of the research and writing I have done these past months, he feels to me now both like an old friend and a new love: somehow the fresh revelation of a savior I have known since my own childhood.

December 12, the Second Sunday in Advent, 2010

Introduction

WHY COMPARATIVE THEOLOGY?

Baby Krishna

In my office, I have a small statue of Krishna sitting next to my computer. He has blue skin—a clear sign of his identity as an *avatar*, or incarnation, of Vishnu—a peacock feather tucked in his hair, and a playful expression. He looks to be about three years old. He sits with his right hand in a clay jar he has tipped over, out of which he is scooping handfuls of rich, creamy butter. His left hand is in his mouth, and he seems to be sucking the last bit of butter off his first two fingers.

This statue would be instantly and universally recognizable as Krishna to practically any Hindu, and it would call to mind any number of beloved stories of Krishna's youth. By all accounts, he was a mischievous baby, always misbehaving, and one of his favorite pastimes was stealing butter. In story after story, we read how his mother, Yashoda, had to punish him for this and other misdeeds; but even while punishing him, she could not help but be delighted at her son, whom she loved so deeply. What's more, because Krishna was no ordinary child, any straightforward interaction between mother and son had the potential to turn into a profound lesson about the true nature of reality.

Here is one example, as told in the *Bhagavata Purana*, book 10.

On one occasion, picking up the child [Krishna] and raising him on to her lap, the beautiful Yashoda suckled him at her lactating breast, full of affection. When her son had almost finished drinking, the mother began caressing his sweetly smiling mouth. As he yawned . . . she saw in there the sky, heaven and earth, the host of stars, space, the sun, the moon, fire, air, the oceans, the continents, the mountains and their daughters [the rivers], the forests, and moving and non-moving living things. Seeing the universe so suddenly . . . she began

1

to tremble. Closing her two eyes, the doe-eyed woman was completely astonished.[1]

This is only one example of many that illustrate how important the stories of baby Krishna—and of Krishna as a young boy—are in understanding the role of Krishna as savior and the saving relationship he has with his devotees. Of particular importance here is the concept of *lila*, or "play." It is in these stories in particular, in which Krishna relates to his mother and the *gopis*, the cowherd girls, with flirtation and affection, that we see Krishna as a great lover, in an intimate, joyous relationship with those who return his love. For this reason, it is said that it is this Krishna, as opposed to the more regal figure of the adult Krishna, presented in the *Mahabharata* and *Bhagavad Gita*, for example, "who has provided the themes that have been the most prominently depicted and represented in the devotional art forms that are so fundamental to Indian culture."[2]

Infant Christ

This small statue of Krishna is not the only image of a savior I have in my office, however. As might be expected of a Christian theology professor, I also have a variety of pictures of Jesus: an image of Jesus breaking the gates of hell and freeing the captives inside, and an image of a nativity scene—although in this particular picture the baby Jesus wrapped in swaddling clothing has the unmistakable face of a grown man. (This particular way of depicting Jesus—in the body of a baby but with the face of man—is not uncommon, particularly in images depicting the adoration of the three kings.) Finally, of course, I have several images of Jesus on the cross—including a stained glass representation by Chagall and an image of the San Damiano cross of St. Francis.

As I scrutinize my little collection, the fact that images of the crucified Jesus predominate should come as no surprise. I think it is fair to say that such would be the case for most, if not all Christians who have images of Jesus Christ on a wall, on a table, or on a shelf. Such images sometimes show just the face of Jesus, with a crown of thorns on his head, but more often, the picture depicted in crucifixion images is the full-body image of Christ hanging on the cross. Jesus might be suffering—bloody and in agony, or he might have a regal bearing, resigned to his fate and clearly in control; either way, however, the event of the crucifixion, and the corresponding centrality of the cross, is emphasized.

Over the centuries, this emphasis on the crucifixion as the focal point of Jesus' life, death, and resurrection, and correspondingly, as the central image of salvation in Christianity, has been taken to its logical conclusion, resulting in the fact that the Christian image most people have in their homes is either a crucifix or an empty cross, the latter suggesting by his very absence the crucified and resurrected Jesus. Regardless of the particulars, then, it seems safe to say that the Jesus with whom most Christians relate, the Jesus to whom Christians owe their salvation, is the crucified Jesus, and this is the Jesus that has the most visible presence in the Christian church as a whole.

What I do not have in my office, however, or anywhere else, for that matter, are any images of Jesus' youth—and in churches and museums I only rarely see such images. Christians take this fact for granted and do not question it, but on the surface, it does seem a bit odd. Why aren't there any stories in the Bible of Jesus as a young child? It's not as though he simply entered the scene as an adult; Luke and Matthew both have detailed accounts of his birth, and so it seems natural that they also would have recorded some stories of him as a young boy. However, apart from one brief, tantalizing story about the twelve-year-old Jesus wandering off from his parents in Jerusalem—a story found only in Luke—the gospel accounts are silent about Jesus' life until he begins his public ministry when he is around thirty years old.

Continuing this line of inquiry leads us to notice that even the birth narratives about Jesus are somewhat strange; in both Matthew's and Luke's accounts, Jesus is entirely passive—the object of attention and the cause of activity by others, but not doing anything himself. In fact, at various points in the stories his very existence seems to hang by a thread. Mary is really the focus of the story in Luke, and the only person who does anything miraculous in that account is Jesus' cousin John, who leaps in his mother's womb when Mary comes to visit Elizabeth.

In Matthew's gospel, it seems that Jesus would have been lost several times over had not an angel come to Joseph, first instructing him not to divorce Mary and send her away, and second, commanding him to take Jesus away to Egypt so that he would not be killed by an angry Herod. Of course, Jesus is just an infant, so one might rightly question what he should or could have done at such a young age. However, he is also God incarnate, and so it does not seem to be unrealistic to expect that he could have done something unusual, particularly when his own life was threatened. Such a probability is not necessarily so far-fetched, especially when we consider

the miraculous stories of other savior figures in other religious traditions, like Krishna, for example.

The fact is, however, that there are sources other than the Bible
where stories about Jesus' youth can be found. When Christians go
outside the canonical literature, they can find other stories—although
it takes some digging—particularly in what has come to be called the
Infancy Gospel of Thomas (to distinguish it from the Gnostic Gospel
of Thomas, found at Nag Hammadi in the sensational discovery of
1945). In that apocryphal gospel, we find a wide variety of miraculous stories from Jesus' youth, stories that, not unlike the stories of
Krishna, depict Jesus as a somewhat capricious and willful child.

Let me offer just one example. Chapter 2 of the Infancy Gospel
reads as follows:

> When this child Jesus was five years old, he was playing by
> the ford of a stream; and he gathered the flowing waters into
> pools and made them immediately pure. These things he or-
> dered simply by speaking a word. He then made some soft
> mud and fashioned twelve sparrows from it. It was the Sab-
> bath when he did this. A number of other children were also
> playing with him. But when a certain Jew saw what Jesus had
> done while playing on the Sabbath, he left right away and re-
> ported to his father, Joseph, "Look, your child at the stream
> has taken mud and formed twelve sparrows. He has profaned
> the Sabbath!" When Joseph came to the place and saw what
> had happened, he cried out to him, "Why are you doing what
> is forbidden on the Sabbath?" But Jesus clapped his hands
> and cried to the sparrows, "Be gone!" And the sparrows took
> flight and went off, chirping. When the Jews saw this they
> were amazed; and they went away and reported to their lead-
> ers what they had seen Jesus do.[3]

If stories such as these are to be believed, both Joseph and Mary had
their hands full as Jesus was growing up.

However, many would argue that this is just the point: such stories about Jesus are not to be believed. While they may have been circulated orally from the second century CE on, they were not written
down until later, and their apostolic authority is dubious at best.
Thus, while these stories existed during the time of the formation of
the church, for all practical purposes, they played no role (or perhaps
more accurately, they played only a negative role) in the early
church's theological construction of who Jesus is and how he saves.
That is, they did not affect the traditional picture of Jesus as savior,

and they did not influence the traditional understanding of the relationship Jesus has with his followers.

It is hard to ignore the logical conclusion of this glaring absence:
neither the writers of the gospels, nor the later followers of Jesus, nor
the church fathers who both defined the Bible as we know it today
and constructed what have come to be the orthodox doctrines of
Jesus' humanity and divinity thought that what Jesus did as a child
had any relevance to his identity as the messiah. Clearly, it was decided that such stories were untrustworthy, inaccurate, perhaps even
blasphemous; and the Christian community would be better served if
their existence were simply ignored.

Exploring the Difference

A greater contrast between savior figures then—at least in this
particular area—would be hard to find. In Hinduism, one can argue
that Krishna is most beloved in his childhood form, and that it is the
stories of his infancy and youth that reveal the key insights into the
nature of reality, Krishna's own true nature, and the saving relationship he has with his followers. By contrast, in Christianity, the childhood of Jesus is all but lost to Christians, and those stories that do
exist have been deemed entirely irrelevant both to the Christian faith
as a whole and to the understanding of who Jesus is as savior of the
world.

I would argue that one of the key reasons for this neglect relates
to differences in the theological understanding of the humanity of
Krishna and that of Christ. In particular, I suggest that for Krishna
one of the key soteriological insights about his nature is that he is not
human like we are human. While he looks human and acts human,
ultimately he does not share our true human nature; in fact, part of
his role as savior is to call us out of our human nature into oneness
with him and the true divine nature he embodies. Thus, the stories of
Krishna's infancy and youth highlight that while he appears to be
"one of us," he actually is not; and part of the process of salvation is
realizing that this finite human nature to which we cling is illusory.
Instead, what we are called to is loving union with the Divine that
transcends our finite limitations.

With Jesus, on the other hand, things are quite different. Jesus'
true human nature, which he pointedly and explicitly shares with us,
is a central component both to his being and to his saving work in
the world. The church as a whole has consistently affirmed from its
very inception that Jesus could not be a savior unless he was truly

human, and some of the most trenchant, heated controversies in both the early church and in later centuries centered around this very point. Insistence on this affirmation led Gregory of Nazianzus to maintain, in language that has become a key part of traditional Christian atonement theology, "that which has not been assumed cannot be redeemed."

Consequently, the seemingly magical and fanciful stories of Jesus' infancy and youth seemed to threaten this central soteriological affirmation, as they raised doubts about Jesus' true humanity. How could the church affirm that Jesus had a truly human infancy and youth when he was doing such amazing deeds even as a young boy, having not yet attained the human capacity to truly understand who he was and what he was called to do, nor having been baptized with his divinity proclaimed by God the Father? Such stories did nothing to enhance a soteriological picture of who Jesus is, and instead, seemed to compromise it. Thus, such stories were marginalized, ignored, and repudiated.

An Outline of the Argument

However, I would like to revisit this assumption, asking the question: What might be learned about who Jesus is and how he saves, not only by examining theologically the stories about his infancy and youth—both canonical and noncanonical—but also and particularly through an explicit comparison with "baby Krishna"? In this way, I hope to generate some new insights about the God who is revealed in Jesus Christ, "flesh out" the picture of Jesus' life and ministry in new ways, and then explore some positive ramifications of these new insights as to how Christians understand Jesus as savior.

This book, then, proceeds as follows. The first short chapter introduces and explains my methodology, in particular, what I mean by "comparative theology" and what that task entails. I include here my argument for why and how this exercise of comparing Jesus and Krishna contributes positively to the formation of Christian theological doctrines, and why it is both acceptable and even helpful for lay Christians to engage in this type of interreligious dialogue. I explain how, in what follows, the Christian reader will come to understand Jesus in a new way, and learn new things about what it means to call Jesus savior.

This chapter is followed by Part 1, which consists of two chapters devoted to an exploration of Krishna as an infant and youth. In the first chapter (chapter 2), I introduce Krishna, setting him in the larger context of the Hindu faith and then elaborating on several key stories that take place during his infancy and youth that have been heavily accentuated in the Hindu tradition and are formative for understanding who Krishna is and how he saves. In the next chapter, chapter 3, I explain the theological significance of these stories, emphasizing what they say about Krishna's relationship with his devotees, and how these stories exemplify the soteriological dimension of Krishna's identity. More plainly, in this chapter I examine how these stories contribute to an understanding of Krishna as savior, and how they exemplify his saving work in the world.

Part 2 parallels Part 1 in structure, with the focus there being on the infant/youth Jesus rather than Krishna. In the first chapter in Part 2 (chapter 4), I do two things. First, I analyze the birth narratives found in Matthew and Luke and discuss the brief story of the boy Jesus in the temple. Second, I recount some of the stories of Jesus as a young child that are found only in the noncanonical literature (the texts that were not included in the Bible Christians know today). I suggest some theological rationale as to why certain stories of Jesus were rejected by the tradition, and what the decisions about which stories to include/not include reveal about the church's nascent Christology—that is, its understanding of Jesus. Following up on that analysis then, in the subsequent chapter, chapter 5, I examine the significance of these stories (and their absence) for understanding Jesus' role as savior; what they might have meant then, and what they might mean for Christians today.

I conclude with a final section, Part 3, in which I look beyond infancy to adulthood for both Krishna and Jesus, examining how the picture of both figures as babies/young children relates to their adult character, using certain paradigmatic stories of Jesus and Krishna as adults. Here I look particularly at the stories of Jesus' life and ministry and his crucifixion and resurrection in the Gospel of Luke, and Krishna's role in the *Mahabharata*, particularly the *Bhagavad Gita*, linking the theological ramifications of those narratives with what has already been seen in the previous stories.

Finally, in chapter 7, the concluding chapter of the book, I bring together all the threads that have been discussed thus far, examining what has been learned through the comparison and how that information sheds new light on a Christian understanding of who Jesus is and how he saves. I conclude by returning to the themes discussed in chapter 1, noting the importance of comparative theology and suggesting possibilities for further study and research.

1

Comparative Theology and Learning about Jesus

This first chapter introduces readers to the discipline of comparative theology and makes the following three arguments. First, Christians can and should learn something about non-Christian religious traditions for the sake of the religious other; in fact, both the license and the imperative to do so rest on a biblical foundation. Second, Christians can and should expect to learn something about God in the course of that exploration, and the basis for such a belief can be found in who God has revealed Godself to be and how Christians have traditionally understood that divine self-revelation. Third, Christians can and should expect that their understanding of their own faith tradition will be stretched and challenged, but at the same time deepened and strengthened through such interreligious dialogue. In the final section of this chapter I describe how the exercise of comparing Jesus and Krishna contributes positively to the formation of Christian theological doctrines and explain how, in the chapters to come, the Christian reader will come to understand Jesus in a new way and learn new things about what it means to call Jesus savior.

What Is Comparative Theology?

This book is an exercise in comparative theology, a discipline that, for Christians, falls under the umbrella of Christian systematic theology. Scholars and religious leaders engaged in this particular enterprise learn about and are in conversation with other religious traditions, as are many people who are involved in different aspects of interreligious dialogue. However, what sets this particular discipline apart is that those involved in comparative theology are open and up front about their own religious commitments and their own loyalties to the faiths they practice. They have particular religious truth claims and they use particular religious language and symbols. They have an opinion about the practices and beliefs under discussion; they are not "unbiased observers."

One of the well-known scholars in this field, James L. Fredericks, defines comparative theology this way: "Comparative theology is the branch of systematic theology which seeks to interpret the Christian tradition conscientiously in conversation with the texts and symbols of non-Christian religions."[1] In order to better define what comparative theology is and how it functions, Fredericks argues that it is situated on a healthy, constructive middle ground between two ends of a spectrum: *liberalism*, a term that he uses to refer to those who follow in the footsteps of Friedrich Schleiermacher and interpret religious phenomena using the category of "experience," and those who follow George Lindbeck's "*postliberal alternative.*"

According to Fredericks, Schleiermacher and others promoted a "turn to experience," arguing that there is a "universal religious experience" that allows one to minimize evident differences between religions by interpreting them as "*expressions* emanating from a universal religious experience."[2] The strength of this position is obvious, as it allows members of different religious traditions to downplay their divergences in belief and practice in favor of the greater category that they have in common—an experience of the same Divine. In this interpretation, what we all share trumps what is different or unique, and it is this common ground that makes dialogue possible.

However, Fredericks notes some potential problems with this perspective. He argues that such an idea can promote theological indifference toward the particular doctrinal claims of other religious traditions (again, these are seen as less important in light of the greater truth of one shared religious experience), a subtle theological imperialism (if I categorize and describe your experience with my particular theological lens and vocabulary), and an uncritical syncretism that obscures real differences in favor of a "can't we all just get along" mentality.

At the opposite end of the spectrum, Fredericks puts what he calls George Lindbeck's *postliberal alternative*, which he takes from Lindbeck's important work, *The Nature of Doctrine.*[3] In this text, Lindbeck uses the work of the philosopher Ludwig Wittgenstein, among others, to argue that each religion functions as a different "language" and that each religious language offers a different way of perceiving the world. Most importantly for Frederick's argument, these languages are not interchangeable or reducible to some common norm. Thus, in this view, "Christianity's notion of *agape* should not be taken as an alternative interpretation of what Buddhists know as *karuna*, or for that matter, what French revolutionaries called *fraternité*. On the contrary, all three are different ways of configuring the self and the world."[4] For Lindbeck, in contrast to Schleiermacher, there are no "uninterpreted experiences": "different religions do not thematize the same experience in different ways because 'the experiences that religions evoke and mold are varied as the interpretive schemes they embody.'"[5]

The strength of this position is that it does not gloss over important differences between religious traditions, and it validates the way in which one's entire worldview is colored by one's religious background. It recognizes that these different backgrounds result in quite divergent ways of seeing the world, understanding the human condition, and deriving ethical norms of behavior. These are central aspects of any interreligious dialogue, and if they are ignored or marginalized there is great risk that a tradition will be distorted beyond recognition in the course of finding common ground.

However, this position also has drawbacks. Fredericks notes that this way of understanding different religions offers no reason or impetus for interreligious dialogue; such conversation is irrelevant to the development of one's own faith. Thus, other religions are neither right nor wrong but meaningless "as interpreted from within the universe of discourse established by Christian texts."[6] Therefore, if pushed to its logical conclusion, this viewpoint renders discourse about religion private: as English-only speakers cannot have a deep, meaningful conversation with Russian-only speakers, so too Christians are able to talk only to other Christians about significant religious issues. Christian-Hindu dialogue, for example, would be impossible.

In contrast to these options, then, Fredericks argues that comparative theology walks a middle path, proceeding "by means of limited case studies in which specific elements of the Christian tradition are interpreted in comparison with elements of another religious tradition."[7] This methodology avoids positing grand, unifying theories and instead offers more focused, specific engagements and comparisons. I maintain that this is more authentic to the situation we find ourselves in today, because, as Francis Clooney, another distinguished scholar in this field, argues, "the information on religions now available to us is far too complex and far too concretely situated to be accounted for justly by one or another of these [grand explanatory] theories and because, by extension, there is, in fact, no universal position from which one could adequately articulate such a theory."[8]

The practice of comparative theology is not without its own set of risks, however. Fredericks notes that the openness to which the comparative theologian is called and the resulting changes in one's perspective can be both "disruptive and destabilizing." Nonetheless, this is only one side of the coin. He goes on to say, "Although other religions pose a threat to the security of our present theological understanding, they also offer an opportunity for revising those understandings."[9] For this reason, "The comparative theologian is a believer in a crisis of understanding fomented by the intrusive presence of the Other. This means that the comparative theologian operates within a tension defined by 1) vulnerability to the transformative power of the Other and 2) loyalty to the Christian tradition. *All temptations to overcome this tension should be resisted.*"[10]

This second pole of the tension raises a good point that needs to be emphasized. Because of their loyalty to their own tradition, comparative theologians do not simply engage in dialogue for their own individual gain. Instead, they also seek to transform their own faith communities, applying what they have learned to their own tradition and seeing how that might result in deepened, enriched religious understanding not only for themselves but for the community as a whole.

One of the main differences, then, between comparative religion and comparative theology is that those who engage in comparative theology are active participants in a particular religion, whereas those in comparative religion may or may not be—and if they are, they do not assume that their personal religious beliefs shape their analysis. As Francis Clooney notes,

> The distinction between comparative theology and the range of disciplines collected under the title of "the study of religion" points to the fact that comparative theology, like theology in general, is invested with the dimension of faith. The faith of the inquirer cannot be separated from the faith claims of the inquirer's community; this faith is explicitly at issue in the comparative exercise . . . Comparative theology differs in its resistance to generalizations about religion, its commitment to the demands of one or another tradition, and its goal of a reflective retrieval, after comparison, of the comparativist's (acknowledged) own community's beliefs in order to restate them more effectively.[11]

In my view, this insight of Clooney's points to one of the great advantages of both the method and practice of comparative theology.

Simply put, comparing religions is not an activity for the science lab, so to speak. That is, it is not an activity best served by observing different practices or beliefs under a microscope, recording their similarities and differences on a chart, and, once the experiment is over, putting down one's pencil and going home, untouched and unmoved by any new information or insight that has been uncovered. The obvious reason for this is that, at their core, religions connect with and express the deepest, most profound human thoughts and emotions; they claim our most passionate allegiances, and they speak a most important word about the truth of our existence.

Without being part of a religious tradition oneself, it is much more difficult, if not impossible, to understand the passion and profundity in another tradition and thus fully appreciate it. In addition, without being part of a religious tradition oneself, there is no possibility for transformation—either for an individual or a community. Instead, the comparison remains purely an academic endeavor—a "head" exercise without any "heart" component. It is my conviction that, because of the subject matter, a comparison between religious traditions must be more than that. The activity of comparative theology makes the "more" possible, in spades.

A Rationale for Engagement

For the sake of the religious other I maintain that Christians can and should learn something about non-Christian religious traditions and, in fact, both the license and the mandate to do so rest on a biblical foundation. In his book, *The Immanent Divine*, John Thatamanil writes: "Let me suggest that comparative theology can be understood as motivated by two ancient biblical imperatives: the injunction prohibiting false witness against our neighbors and the deeper injunction to actually love our neighbors."[12] This is an important insight into the rationale all Christians can and should use to learn more about different religious traditions.

First, what does it actually mean to "bear false witness" against someone? Here, I rely on my own Lutheran tradition and cite Martin Luther's explication of the eighth commandment as found in his Small Catechism. Luther writes, "We are to fear and love God, so that we do not tell lies about our neighbors, betray or slander them, or destroy their reputations. Instead, we are to come to their defense, speak well of them, and interpret everything they do in the best possible light."[13] Note the connections Luther makes in this brief explanation. First, the way Christians treat their neighbors is directly related to their relationship with God: because Christians love God, so also they are called to live out that same love in their relationship with their neighbors.

Second, bearing false witness goes beyond simply holding one's tongue and not speaking ill of another; it also includes the directive to speak out in another's defense and come to her aid when she is being slandered or maligned. Third, when one sees one's neighbor engaged in behavior one doesn't understand, the imperative is to assume the best rather than the worst and, in all cases, to give her the benefit of the doubt and assume the most favorable possible interpretation.

In Luther's view, this prohibition against bearing false witness is intimately connected to the prohibition against murder (the Fifth Commandment), which makes his argument even stronger. In that explanation, Luther writes, "First, we should not harm anyone, either by hand or deed. Next, we should not use our tongue to advocate or advise harming anyone, whereby anyone may be mistreated. Finally, our heart should harbor no hostility or malice against anyone in a spirit of anger and hatred . . . *Therefore it is God's real intention that we should allow no one to suffer harm but show every kindness and love.*"[14]

What might this imperative look like in a relationship with a neighbor of a different religious tradition? Perhaps when you are at work and you hear your colleagues characterize all Muslims as terrorists, you would speak up and note that terrorists are extremists, and that while there are extremists in all religious traditions, including Christianity, the vast majority of Muslims reject terrorism. Or, perhaps when your daughter says that her Jewish friend is boring because she can't ever come over on Saturdays or sleep over on Friday nights, you could talk to her about what it means for certain Jews to keep the Sabbath, and work with her to find a different time for the girls to play together. Or, perhaps when you notice several small religious statues in a neighbor's home, you could ask her to tell you about them and explain how they relate to her practice of Hinduism, instead of going home and making fun of her to your friends. Responding faithfully in these situations, however, requires that one take the time and effort to learn something about Muslims, Jews, and Hindus, and equip oneself to combat lies and misinformation with insight, compassion, and invitation—hence the need for engaging other religious traditions.

Now let me turn to the second mandate, the command to love our neighbors. Many, many passages in scripture reinforce this command; let me mention only two. First, in the Gospel of Matthew, a lawyer asks Jesus, "Teacher, which commandment in the law is the greatest?" Jesus replies, "You shall love the Lord your God with all your heart, and with all your soul and with all your mind. This is the greatest and first commandment. And a second is like it: you shall love your neighbor as yourself. On these two commandments hang all the law and the prophets" (Mt 22:36–40).

The second passage comes from the Gospel of John. In the hours before Jesus' arrest, after Jesus has washed his disciples' feet and is preparing for his betrayal and death, he says to his disciples, "I give you a new commandment, that you love one another. Just as I have loved you, you also should love one another. By this everyone will know that you are my disciples, if you have love of one another" (Jn 13:34–35).

These two verses make clear that love is a primary (if not *the* primary) mode of being in which Christians are to live their lives; it suffices as a summary of all the other commandments and prophetic words of the Lord. It is an indispensible core component of fidelity to God, and it is the defining characteristic of one's identity as a follower of Jesus. Thus, it can be argued persuasively that it is impossible to love God without loving one's neighbor, and that calling oneself a Christian while hating others (even, as you will recall, hating your enemies) is a fundamental contradiction.

So, how does this relate to interactions with members of other religious traditions? Obviously, if you love someone, you want to know something about him: you want to know who he is, what he values, and how he orients his life. If you love someone, you take the time to talk to her, you get to know her, and in so doing, you share yourself as well. Love shows itself in attention to another, in accepting another on her terms, in a willingness to learn something new, to think about things in a new way, and to grow together in friendship and harmony. When I say Christians are called to love their Hindu, Muslim, Jewish, and Buddhist neighbors, I mean they are called to develop relationships of mutual affection, understanding, and appreciation. This cannot occur without interreligious dialogue.

A statement from the World Council of Churches ties together both imperatives:

> Dialogue can be recognized as a welcome way of obedience to the commandment of the Decalogue: "You shall not bear false witness against your neighbor." Dialogue helps us not to disfigure the image of our neighbors of different faiths and ideologies... Dialogue therefore is a fundamental part of Christian service within community. In dialogue Christians actively

respond to the command to "love God and your neighbor as yourself." As an expression of love engagement in dialogue testifies to the love experienced in Christ. It is a joyful affirmation of life against chaos, and a participation with all who are allies of life in seeking the provisional goals of a better human community.[15]

What Can Be Learned about God?

A second point to note is that Christians can and should expect to learn something about God in the course of interreligious exploration, and the basis for such a belief can be found in who God has revealed Godself to be and how Christians traditionally have understood this divine self-revelation. One of the core beliefs of the Christian faith is that God is the creator of all. All that exists has come into being through the word and the hands of God, and all that exists relies on the continuing creative activity of God for subsistence moment to moment. Augustine and others in the Christian tradition have described this dependence using the metaphor of God's hand constantly undergirding the cosmos. If God were to withdraw God's hand for even an instant, creation would fall immediately into nothingness. Another common metaphor that expresses this idea is derived from descriptions of the Spirit who moved over the face of the waters at the beginning of creation, the same Spirit breathed into the creature God molded from the clay, bringing the first human to life. It is this divine aspiration that gives life to all beings. As God inspired Ezekiel's dry bones, so also is all creation simply parched and withered without the constant flow of God's breath.

Both metaphors point to the continued relationship that God has with God's creatures. From the existence of this ongoing relationship we can conclude that each creature manifests something of God in his or her very being. This is true even of the cosmos itself; indeed, this is the conviction behind the category of "general revelation." General revelation is referred to as the unveiling of God that is self-evident, that is visible and obvious to anyone who has eyes to see, not simply to those who are Christians. God, the creator and mother of the universe, has stamped God's presence on all things made by God's hand and through God's word. Thus, it is possible to discern something of God's nature through the observation and contemplation of creation. It is something akin to recognizing the hand of Michelangelo in the Sistine Ceiling, for example, or hearing the distinctive voice of Shakespeare in *Romeo and Juliet*. The creator leaves a mark on creation and thus the world in all its beauty and diversity bears the mark of the One who created it.

In the Bible, this type of revelation is witnessed to most often by the psalmist. For example, Psalm 8 begins, "O LORD, our Sovereign, how majestic is your name in all the earth! . . . When I look at your heavens, the work of your fingers, the moon and the stars that you have established; what are human beings that you are mindful of them, mortals that you care for them?" Psalm 19 states, "The heavens are telling the glory of God; and the firmament proclaims God's handiwork. Day to day pours forth speech, and night to night declares knowledge. There is no speech, nor are there words; their voice is not heard; yet their voice goes out through all the earth, and their words to the end of the world."

Indeed, then, if something of God can be seen and known in creation itself—the mountains, the stars, and the oceans—how much more so must something of God be found in worshipers in other faith traditions? Christians affirm that every single human being has been created not just by the hand of God but in the very image of God (*imago Dei*). In many ways, the twentieth-century foundation for this argument was laid during the Second Vatican Council, which produced several documents that explicitly affirm God's active presence and salvific work in other religious traditions. For example, in the document *Nostra Aetate* we read, "The Catholic Church rejects nothing of what is true and holy in these [non-Christian] religions. She has a high regard for the manner of life and conduct, the precepts and doctrines which, although differing in many ways from her own teaching, nevertheless often reflect a ray of that truth which enlightens all men."[16] Similarly, the document *Lumen Gentium* states that God is not remote from "those who in shadows and images seek the unknown God, since he gives to all men life and breath and all things."[17] Both of these documents emphasize that the God Christians worship in Jesus Christ can, in fact, be known and experienced in other religions, and even salvation can be found there as well. *Lumen Gentium* continues, "Those who, through no fault of their own, do not know the Gospel of Christ or his Church, but who nevertheless seek God with a sincere heart, and, moved by grace, try in their actions to do his will as they know it through the dictates of their conscience—these too may achieve eternal salvation."[18]

The great twentieth-century theologian Karl Rahner argues that the grace of God comes to all humans universally and creates in all of us a searching for God, a longing for God. This means that ontologically, fundamentally, and inherently, humans are "oriented towards God."[19] Rahner further argues that because God wills the salvation of all and comes to all through the Holy Spirit, those who seek God and respond to the movement and work of the Spirit in their own faith traditions actually have a saving relationship to God—and indeed, to Jesus Christ.[20] John Cobb notes that, from this standpoint, "the person who is not a Christian is approached not merely as unbeliever but also as one in whom and through whom the everlasting Word acts and speaks."[21] Thus, Christians can and should expect to find something of God in their encounter with non-Christian religions, but how exactly God will be experienced, however, can never be predetermined or foreseen.

How Can One's Own Faith Be Strengthened?

Finally, Christians can and should expect that their understanding of their own faith tradition will be stretched and challenged in interreligious dialogue, but also deepened and strengthened. To elaborate, a parallel from a different aspect of human life is useful. Imagine that you find yourself faced with one of life's big decisions: whether or not to take a new job, move to a new city, marry, divorce, or have children. If you are like most people, you will discuss the pros and cons of that decision with a wide variety of people: family members, friends, coworkers, fellow church members, the woman who does your hair, the guy at the gym—sometimes even virtual strangers will be brought into the conversation. Why do this? Why solicit so many opinions and ask for advice from so many different people?

Most of us engage so many different people about the potentially life-changing decisions we face because we know intuitively that everyone sees things from a different perspective, and thus everyone brings something new to the table. A free spirit might leap at the opportunity to take a new job, regardless of the potential pitfalls, just for the excitement of a new experience. A happy father of four children might strongly encourage fatherhood for all of his friends, confident that being a father is one of life's greatest joys. A woman who has just come through a bitter divorce and custody battle might well caution a potential bride to wait awhile before jumping into marriage. Are some of these opinions wrong and others right? Of course not; all are equally valid viewpoints, depending on one's current standpoint and the life experiences that have shaped it.

Thus, the reason for soliciting so many different ideas is not to choose the "right" one out of the many "wrong" ones, or even to decide which person's view you are going to adopt as your own. Instead, the point is to expand your own vision of the situation as a whole, using the insights of others to gain a deeper perspective on everything involved in your decision. A person from a small town considering a job in a big city might not have imagined that urban housing costs would be so high that owning a home would not be possible. A starry-eyed bride might not even consider discussing a prenuptial agreement or separate checking accounts, something a wife in her second marriage may well suggest.

The many and various conversations we have with other people enrich our own perspective on life in general. They open our eyes to new things, they invite us into a different experience than we could have on our own, and they challenge our deeply held convictions by presenting another side of the issue. These conversations are not always easy; sometimes they make us very uncomfortable because they reveal shortcomings in our own opinions and ramifications that we were hoping to avoid. But they also can be wonderfully enlightening if the fresh beam they shine on a situation illuminates new possibilities or insights that had previously gone unnoticed. Being open to the views and ideas of others is risky and can be painful but, ultimately, such openness proves to be both rewarding and even indispensible in the end.

What is true for life in general is also true for religion in particular. In the same way that my understanding of the world is deepened through my conversations with others, so too are my religious understanding and my faith life deepened through dialogue with others, particularly those who have differing views from my own. These conversations also are risky, and can be painful, as they can challenge some of our most cherished religious convictions. However, ultimately, such dialogue can transform our faith for the better. Such dialogue brings new insights into the familiar old stories we thought we knew inside and out, and it brings new life into the desiccated skeleton of beliefs and practices we had ceased to reflect on years ago. Even if we find ourselves with pretty much the same convictions after the dialogue is over, certainly the ground on which we are standing will be different, and our interpretation of those convictions will be richer and more complex. We cannot undertake this process on our own or even with only those who share our beliefs. We need the religious "other" to produce these fruits. While I would not argue that someone who knows only her own faith is not a "good" Christian, or cannot truly worship God, I do believe that there is some truth to the expression that "she who knows one religion, knows none."

The Specific Task Ahead

Thus, this book will compare the two savior figures of Jesus and Krishna primarily through the lens of the stories that were told around their infancy and youth by examining the role these stories play (or do not play) in their disciples'/devotees' understanding of how each figure is the bearer of salvation. I ask what salvation means in each context, and what the stories about each figure might reveal about what constitutes salvific activity. This comparative work is done, in the end, in the service of contributing positively to the formation of Christian theological doctrines, particularly a Christian understanding of salvation and of the person and work of Jesus Christ. It is my hope that the Christian reader will come to understand Jesus in a new way, and learn new things about what it means to call Jesus savior.

And, yet, I dare hope for more than that. As Francis Clooney writes, in his wonderful introduction to *Hindu Wisdom for All God's Children,*

> Readers may eventually find their own, personally better ways to encounter Hindu wisdom, to study it, to present it to others, and some may even go to India themselves, to observe how all this works out at the beginning of the twenty-first century. My hope is that in the end all readers will strike out on their own and then encounter and integrate wisdom ever more widely, and from still other religious traditions.[22]

May this book be for you the beginning of a long, rich, rewarding interfaith journey.

PART I

Baby Krishna

2

A Savior in Disguise

THE STORIES

What Is Hinduism?

In order to present a clear description of who Krishna is and how he saves, it is necessary to give a brief overview of Hinduism, including a discussion of the god Vishnu. Only then will the reader be prepared to learn about Krishna.

Of the five major world religions (Hinduism, Judaism, Buddhism, Christianity, and Islam), it is certainly the case that Hinduism is both the least understood and the least experienced by most Americans. This state of ignorance will not continue, however, as the Hindu population both in the United States and worldwide continues to grow. The website for Diana Eck's well-regarded Pluralism Project (based at Harvard University) cites the following statistics regarding Hinduism: "The 1990 U.S. Census indicated that the number of Asian Indians in the United States (not all of them Hindus) increased 125 percent during the 1980s, rising to 815,000 (about 0.3 percent of the U.S. population). When non-Asian Hindus are incorporated into the equation, one arrives at a total of well over 1 million Hindus residing in the United States."[1] What's more, the Pluralism Project directory lists 723 Hindu temples and centers in the United States, and notes that there is a Hindu center and/or temple in every state, with the exception of Montana, Wyoming, North Dakota, South Dakota, and Vermont.[2] If Christians want to follow the two imperatives discussed in chapter 1—not bearing false witness against one's neighbor, and loving one's neighbor—then it is incumbent upon Christians to learn something about Hinduism, particularly in light of the many misconceptions having to do with Hindu worship and the concept of the deity in Hinduism.

A Religion of Great Diversity

The first thing that must be stated is that, in fact, Hinduism is not one religion. Instead, it is more accurately seen as a medley of religious traditions that originated in India, best described not as "a monolithic entity but rather a conglomerate of religions that share certain traits in common."[3] The word Hinduism itself is an artificial word, coined by scholars in the West in an effort to name and categorize Indian religion on the model of Christianity.[4]

To offer an analogy from the Western context, imagine if someone from India had come to the Middle East around the tenth century and determined that Judaism, Christianity, and Islam were all variations of the same religion—let's call it "Arabism"—simply because they all were founded in the same general area, and they all had their roots in the same mythology, sharing similar stories and similar ideas about the world, God, and humanity. To some degree, this is what happened in India. While today we are left with a word that is almost impossible to do without, we must recognize that it does not carry nearly the specificity of meaning once assumed. In light of this, many scholars would agree with the statement that "Today without wanting to admit it, we know that Hinduism is nothing but an orchid cultivated by European scholarship. It is much too beautiful to be torn out, but it is a greenhouse plant: It does not exist in nature."[5]

Hinduism has several unique features that set it apart from the other religions mentioned above and that contribute to Hinduism's diversity of belief and practice. First, while there is no shortage of historical scholars, sages, and teachers in Hinduism, there is no historical founder of the religion as a whole, no figure comparable to Jesus, the Buddha, Abraham, or Muhammad. Consequently, there is no firm date of origin for Hinduism. Scholars agree that Hinduism is the oldest living major religious tradition, but beyond that simple fact there is much debate, since it is clear that what we today call Hinduism is made up of different beliefs and practices that were handed down orally for millennia before they were finally written down. Thus, because the oral transmission of tradition is notoriously difficult to establish conclusively, there are wide variances even among scholars as to when certain texts, specific practices, and key doctrines originated. For example, the earliest known sacred texts of Hinduism, the Vedas, date back to at least 3000 BCE, but some scholars date them back even further, to 8000 to 6000 BCE, and some Hindus themselves believe these texts to be of divine origin and therefore timeless.

Second, there is no clear established religious hierarchy that determines official Hindu doctrine or practice. Thus, there is no one who can speak for Hindus as a whole and no single authority regarding what is orthodox and heterodox. This is perhaps one reason why, unlike members of most other religious traditions, "most Hindus would not define their religion in terms of a single creed that embodies the faith because different Hindus believe in many different things."[6] This is not to say, however, that there are no general characteristics of Hinduism that can be articulated. For example, here is one list of principles that, by practitioner consensus, characterize one as "Hindu:"

- Belief in the divinity of the Vedas
- Belief in one, all-pervasive Supreme Reality
- Belief in the cyclical nature of time
- Belief in karma
- Belief in reincarnation
- Belief in alternate realities with higher beings
- Belief in enlightened masters or gurus
- Belief in non-aggression and non-injury
- Belief that all revealed religions are essentially correct
- Belief that the living being is first and foremost a spiritual entity
- Belief in an "organic social system."[7]

Another example of a similar list comes from the Indian Supreme Court, which produced the following set of workable criteria as to what it means to be a Hindu:

- The Vedas should be accepted and revered as the foundation of Hindu philosophy
- One should have a spirit of tolerance, and recognize that the truth has many sides
- One accepts belief in recurring cosmic cycles of creation, preservation and dissolution
- One accepts belief in reincarnation
- One recognizes that there are numerous paths to truth and salvation
- One recognizes that although the worship of idols may be deemed unnecessary, there may be many deities worthy of worship
- In distinction from followers of other religions, one does not believe in a specific set of theological or philosophical conceptions.[8]

Clearly, the breadth of these criteria goes far beyond what is found in Christianity. However, as should be evident from the emphasis on tolerating the different beliefs of others, respecting the pluriformity of truth, and recognizing the diversity of belief and practice, any talk of Hinduism as a whole needs to keep this multiplicity in mind. One scholar has suggested the following metaphor: "If the essence of Hinduism could be summarized in a few words, those words might be 'structured diversity.' We might think of Hinduism as a rainbow in which all the different colors are represented, but in which each of these colors has a very distinct place in the spectrum."[9]

Sacred Texts of Hinduism

Another feature of Hinduism is the fact that there is no single, authoritative text in Hinduism that functions like the Bible for Christians or the Qur'an for Muslims. Instead, there are several different collections of texts that have authority.

First are the Vedas. The Vedas represent the most important category of sacred writings. In the narrowest sense "Veda" refers to the four samhitas (collections) of sacred texts of ancient India. They are the oldest body of literature and are traditionally held to be eternal and of non-human origin. The most important of the Vedas and the most well-known in the West is the Rig Veda, which comprises a large collection of hymns praising various gods and goddesses and telling various stories of creation.[10] The Vedas are the collection of writings held to be the basis of true belief and practice among Hindus.

Second are the Upanishads, which do not share the Vedas's focus on ritual and sacrifice but instead describe a more philosophical and theoretical approach to the practice of Hinduism.[11] The primary teaching of the Upanishads is that the self (atman) is identical to the Ultimate ground of reality (Brahman), and the person who realizes this sacred truth (through disciplined practice and meditation) finds liberation (moksha) from the endless cycles of rebirth (samsara). It should be noted that in the Upanishads themselves, Brahman, the Ultimate Reality, is not personified or personalized; however, some later schools of Hindu thought did personalize this unified One Supreme Being, most typically as Shiva, Vishnu, or the Goddess.

Third are the two great Indian epics, the Mahabharata and the Ramayana. The Mahabharata, the oldest, has existed in various forms for well over two thousand years. It is the longest epic poem in the world, and is said to have been written by the great sage Vyasa. However, it is clear that the epic as it exists today has been redacted by many hands over the centuries. The main plot narrative concerns the rivalry between two sets of paternal first cousins: the five sons of Pandu (the Pandavas), led by Yudhishthira; and the one hundred sons of the blind King Dhritarashtra (he and his sons are called the Kauravas). However, within this overarching story, the reader finds elaborate side narratives on philosophy, ethics, and politics, and other stories only tangentially related to the main characters.[12]

The most well-known portion of the *Mahabharata* is the *Bhagavad Gita*, and it is a particularly important text for this study of Krishna, as the story revolves around him. More will be said about both these texts in coming chapters; for now, let me simply summarize the action. After years of trickery, intrigue, and behind-the-scenes maneuvering, the Pandavas and the Kauravas find themselves on the brink of all-out war. The two massive armies face off on the *Kurukshetra*, "Kuru's field," for what will be the decisive battle for the entire Indian kingdom; it is clear the death-toll will be monstrous. At the very moment the battle is to commence, Arjuna, the Pandava's champion, loses heart: looking out across the field of battle he sees cousins, friends, and mentors, and the thought of killing them overwhelms him. Discouraged, he sits down in his chariot and refuses to fight. At this point, Krishna, who is acting as Arjuna's charioteer, preaches the most famous sermon in Hinduism, explaining to him why it is his duty to fight and why fighting in the battle will be an act of great religious significance. In the course of this sermon, Krishna reveals his true self to Arjuna as the one supreme reality—creator and destroyer of all. Arjuna then goes on to fight, helping his brothers win the war and the kingdom.

In his book, *Arrow of the Blue-skinned God*, Jonah Blank writes,

> Imagine a story that was the *Odyssey*, *Romeo and Juliet*, the Bible, and a Hollywood blockbuster all rolled into one. Imagine a story that combined adventure and aphorism, romance and religion, fantasy and philosophy. Imagine a story that could make young children marvel, grown men weep, and old women dream. Such a story exists in India, and it is called the *Ramayana*."[13]

Along with the *Mahabharata*, the *Ramayana* is one of the most important epic poems in Hinduism. Its earliest form is a Sanskrit poem attributed to the sage Valmiki, and scholars believe that it was composed sometime between 500 BCE and 400 CE. However, as in the case of other texts, Hindu tradition places the date of composition much earlier. The story itself is about Prince Rama of Ayodhya, his wife Sita, her capture by the demon Ravenna, and her subsequent rescue by

Rama, his brother Lakshmana, and their monkey helper Hanuman.[14] More broadly, however, the story models proper *dharma*—that is, the proper actions and behaviors required to maintain or uphold one's place in the world and to support the proper functioning of the cosmos as a whole. Rama, Sita, and the other main characters all exemplify proper *dharma* through the way in which they live as a husband, a wife, a brother, a king, a son, and so on. In all of their relationships, they demonstrate ideal social behavior. Thus, people today still model their own behavior on that of Rama and Sita.[15]

Finally, I want to mention the Puranas, a series of texts that describe specific gods in great detail, specifically Vishnu, Shiva, and Brahma, along with the way in which they are to be worshiped and what rewards devotees can expect to receive from them. As with the other sacred texts in Hinduism, a date of composition for the Puranas is difficult to establish. Freda Matchett surveys several different scholarly opinions, concluding that "It would be hard to disagree . . . that 'the most reasonable date' for the *Bhagavata* [the particular Purana that concerns Krishna] is 'the ninth or early tenth century.'"[16] However, she also agrees with Friedhelm Hardy, who writes, "On the whole, it is meaningless to speak of 'the date' of a Sanskrit *purana*, because many generations of bards, etc., have been involved in the accumulation of material which at some stage has been given a name."[17]

While the list of Puranas is seemingly endless—"vast in extent and miscellaneous in content"[18]— the major Puranas are typically listed at eighteen, and these books are subdivided into three sets of six books each, with each set corresponding to one of the three gods mentioned above, although many texts also are devoted to worship of the goddess. One of the reasons why the Puranas are important for this particular study is that many scholars would agree that "it is an undeniable fact that the most popular and loved of the Puranas is the *Bhagavata Purana*,"[19] also called the *Shrimad Bhagavatam*, which describes all of the ten principal avatars of Vishnu but at the same time gives primacy of place to Krishna. Obviously, this text is of particular concern here, and it is on this text that the biography of Krishna presented below will be based.

A New Mindset

This diversity points to the fact that, for Christians, a new mindset is required to get into a study of Hinduism, as practitioners of Hinduism do not share many of the core ontological and epistemological beliefs of Westerners. What I mean by this is that a Hindu understanding of the cosmos, human nature, and God is radically different from what is found in Christianity—and, for that matter, what is found in Islam and Judaism as well. In other words, "What we label 'Hinduism' ranges from monotheism to polytheism, from monism to materialism and atheism; from nonviolent ethics to moral systems that see as imperative elaborate blood sacrifices to sustain the world; from critical, scholastic philosophical discussion to the cultivation of sublime, mystical, wordless inner experiences."[20] Nowhere is this more obvious than with the understanding of God. Any introductory text on Hinduism must deal with the difficult question of how to explain the characterization of the Divine in Hinduism in a way Westerners can understand.

Hinduism accommodates a vast assortment of dynamic and multifaceted concepts of god. For the most part, gods can be categorized under two broad headings: *nirguna* Brahman, a formless, impersonal supreme reality without qualities or attributes—comparable in some general way to what Christians call an *apophatic* understanding of the Divine; and *saguna* Brahman, the personified, personal form of the supreme reality that is worshiped as god—what Christians call a *kataphatic* understanding of the Divine.

It is important to note that these are not two different realities, but rather two different ways of perceiving the one true ultimate reality: the first is perhaps more the subject of philosophical and intellectual speculation and meditation, while the second is more the object of adoration, sacrifice, and devotion. This particular study is more concerned with the personified conception of supreme reality and the consequent relationship that results between the god and the individual. Therefore, it is important to expand on the notion of *saguna* Brahman, the idea of a personified god in Hinduism.

In order to appreciate a Hindu understanding of god, one must first move beyond the "either/or" of monotheism and polytheism: that is, one must let go of the idea that there are only two options—either people worship one god (monotheism) or they worship many gods (polytheism). Instead, in Hinduism, it is both/and. Hindus see no contradiction in believing that there is one god and believing that there are many gods. In addition, for some, the tension between the one and the many actually generates deeper insight into the true nature of the Divine than either one could produce on its own. Hence, Steven Rosen writes,

> To the Hindu mind, opposites are, in a sense, the same thing. They are different sides of the same coin—inseparable and fundamentally related... Thus, in Hinduism, the One and the Many might even function as *synonyms*—the One, say ancient

Hindu texts, only fully reveals itself when in relation to the Other... This is to say, the Other gives meaning to the One, and vice versa. A fundamental Hindu perception: Opposites attract and interpenetrate each other. Ultimately, then, the One and the Other coalesce in a higher spiritual reality. This is expressed in various ways in the Hindu tradition.[21]

Hindu doctrine and practice, then, have a wide variety of ways of conceptualizing the Divine, including the following: *monolatry*, which points to the worship of one greater god among many lesser gods; *kathenotheism* or *henotheism*, which refer to the worship of different gods, but only one god at any given time; and finally, *polymorphic monotheism*, which signifies the worship of one supreme god who reveals him/herself in many forms in different times and places in the world.[22]

Part of the reason for this complexity is that the history of the various gods in Hinduism is very complicated, and the depiction of many, if not all, of the major deities has evolved over time, differing greatly depending on which sacred texts are being cited. This chronological diversity is accompanied by an equal geographical diversity: depending on where one is located, the actual worship of the different deities varies widely—not only across the globe, but even from north to south India. Finally, as noted above, the theology that informs people's understanding of the various gods in Hinduism is polyvalent: some people believe that all gods are simply different faces of the same one supreme being; others reject all personified forms of this one; some are devoted to one god exclusively; and others worship many different gods simultaneously.

While this can seem terribly complicated and confusing—perhaps even heretical—to Western Christian ears, perhaps another way in which the concept of the Divine in Hinduism can be viewed is through the lens of hospitality. Steven Rosen argues that "The multiplicity or diversity of Hindu deities points to the tradition's *spiritual hospitality*, its willingness to accommodate personal proclivity, and tastes innumerable."[23] Perhaps Christians can practice their own version of spiritual hospitality here and attempt to understand this new way of thinking, and possibly even come to appreciate it.

Who Is Vishnu?

Unlike Christianity, which is grounded in a linear understanding of time, Hinduism has a cyclical understanding of time, in which the universe continually cycles into and out of existence over many eons. In most descriptions of this process, instead of there being one single divinity behind it all, there are three: Brahma is the creator, the one who brings the universe into being; Shiva is the destroyer, the one who, at the right time, causes the universe to fall into nothingness; and during the in-between-time stands Vishnu, the preserver, the god who sustains the universe and protects it from evil while it is in existence. Together, these three gods make up what is sometimes (and somewhat confusingly) called the Hindu "trinity," but the more accurate name in Hinduism is *trimurti*, which translates roughly as "three faces."

As should be expected, there are different understandings of what these gods represent and how they function. Some Hindus see all three gods as simply manifestations of one supreme being that is above all personification, but they still honor and worship the different manifestations individually as genuine representations of god—although it should be noted that today there is hardly any direct worship of Brahma alone. By contrast, both Shiva and Vishnu, as well as the goddess, who is personified with different names and in different forms, have millions of followers who worship him/her as the single supreme deity, the highest embodiment of the Divine. It lies outside the scope of this chapter to discuss how this worship functions in relationship to the goddess and Shiva, but Vishnu is a different case altogether, as is it impossible to understand Krishna without knowing something about Vishnu.

According to Rosen, "two-thirds of the known Hindu world identifies themselves as Vaishnavas,"[24] that is, worshipers of Vishnu. As noted above, Vaishnavas believe that Vishnu is the personal embodiment of the Divine—the highest form of the one supreme god himself who is the ground and source of all being. In terms of Hindu iconography and statuary, Vishnu is always depicted with dark skin—typically blue. He is usually shown with four arms, one holding a lotus flower, another holding a conch shell, another holding a disc or wheel, and the final arm holding a mace. Sometimes he is shown resting on the coils of a many-headed serpent, called *Sheshanaga*, and sometimes his consort, Lakshmi, is rubbing his feet—or sometimes she is sitting next to him. He also is depicted riding his "vehicle," the great eagle *Garuda*. Hinduism knows no prohibition against imaging the Divine, and in no other religion in the world is there such a profusion of depictions of the gods, in all manner of art forms, in all possible materials, from great stone statues to children's comic books.

The primary aspect of Vishnu's mythology that makes him relevant for this particular study is the doctrine of the *avatar*. *Avatara* is a

Sanskrit word that refers to a divine incarnation (literally it means "one who descends"), and it is almost always associated with Vishnu. The word "incarnation" must be read and interpreted by Christians with care, however. Certainly, it is true that there are some general similarities with the concept of incarnation in Christianity, insofar as both refer to a divine decision to "come down" and dwell in creation. Nevertheless, there are many important differences as well, most notably the fact that, unlike Jesus, who according to Christian tradition was truly fully human (and fully divine), the *avatar* is more correctly viewed as an appearance of the Divine, something akin to the Greek god Zeus coming down from heaven disguised as a mortal, but ready and willing to throw off his human camouflage at a moment's notice if the need arises. Further, while Jesus is believed to be the unique incarnation of God, Vishnu is believed to have many, many different *avatars*.

The purpose for this "divine descent" is also different in Hinduism, having nothing to do with a doctrine of sin or human alienation from God. Instead, Hindus believe that at various times in the endless cycles of history Vishnu descends into the world in the form of some created being in order to save and preserve creation from a particular demonic force threatening the very existence of the cosmos. While, as noted above, there are many different *avatars* in Hinduism, tradition holds that there are ten primary *avatars* of Vishnu and their stories are told in elaborate detail both in the Puranas and in a variety of other sacred Hindu texts.

The ten are as follows: first, the fish, Matsya, who saved the world from a great flood; second, the tortoise, Kurma, who allowed the gods and demons to churn up valuable objects from the ocean of milk using a pivot resting on his back; and third, the boar, Varaha, who also rescued the earth from a flood by raising it up on one of his trunks. Fourth is the man-lion, Narasimha, who came to deliver the world from a terrible demon who had obtained from the gods a special boon that prohibited him from being killed by a god, an animal, or a human; Narasimha was a combination of all these, and thus succeeded. Fifth is the dwarf, Vamana, who confronted another demon who had conquered the entire universe. He begged the demon-king for just as much land as he could cover with three of his dwarf steps, and the king, scoffing at such a request, granted it. Imagine his surprise when the dwarf covered the entire universe in his first two steps, placing his last step on the king's own head. Sixth is Parashurama, the man called "Rama with the axe," the hero who destroyed the entire *Kshatriya* class of warriors who were exploiting others.

The next two *avatars*, numbers seven and eight, are the most famous. First is Ramachandra—simply called Rama, the hero of the aforementioned *Ramayana*, who embodied in his person perfect obedience, *dharma*, filial love, and righteousness. He is still seen as the example *par excellence* for human conduct in Hinduism today. The eighth *avatar* is Krishna, who is not only viewed as the perfect and highest incarnation of Vishnu, but whose position in relation to Vishnu, according to many devotees, is reversed, with Krishna being worshiped as the one supreme god and the source of all incarnations, including Vishnu himself.[25] More will be said about this shortly.

Finally, the last two *avatars* are ninth, the Buddha—in this way, Hinduism was able to enfold Buddhism as a whole under its large umbrella; and tenth, Kalki, the form of Vishnu who is still to come, and whose arrival will signal the end of the present age.

Krishna's Life: An Overview

Having bathed and cleaned himself, good Govinda [another
    name for Krishna] is walking: look at him!
He has a golden pot and is offering water: look at him!
He is playing a golden flute in his hand: look at him!
He has a golden anklet on his ankle and is making a ringing
    sound with it: look at him!
He has a shiny, golden *sehara* [a type of headpiece] on his
    head: look at him!
The *pitambar* [a type of yellow garment associated especially
    with Krishna] that he is wearing is flapping: look at him!
He is chewing *pan* [a mixture of betel nut and spices rolled in
    a betel leaf] in his mouth: look at him!
He has put black eyeliner [*kajal*] on his eyes: look at him!
He is wearing golden sandals and tapping them: look at him!
Oh Krishna, Oh Narayan [another name for Krishna], take
    away my worries![26]

Barbara Powell notes that "Krishna's significance in Hinduism cannot be underestimated... He is believed by some to be among the several incarnations of Vishnu, by others to be a divine incarnation of unique and singular importance (as Jesus is to Christians), by others the highest and most perfect manifestation of Brahman, and by still others simply God, the Original and Supreme."[27] For those outside

Hinduism, however, if they know anything about Krishna at all, it is typically through exposure to the great Hindu epic, the *Mahabharata*, where the *Bhagavad Gita* is located. This text reveals Krishna to be the Universal Divine Being, the reality containing all existence in himself. This is a key lens through which to view Krishna's salvific character, and this text, and his role in it, will be discussed in a later chapter.

However, Steven Rosen notes that "while these images of Krishna are highly regarded by Hindus worldwide, his early life as a child and as a young lover is often held in greater esteem. Frolicking in the simple bucolic atmosphere of Vraja, in northern India, he captured the local people's hearts, and their descendents have been retelling his extraordinary pastimes ever since. It is *this* Krishna that is most loved in the Indian subcontinent."[28] It is *this* Krishna, then, who is the focus here.

The bulk of this material of the life of Krishna can be found in book [or canto] ten of the *Bhagavata Purana*,[29] a text that has been described by more than one scholar as a kind of Hindu New Testament.[30] This particular Purana, which, as I noted earlier, details the various avatars of Vishnu, is believed to have been composed sometime between the sixth century and the eighth or ninth century CE., although some scholars date the earliest pieces of the text to the fourth century CE and the final composition to as late as the tenth century.[31] The Purana comprises 18,000 stanzas and is divided into twelve books, or cantos, all of which laud Vishnu and his different avatars.

Even in the context of the whole of this large text, Krishna receives special treatment: he is "uniquely exalted here as the most perfect and complete earthly and transcendental manifestation of the Divine."[32] This is true of the whole, but it is particularly and inimitably true of the tenth canto. Here is how one scholar describes this particular section of the text:

> It has a magic about it. There is nothing you will ever read which quite resembles it, for it is unique in all world literature, sacred or secular. From a strictly aesthetic standpoint it is gloriously beautiful, but from a philosophical and religious standpoint it accomplishes something more amazing: it describes that which is indescribable, captures in time and space that which is eternal and infinite, makes understandable that which is inconceivable. The eternal Reality which the *Upanishads* suggest through abstraction and metaphor is made tangible in the person Krishna. We can, without performing a single meditation or making one inch worth of

spiritual progress see, hear, feel and come to intimately know the Ultimate Truth."[33]

The tenth canto itself is divided into two main parts. Part one, which is our primary concern here, describes Krishna's birth and childhood in Braj (also written as Vraja) or, more specifically, Vrindavana, and part two describes Krishna's adult life after leaving Vrindavana, his many marriages, and his vanquishing of many demons. The picture painted in part one in particular is of a beautiful, loving god at play, enjoying time with his devotees purely for the joy of it, without any hidden agenda or higher purpose.

This concept of play, or lila, is one of the key characteristics of Krishna, and one that will be discussed in depth in chapter 3. In fact, although the ostensible purpose for Krishna's incarnation, described in more detail in the Mahabharata and the Bhagavad Gita, is to rid the world of the increasing number of demons and demonic forces, another equally important purpose described in the Bhagavata Purana is to encourage loving relationships of devotion that ultimately lead to salvation. One of the primary means by which Krishna facilitates these relationships is through his acts of lila with his devotees.

A Dangerous Birth

What is recounted in the Bhagavata Purana is presented as having occurred just before the onset of the kaliyuga, the final age in the winding down of creation before its eventual destruction. It is believed that the inauguration of the kaliyuga was, in fact, Krishna's departing this world and returning to his divine abode. The Bhagavata is told in the form of various narrations by the sage Suta, who has been asked to tell about Krishna's activities, since both the hearing and the speaking of Krishna's name are said to bring liberation, and meditation on his deeds is particularly auspicious.

The story begins with an explanation of why Krishna chose to become incarnate at that particular time. Suta relates that at one time the earth was greatly oppressed by wicked kings and demons. Taking the form of a cow, she appealed to Brahma, the god of creation, for assistance. Then Brahma, with Shiva and the other gods, prayed to Vishnu/Krishna, who is identified as "the supreme being, the Lord of the universe, the God of all gods."[34] He replied that the distress of the earth was already known to him, and he had already made plans to incarnate himself as the son of Vasudeva, along with his amsha, who becomes Balarama, his brother and his constant companion.

A quick word about this concept of *amsha*, which refers to a "portion" or "partial incarnation." Describing this idea, Edwin Bryant writes,

> the sense of the term is that the supreme Godhead [who in the *Bhagavata Purana* is unquestionably Krishna] can maintain his (or her) own presence while simultaneously manifesting some aspect of himself (or herself) elsewhere in a separate and distinct presence (or any number of presences). That secondary, or derivative manifestation, which exhibits a part but not the full characteristics or potency of the source being, is known as an *amsha*.[35]

Balarama, then, is a partial incarnation of Krishna, a secondary manifestation that Krishna creates alongside his full incarnate form.

As the story begins, Vasudeva, the man who becomes Krishna's father, has just married a woman named Devaki, and she has a brother named Kamsa. As Vasudeva and Devaki are riding away from the marriage ceremony in their chariot, with Kamsa at the reins, a voice from the heavens announces that the eighth offspring of Devaki will become Kamsa's killer. (As the reader finds out soon enough, Kamsa is one of those wicked kings *par excellence* of whom the earth was complaining about to Brahma.) Kamsa comes close to killing Devaki right then and there, but Vasudeva, hoping to save his wife's life, promises that he will hand over to Kamsa every child that Devaki bears. Kamsa then agrees to spare Devaki, but imprisons both her and her husband, and kills each one of their children as they are born.

After six of the infants have been killed and Devaki is pregnant with her seventh child, Krishna puts his master plan into action. He goes to *Yogamaya*, a feminine power of illusion that serves Krishna during his incarnation, and instructs her to spirit away the unborn child that is in Devaki's womb. This child is born as Balarama by another mother, Rohini, and everyone believes that Devaki has miscarried.

Finally, Devaki becomes pregnant with Krishna, not by means of sexual intercourse, but by the "mental transmission" of Vasudeva. Simply by the change in Devaki's appearance—her radiance and glow—Kamsa knows that the child she is carrying is Krishna, and he waits with impatience until Krishna is born, sure that he will be able to kill Krishna while he is an infant.

When the time of Krishna's birth finally comes, Suta relates in detail the many auspicious signs that herald the birth of the supreme god of the universe: the sky was clear and full of stars, a fresh breeze blew, the minds of the sages were peaceful and calm, the birds were singing, and flowers rained down from heaven. Krishna was born at midnight, and although his parents for a brief moment saw him in his true form—four arms bearing weapons, a magnificent jewel around his neck, arm and wrist bracelets, beautiful earrings, and wearing a yellow garment—Krishna quickly cloaked himself in the guise of an ordinary child by the power of his *Yogamaya* illusion. One source describes the scene this way:

> At the moment of His birth, the prison was filled with a soft light, streaming out from the Babe Himself, and as He lay back in His mother's lap, they saw shining out from behind Him four arms. One hand held the Shankha or battle-trumpet; another the discus; a third the mace; and in the fourth was a lotus on its stem. Then Devaki and Vasudeva knew these for the signs of Vishnu, and they worshipped the child, saying the salutations, as Narayana, Savior of the World. But as the salutations ended, the veil of Maya descended upon them once more, and the Child appeared to them as their own babe.[36]

The baby Krishna then instructs Vasudeva to remove him from the room (Krishna opens the bolted doors himself) and carry him to Vraj, to the house of Nanda and Yashoda. There, *Yogamaya* has just been born as a child of Yashoda; in the darkness, as everyone is sleeping, Vasudeva switches the children, laying Krishna in the arms of Yashoda and taking the infant girl, who is really the goddess *Yogamaya*, back to Devaki. As soon as the cries of the girl are heard in the household, Kamsa comes to kill the child. Taking her by her feet, he dashes her against a rock, and is astonished when *Yogamaya* reveals her true form, flying into the air and manifesting herself as a goddess. She then warns Kamsa that Krishna has already been born somewhere else. Kamsa responds by ordering all the babies who are ten days old or less in and around the area to be killed. Notwithstanding this order, Krishna survives, and embarks upon a marvelous childhood.

A Divine Childhood

Krishna's childhood is marked by mischievous play with Balarama (the seventh child conceived by Devaki), which both exasperates and delights his mother, Yashoda. Throughout, however, Krishna repeatedly gives glimpses of his true form, which reminds both readers and the other inhabitants of Vraj that, while he "behave[s] as humans do," he does not, in fact, share true human nature.[37]

One of the first examples of Krishna's power comes in the form of his vanquishing the demoness Putana. One day, Putana changed into a beautiful woman who walked through Vraj, looking for children to kill. She came into Yashoda's house and offered to nurse Krishna. Yashoda, believing her to be an eminent woman because of her beauty, agreed; but when Putana put Krishna to her breast, Krishna sucked not only the poison from her breast, but took her life breath as well. As she was dying, she turned back into her original form, horrible and terrifying to behold. The story, however, concludes with an unusual twist: in spite of her evil intention, because Krishna had suckled at her breast, she was immediately transported to *svarga*, the highest heaven. This illustrates that any type of contact with Krishna—indeed, even Kamsa's evil fixation on Krishna—can be salvific, because of who Krishna is.

This echoes another nursing story (recounted in full in the introduction to this book) in which Krishna's true nature and power are revealed when Yashoda sees the whole universe in sleepy Krishna's yawning mouth.[38]

There are many stories like this in which Krishna reveals his true form to his mother—if only for a moment. One more tells of a time when Yashoda was churning butter, which Krishna especially loved. While she was churning, Krishna got hungry, grabbed the stick and got in her way. She took him onto her lap and let him nurse for a bit until she realized that the milk on the stove was boiling over, and so she put him down before he was full. This made him angry, so he picked up a rock and broke the butter churn, running with the butter into his hiding place so he could eat it. When Yashoda came back and saw what he has done, she laughed—she couldn't help it—and she found him feeding some of the butter to a monkey. When she finally caught him, she tried to bind him with a rope, so he couldn't do any more harm, but although she used rope after rope the length was not enough to contain him: "Krishna has no beginning and no end, no inside and no outside. He is the beginning and end and inside and outside of the universe. He is the universe."[39] At last, Krishna took pity on his mother and allowed himself to be bound.

A Happy Cowherd

In such manner, Krishna spends his first few years—"in youthful games such as playing hide-and-seek, building dams and jumping about like monkeys."[40] Shortly after this, when he is still a little boy, he and Balarama, "the sole keepers of the whole universe," become the caretakers of the calves in the forest of Vraj, "a place which brings happiness in all seasons."[41] During this time, it is clear how beloved Krishna is, not

only by his human followers, but indeed by the whole creation—particularly by the calves he tends with the other cowherd boys. It is said:

> Even the grazing animals had a special love for the Lord, and
> lowed happily, whenever he caressed them, or came near,
> gathering about Him in a ring, to listen, whenever—standing
> with feet crossed beneath the beautiful Kadamba tree—He
> played upon His flute. Some say, indeed, that at such mo-
> ments the lotus-buds lying on the Jamuna waters opened,
> and the river itself bent out of its straight course.[42]

While in the forest, he continues his playful antics, performing
all sorts of amazing feats on a regular basis. For example, he kills the
demon Baka, who has assumed the form of a great crane. The demon
actually swallows Krishna, but only for a moment: Krishna is furious,
and burns Baka's throat like fire, causing him to be disgorged. As
Baka comes toward him again, Krishna effortlessly tears him apart by
his beak, to great rejoicing by the other cowherd boys.

Another interesting episode during this time illustrates how, in
the *Bhagavata Purana*, Krishna is depicted as the supreme god above
all gods. At one time, Brahma, the creator, comes to Vrindavana and
leads away all the other young calf-herders and their calves. Krishna
searches all over for them and cannot find them; immediately, he realizes what Brahma has done, and provides an astonishing solution:

> Thereupon Krishna, the Lord and maker of the universe,
> transformed his own self into both [the calves and the boys]
> in order to give pleasure to the mothers of those [calves and
> calf-herders] as well as to Brahma. He took the form of as
> many little bodies of calves and calf-herders as there were
> calves and calf-herders, with as many hands and feet and
> bodily parts...Then Krishna took care of his calves, who
> were his own self, by himself in the form of the calf-herders.
> The Self of everything entered Vraj, playing games with him-
> self [in the form of the calves and boys].[43]

In other words, to avert any anxiety about the missing children
and cows, Krishna manifests himself as each and every calf and boy
for an entire year, fooling their mothers and all the people of Vraj.
Brahma, seeing what Krishna has done, pays him homage, confessing
that even he is not able to understand Krishna's greatness. Brahma
worships Krishna, praising him as "the one self, the supreme being, ancient, the truth, self-effulgent, unlimited, original, eternal, imperishable,

perpetually happy, immaculate, complete, without a second, and free from limitations and death."[44]

Another famous story from this period of Krishna's life tells of his battle with Kaliya, the snake demon who was polluting the Yamuna River with his poison. The problem came to Krishna's attention when his fellow cowherds and their cows, made thirsty by the heat of the day, drank from the poisoned river and immediately fell down dead. Krishna did not let them lie lifeless for long: "A few minutes passed, however, and the tears of Krishna brought them all back to life. For His mercy and love could not fail to give life and strength, and He poured them out in abundance over His fainting friends."[45]

His friends thus restored, Krishna took steps to purify the river and banish the snake. He climbed a tall tree, dove into the river, and immediately began to wrestle with the demon. Kaliya bit Krishna in his "tender parts" and coiled his body around him, distressing Krishna's friends on the shore who were watching the action. All of this was nothing but sport to Krishna, however, and the text makes clear that Krishna was never in any real danger. Instead, entirely without fear, he toyed with Kaliya, like a child plays with a rubber snake. Finally, Krishna climbed up on Kaliya's hoods (from this we assume Kaliya to be a many-headed cobra) and began to dance, his powerful feet crushing Kaliya's heads with each rhythmic step. Kaliya is thus "danced" into submission; recognizing Krishna's power, he worships Krishna and retreats to the ocean. The story concludes that the Yamuna river is freed from poison by the great lord who "assumed a human form for sport."[46]

Stories like this fill Krishna's biography, consistently surprising those who forget that Krishna only *appears* to be a young boy; but for those who know his true identity, "there is nothing in this that is astonishing for Krishna. By his *maya* potency, he [appeared] as a small human boy, but he is the supreme creator of both the highest and the lowest."[47]

Another key component in Krishna's life as a cowherd can be found in his relationship to the *gopis*, the cowherd girls who are devoted to him. One story in particular, in which Krishna dances with them, will be discussed at the end of this chapter; it is one of the two paradigmatic stories that will be mined for their salvific efficacy in the following chapter. However, a similar story can be told here. One day, the *gopis* were bathing naked in the river at sunrise, singing songs about Krishna, and thinking only of him. When Krishna and his young companions came upon them, he gathered up their clothes and climbed up a tree. The *gopis* were shivering in the water, but did not dare come out and retrieve their clothes and show their nakedness. Krishna laughed and teased them, telling them that if they were really his servants, they would do as he said and come out to get their clothes. At this, the *gopis* covered themselves as best they could with their hands and came out of the water. Krishna was pleased at this, and gave them back their clothes. The text says that while they certainly had cause to be angry, "they were not really upset with Krishna. They were delighted to be in the company of their darling."[48] This erotic play is a central way in which Krishna interacts with his devotees and reflects the passionate love he engenders in those who worship him—both men and women.[49]

Krishna passes the rest of his childhood this way—enjoying the company of his brother Balarama, dispatching demons, playing with the *gopis,* and just generally delighting in his friends, the forest, and his own being. What's more, it is this "delight" that is at the heart of Krishna's existence during this time. The text is clear that Krishna's play is his purpose—it is not a means to an end, but the end itself: "Krishna's entire sojourn in Vrindavana serves no 'purpose.'...Only when demons appear, in most cases sent by Kamsa to kill the child, are we reminded of Krishna's ostensible mission. The way in which Krishna deals with these adversaries, however, does not break the mood of playful freedom that fills Vrindavana while Krishna is there."[50]

Krishna's Adult Life and Death

The event that marks the end of Krishna's childhood and the beginning of his adult life is his killing of Kamsa, the evil king who had tried to kill him at birth and never stopped trying to destroy him throughout his youth. Kamsa has decided to summon Krishna and Balarama to the city of Mathura, under the pretext of a public wrestling competition. Once they arrive, Kamsa plans to have them killed, one way or another, and then he will kill their relatives and all his enemies along with them. When Kamsa's messenger, Akrura, comes to the boys to explain what Kamsa wants—and what he has in store for them— they simply laugh and agree to come at once. They leave the forest, amidst much weeping by the *gopis,* and as they come into the city, the women immediately fall in love with Krishna and shower him with flowers from their windows.

This scene echoes the same theme that can be found in many of the stories—Krishna is not only the most powerful god, the supreme god of the universe, but is also exceedingly beautiful, which is a central aspect of his perfection. David Kinsley writes,

Another and obvious characteristic of the cowherd Krishna is his surpassing beauty. Beauty is not an attribute of Krishna alone. Many Indian gods are known for their beauty and grace. But Krishna surpasses them all. He is the embodiment of that otherworldly grace, that astonishing divine beauty that transcends the ordinary world and attracts all who behold it. His every characteristic is the most beautiful, the most relishable.[51]

After being adulated throughout the city, the boys come to the wrestling arena and the contest begins. At the gate of the arena, Krishna kills the great elephant, Kuvalayapida, who had been stationed there by Kamsa, and as they enter, it is clear to all that they are invincible, and the entire crowd is dazzled by their radiance: "At the sight of those two singular men, the people on the platforms—both country and city folk—drank in their faces with their eyes but remained unsatisfied... Their faces and eyes bloomed with a surge of happiness. It was as if they were devouring [them] with their eyes, licking [them] with their tongues, smelling [them] with their noses, and embracing [them] with their arms."[52] The wrestling match begins and, one by one, Krishna and Balarama kill each of their adversaries, until the remaining wrestlers run away from the competition. At this point, Krishna confronts Kamsa directly, killing him quickly, ending his evil reign.

This more or less ends part one. The story continues in part two, but in a very different vein. It begins with Krishna meditating on the purpose for his descent to earth—to remove the evil kings, relieve the burden of the earth, and protect the righteous. (It should be noted that this purpose complements, but does not supersede, the "purpose" of play for which Krishna also came to earth. Even in part two, Krishna is described as the one "whose human form is for the purpose of sport."[53]) This part of Krishna's story climaxes in the events of the *Mahabharata*, particularly the *Bhagavad Gita*, but part two also describes at length how Krishna defeats the various wicked kings who cross his path.

In addition, part two also is taken up with the description of Krishna's various marriages, as he seems to fulfill the proper dharma of a householder. However, as in part one, the reader is reminded repeatedly that Krishna only *appears* to be a mortal husband; in reality, he is perfectly self-contained and only acting a part—or, more accurately, acting 16,000 parts, which is the number of wives Krishna takes. With the same powers of illusion he showed as a boy, he manifests himself to each wife individually so that each thinks that he is hers alone. The text reports that Krishna has his own private inner city in Dvaraka, in which were found 16,000 different palaces, where Krishna lived simultaneously with each wife: "Thus, following the ways of humans, [Krishna] manifested his *shakti* powers for the liberation of everyone. He enjoyed himself with 16,000 of the choicest women . . . delighting in their laughter, their glances, their affection and their shyness."[54]

Book ten of the *Bhagavata Purana* ends with an exhortation to surrender to Krishna and to listen to a retelling of his deeds: "By thinking about, reciting and hearing the beautiful stories of [Krishna], which constantly become more in number, a person [attains to] his incomparable abode, and overcomes death."[55]

The Death of Krishna

An account of Krishna's death appears in book eleven, which recounts that after Krishna had fulfilled the mission for which he came to earth, the creator god Brahma and the other gods came to see him at his home in Dvaraka. After a lengthy discourse of praise and adulation, Brahma said,

O master, we previously asked you to remove the burden of the earth, a task which has now been accomplished, O unlimited soul . . . Assuming an incomparable form, you incarnated in the Yadu dynasty and performed extraordinary deeds for the benefit of the world . . . Nothing of the world of the gods remains to be done, O support of everything . . . Therefore, return to your supreme abode, if you care to, and protect us, the rulers of the worlds, along with the worlds.[56]

Krishna agrees that the time is right for him to return to the heavens. After a long discourse to his faithful follower Uddhava about the nature of reality and the means to liberation, Krishna allows events to unfold that he knows will lead to his death. It is important to note that in what follows, at every step of the way, Krishna is in full control of the proceedings: nothing happens that he is not aware of, and nothing occurs that he does not permit. There is no question of assuming that somehow Krishna is overpowered or surprised by forces beyond his control. Even in death, Krishna remains the supreme ruler of the cosmos.

First, through his power of illusion, Krishna allows the warriors of his own dynasty, the Yadus, to destroy themselves through infighting. This was to fulfill a curse that had been put on them by a group of sages, a curse that Krishna knew about and permitted, and also to ensure that he did not leave another powerful dynasty upon the earth to become another burden. When this was accomplished, Krishna sat down under a banyan tree in meditation, with one foot crossed over the other, manifesting himself in his true form, just as he did at birth.

A hunter named Jara mistakenly thought Krishna's "reddish lotus foot" was a deer and shot him—another event that Krishna both permitted and desired. As he was preparing to ascend to his heavenly abode, the gods gathered, eager to see his departure from earth. The text records that they were "crowding the sky with rows of celestial vehicles, and filled with great devotion, they showered down streams of flowers."[57] Then, through his powers of concentration, he ascended into heaven, but no one was able to see him, not even the gods, "since his path is unknown. As mortals cannot trace the path of a moving lightning flash which has left a ring of clouds, so the path of Krishna could not be traced by the gods."[58]

Today, Krishna is remembered in the Hindu calendar first and foremost on his birthday, which is celebrated in August or September in a festival called *Janmashtami*. The *Janamashtami* celebration takes place over two days, during which time Hindus are likely to forego sleep and instead sing traditional Hindu songs that celebrate Krishna. It is believed that Krishna was born at midnight and this is when the true festivities commence. Food is prepared from milk and curds, which Krishna particularly favored. Dances and songs are used to venerate and remember him, and plays are also carried out to reenact particularly memorable scenes from Krishna's childhood. In temples, images of Krishna are bathed and placed in cradles, and special mantras are also chanted.

Two Key Stories of Krishna's Childhood

With this background in place, we turn to a soteriological question to reflect upon what is "saving" about Krishna's life, and what is salvific about the relationship that he has with his devotees. Two well-known stories from Krishna's childhood are in many ways paradigmatic for teasing out the theological and soteriological meaning of Krishna's young life.

The Vision of the Universal Form

This first story is easily one of most famous stories in Krishna's biography. Incidentally, it also has important resonances with another theophany (divine revelation) of the same name that occurs in the context of a conversation between Krishna and Arjuna in the *Bhagavad Gita*. That text and that particular episode will be discussed at length in a later chapter.

The background to this particular story is the love Krishna's mother, Yashoda, has for her son and, indeed, the love all the *gopis* have for Krishna, even when they become exasperated at his playfulness. It is clear in the Krishna mythology that Yashoda's love for Krishna is meant to be exemplary, reminding all Krishna's devotees that the sheer joy and delight a mother takes in her child should be part of the love one experiences for Krishna. As Diana Eck writes:

> Hindu Vaishnavas insist that the most spontaneous and unconditioned love is that of parents for a child, and the adoration of the child Krishna in the Hindu tradition is very popular. In every Vaishnava household one would very likely find one particular figure among the *murtis*, the "images," on the home altar: the child Krishna on his hands and knees, crawling with a ball of butter in one hand. He is affectionately called *makan chor,* the "butter thief" who manages to get his little hand into the pot of freshly churned butter no matter how assiduously his mother tries to keep it out of his reach. She scolds him, but even in her scolding it is clear that the naughty little Krishna has stolen more than butter. He has stolen hearts.[59]

The story is told that one time when Balarama and Krishna were playing with the other boys, Balarama and the others complained that Krishna had eaten mud. Yashoda was concerned about Krishna's well-being and, taking him by the hand, she scolded him for what he had done. Krishna, however, protested: "Mother, I didn't eat any mud. They are all spreading false accusations. If you think they are speaking the truth, then you look into my mouth yourself." "If that is the case, then open wide," she said. The story goes on:

> Lord Hari [Krishna], whose supremacy cannot be constrained, but who is God assuming the form of a human boy for play, opened wide. Yashoda saw there the universe of moving and non-moving things; space; the cardinal directions; the sphere of the earth with its oceans, islands and mountains; air and fire; and the moon and the stars. She saw the circle of the constellations, water, light, the wind, the sky, the evolved

senses, the mind, the elements, and the three *guna* qualities [goodness, action, and inertia]. She saw this universe with all of its variety differentiated into bodies, which are the repositories of souls. She saw the time factor, nature and *karma*. Seeing Vraj as well as herself in the gaping mouth in the body of her son, she was struck with bewilderment: "Is this actually a dream? Is it a supernatural illusion, or is it just the confusion of my own intelligence? Or is it, in fact, some inherent divine power of this child of mine? Therefore, I offer homage to his feet, which are the support of this world. From them, and through their agency, this world manifests. Their true nature cannot be known by the senses nor by reason. They are very difficult to perceive by thought, words, deeds or intellect. He is my refuge. Through his illusory power arise ignorant notions such as: I am me; he over there is my husband; and this is my son; I am the virtuous wife, protectress of all the wealth of the ruler of Vraj; and all the *gopis* and *gopas*, along with the wealth derived from the cattle, are mine." Then the omnipotent supreme Lord cast his *yogamaya* [divine power of illusion] in the form of maternal affection over the *gopi* [his mother Yashoda], who had come to understand the truth. Immediately, the *gopi's* memory was erased. She sat her son on her lap and returned to her previous state of mind, with her heart full of intense love. She considered Hari [Krishna], whose glories are sung by the three Vedas, the Upanishads, Sankhya *yoga* and the *Satvata* sages to be her very own son.[60]

The meaning of this story is clear, and emphasizes the same point that was made in the previous infancy narrative, recounted in the introduction: while Krishna might have the appearance of a baby, he is still the supreme lord of the cosmos. For a moment, then, the mind of Yashoda was illumined and she understood the true nature of her son—and indeed the true nature of reality—but only for a moment. This story concludes by explaining how Krishna caused his mother's mind to be erased, so that once again, she understood herself simply to be a mother holding her infant son on her lap.

The Rasa-lila

A second significant story is called Krishna's *rasa-lila*, which means "pastime play," and refers specifically to his dance with the *gopis*, the young girls herding cows. Diana Eck describes it this way:

"In one of the most beloved episodes [of Krishna's life], Hindus recall how Krishna the cowherd used to beckon the milkmaids to the forest in the middle of the night to dance the great circle dance. They came, risking everything, and Krishna miraculously multiplied himself to dance with each and every one of them."[61]

According to Hindu tradition, this episode in Krishna's life is said to have occurred when he was between seven and ten years old. When reading the story for the first time, it is helpful to keep Krishna's age in mind, as well as the purity of his love, since, for Christian ears, there is an erotic flavor to this story that seems quite inappropriate for the Divine. However, it is a misinterpretation to attribute to Krishna any impure or carnal motives in his interaction with the *gopis*. As Steven Rosen writes, "The tradition is clear that Krishna has no prurient interest, nor does he have lascivious motives, at least not as commonly understood. His love for the *gopis*, and theirs for him, is pure."[62]

Indeed, in one account of this story, the love the *gopis* have for Krishna is described in terms of pure joy and light:

> Most wonderful of all was the love that the Gopis had for Him, as they romped and frolicked and tended the herds in the beautiful forests of Vrindaban. It was a love without any selfishness. When Krishna was near, they felt themselves lifted into a golden atmosphere, where all was gaiety and lightness of heart; nothing seemed serious or troublesome; and their happiness bubbled over in the form of gentleness and play.[63]

In the *Bhagavata Purana*, the story of Krishna's *rasa-lila* is told over several chapters, beginning with Krishna playing his flute, enticing the *gopis* to come join him in the forest under the full moon. Upon hearing the music, all the women immediately drop whatever they are doing—milking cows, cooking, eating, putting on makeup—and go to be near Krishna: They are "in a state of rapture." Even those who cannot be with Krishna in person, but only meditate on him from their homes have "left their bodies" and, united with him, relate to him as their supreme lover. Krishna teases them, plays with them, embraces them, and sings with them. At one point, he vanishes, causing the *gopis* to search longingly for him, acting out his miraculous deeds and praising him in song, longing for his return and saying, "Your Lordship is our life." As they continue to sing, weeping, Krishna reappears in their midst—immediately changing their sorrow to joy—and once again delights in their company on the banks of the Yamuna River. At this point, the *rasa* dance begins:

Govinda [Krishna] began the *rasa* pastime there, in the company of those devoted jewels of women, who linked arms happily together. The festival of the *rasa* dance began, featuring a circle of *gopis*. The Lord of all *yogis*, Krishna, inserted himself between each pair of *gopis*, and put his arms about their necks. Each woman thought he was at her side only... There was a tumultuous sound of bracelets, ankle-bracelets and the bells of the young women in the circle of the *rasa* dance with their beloved. Krishna *Bhagavan*, the son of Devaki, was radiant in their company, like a great emerald in the midst of golden ornaments... They were intent on amorous pleasure and overjoyed by Krishna's touch... The *gopis*, with glowing faces, cheeks adorned with locks of hair, and lotus flowers behind their ears, were beautiful. They danced with the Lord in the circle of the *rasa* to the musical accompaniment of the bees complemented by the sound of their anklets and bangles. Wreaths of flowers fell from their hair. Thus Krishna, the Lord of Lakshmi, sported with the beautiful girls of Vraj with freely playful smiles, amorous glances, and with caresses and embraces. He was like a child enraptured by his own reflection... Although content within himself, the Lord became manifest in as many forms as there were *gopi* women, and enjoyed himself with them in *lila* pastimes.[64]

Krishna, it is said, "lives within the *gopis*, their husbands and all living beings. He is the supreme witness who has assumed a form in this world for the purpose of sport. Manifest in a human form, he indulges in such pastimes as a favor to the devotees. Hearing about these, one becomes fully devoted to him."[65] How and why Krishna's interactions with his mother and with the *gopis* are salvific, and what they say about who Krishna is and how he saves will be the subject of chapter 3.

3

Krishna and His Followers

HOW HE SAVES

How radiant!—fresh butter in his hand,
Crawling on his knees, his body adorned with dust,
Face all smeared with curd,
Cheeks so winsome, eyes so supple,
A cow-powder mark on his head,
Curls swinging to and fro like swarms of bees
Besotted by drinking drafts of honey.
At his neck an infant's necklace, and on his lovely chest
The glint of a diamond and a tiger-nail amulet.
Blessed, says Sur, is one instant of this joy.
Why live a hundred eons more?[1]

The previous chapter introduced the reader to Krishna, setting him in context with a brief overview of Hinduism, a short discussion of Vishnu, the god of whom Krishna is believed to be an *avatar*, or incarnation, and then outlining a general biography of Krishna's life, taken primarily from the tenth book of the *Bhagavata Purana*, an unabashedly Vaishnava text.[2] The chapter ended with a detailed narration of two of the most well-known and important stories from Krishna's childhood: the theophany of his universal form to his mother Yashoda, and his *rasa-lila*—his playful dance with the *gopis*. It is now time to examine those stories in light of soteriology, asking what significance they have for understanding how Krishna saves, and what salvation looks like in the life of his devotees.

Three primary soteriological insights can be drawn from these two stories in particular, as well as Krishna's young life as a whole. First, Krishna's *lila*—the playfulness that characterizes so much of his childhood—tells us about who Krishna is and how he saves, and also what this means in the life of his devotees. In particular, I suggest that his playfulness creates a bond with his devotees, calling them

49

into a relationship with him. In more general terms, Krishna's play is what breaks down the barriers that keep individuals from coming to be in relationship with God.

This leads directly into the second point, the kind of relationship Krishna facilitates with those who worship him. I maintain that the young Krishna does not desire to be worshiped in awe, nor does he desire to be feared; instead, Krishna desires that his devotees enter into an intimate relationship of pure love and devotion with him, modeled on the relationships a mother has with her child and a woman has with her lover. This particular invitation is what moves his devotees to love him wholeheartedly and devote themselves to him completely. Again, in more general terms, it is this relationship that allows individuals to give their lives over to God.

Finally, these stories provide an insight into the true nature of reality. The ultimate goal for Hindus is to be released from the endless cycles of rebirth and the suffering that characterizes this existence. In creating this deep devotion among his devotees, Krishna is able to turn people away from the illusory pleasures of this world and their clinging to material existence in order to fix their minds on God and the divine abode that will be their eternal home. In other words, Krishna reveals to individuals the true nature of existence and teaches them to focus their hearts and minds on what really matters, the supreme one who will finally release them from suffering.

The Saving Grace of *Lila*, or Play

As noted in chapter 2, the young Krishna is particularly beloved by Hindus. Even though his adult life, particularly as recounted in the *Bhagavad Gita*, is also well-known and celebrated, by general consensus, "it is apparent, nevertheless, that the Hindu tradition at a very early date bracketed Krishna's childhood and youth...as the most sublime aspect of his biography or revelation."[3] Moreover, when one examines the stories told about that time in Krishna's life, the one word that occurs over and over in the texts is "playful." It is the adjective used to describe him in practically all of his youthful exploits, not only when he is with his family and friends, but also when he is dispatching this or that demon. The stories make clear that even when engaged in such life-and-death matters, Krishna's own playful attitude and the spirit of play that surrounds him are not altered.[4]

Yet, after the end of part one in the tenth book of the *Bhagavata Purana*, the word hardly shows up again—and it never appears in the

Bhagavad Gita. Clearly, then, this word points to a unique quality that characterizes Krishna during this specific time in his life—his infancy and youth. Just as clearly, there is something "sublime" about this playfulness that has been picked up and celebrated by Hindus throughout the centuries.

By contrast, the words "play" and "playful" are never used to describe Jesus in the Bible—and in fact, I would venture to guess that in over two millennia of writing and teaching in the Christian tradition, those words can't have been used in a Christological context over a handful of times, if even that many. All the more reason, then, why Christians should learn more about Krishna, "the divine player *par excellence* of Indian religion,"[5] and come to understand what saving significance such divine play might have. It is helpful, then, to take a closer look at this concept of play and to elaborate on how it draws individuals to Krishna and how it creates the possibility of a loving relationship with him. I maintain that this occurs through two insights: first, the revelation that God is joyful, and second, the transcendence of the distance between God and humanity, which creates feelings of deep affection for God.

What Does the Word "Play" Mean?

In his discussion of the term *lila*, Edwin Bryant notes that "unlike the term 'sport' or even 'game,' then, which might contain a suggestion of drivenness or competition, *lila* is pure play, or spontaneous pastime"—it is God rejoicing in creation simply from "fullness of spirit."[6] Some analogies from human experience can help illustrate what is being described here. *Lila* refers to the exhilaration of children playing in the year's first big snowfall. *Lila* refers to the joy of relaxing in warm ocean waves under bright sunshine. *Lila* refers to the happiness a mother gets from cooing at her infant, making faces at him, and delighting in his returned smile. *Lila* refers to the pleasure lovers feel in each other's company, waking up together in the morning and talking softly about nothing while lying in each other's arms. *Lila*, then, has no ulterior motive and no additional purpose other than the simple experience of joy—far from being simply a means to an end, *lila* is the end: the play is the point.

This is one reason why most children play much better than most adults: once you are an adult, work replaces play as your primary mode of activity in the world. The driving question motivating your doings becomes, "What I am producing?" Adults are taught that their activity needs to have a goal, an assessable outcome, a product, while the very definition of play is opposed to such ends. Children, however, are under no such pressures—and if they are, it is a sad commentary on today's society. Instead, play is integral to the whole concept of what it means to be a child. Children live in the moment and they do not need a reason for playing with modeling clay, watching birds build a nest, riding a bike through the neighborhood, or building a fort with blankets and couch cushions. The sheer enjoyment of the experience is the whole point.

Thus, coming back to Krishna, this applies to his young life as well. In these years, Krishna literally lives for enjoyment, for pleasure, for play, and for delight. During his idyllic time in Vraj, this delight is his *raison d'être*. Without a doubt it is what makes this period in Krishna's life so unique and sets it apart from the rest of his time on earth. While the *Bhagavad Gita* is explicit and emphatic that the purpose of Krishna's incarnation is to rid the earth of evil kings, and while even in the *Bhagavata Purana* as a whole it is clear that Krishna has come to earth to destroy the demons and protect the righteous, part one of the *Purana*, the section that describes Krishna's youth, gives primacy of place to another purpose: "Krishna descends to engage in *lila*, or devotional pastimes."[7]

Lila is the whole point of Krishna's young life, and it has a special function, creating the conditions for a unique experience that Krishna shares with his followers: "*Lila*, then, is an opportunity for Krishna and his devotees to enjoy themselves in the blissful and spontaneous reciprocation of love."[8] In the end, then, it seems fair to say that *lila* is nothing more and nothing less than the unique form of Krishna's love that draws his followers to him, like the flame drawing in a moth. This love creates the conditions for a singular experience of salvation.

Play as the Expression of the Divine Nature

Any revelation of God always reveals something of Godself, even when the revelation itself aims at a different purpose. To take an example from the Judeo-Christian tradition, when God speaks to Moses from the burning bush, (at least) two things stand at the heart of that revelation. Ostensibly, the purpose of the revelation is to give Moses the specific instructions he is to follow in order to lead the Hebrew people out of their slavery in Egypt. But, first and foremost, God reveals something of God's true nature: God is the One who hears God's people in compassion and responds to their prayers; God is the One who is both just and merciful, and God is the great I AM WHO I AM, the God of Abraham, Isaac, and Jacob, who forever remembers the covenant God has made with the people. This revelation, then, not only reveals what God wants of Moses and what God's plan is for God's people, but who God is Godself.

In this same way, then, this divine revelation of Krishna reveals Krishna to be a god of play: playful creativity is Krishna's inherent nature. When we then extrapolate from this particular revelation to a more general concept of God, we can posit that Krishna also reveals play itself as a key attribute of divinity. In his study of Krishna's *lila*, David Kinsley writes, "While play is perhaps not a classic feature of the divine in all religions, in Hinduism it is typical of the gods and represents, I think, an appropriate expression of the unconditioned and transcendent nature of the divine in India."[9] Again, this idea of playfulness as a divine attribute is something we find almost nowhere in the Christian tradition. Thus, it behooves us to ask what the language of playfulness suggests about God's nature and God's activity in the world. Taking Krishna as our example, we can see how his playfulness reveals divine freedom, divine movement, and divine beauty.

Divine Freedom

First, the concept of divine play points to a God who is inherently free, inherently unconditioned, and inherently joyful, taking delight in God's own being, God's own creation, and God's own movement in the world. God does not need a reason for activity, and God does not need to justify God's dynamism with a purpose or a plan. As noted before, the play is the point, and God delights in it just as children do. Kinsley writes,

> Play, just as much as power, knowledge, and eternity, expresses the truth that the gods are not limited. For play expresses freedom; it is carefree and relatively unmotivated. Play is done for the fun of it, for no ulterior reason. As opposed to most other types of activity, it is intrinsically satisfying rather than instrumental. It is an end in itself.[10]

Krishna reveals to us a God who, like a child, laughs simply for the delight of hearing his own voice, runs simply for the joy of feeling her legs beneath her, and splashes around in a river simply for the pleasurable cool of the water on his body. As children take delight in simply being alive, so Krishna takes delight in simply being incarnate in the world.

It is worth noting that the language used in Hinduism to describe this playfulness goes far beyond what is found in Christianity. Take this example, for instance:

> The essential nature of the divine is shown to "exert" itself for no pragmatic purpose. It is shown to revel in its own incomparable joyful being by playing with itself, making love to itself, inciting itself to abandon itself. Krishna, the playful, charming cowherd boy who sports in Vrindavana, expresses the truth that the divine is most completely itself when it dallies aimlessly, overflowing itself in self-delight and self-generated rapture.[11]

It is hard to imagine a Christian theologian describing God as "making love to" Godself, and this sort of ecstatic abandon and "self-generated rapture" is more typically seen as a response to God, rather than God's own action. In the mystical tradition, for example, imagery of love-making, rapture, and delight is common on the part of human beings. However, Christians might have something to gain from this language even as it refers to God's own activity. As banal as it might sound, Krishna's *lila* reveals to us a God who is happy, who enjoys the experiences God has in the world with God's creation, and who takes intrinsic delight in being vibrant in the world. While Christians are used to describing God's "work" in the world, how would our understanding of God change if, taking a page from our Hindu brothers and sisters, we talked instead about God's "play" in the world?

Divine Movement

Second, the concept of divine play suggests a God who is inherently in motion, not detached, impassive, and static. Krishna reveals a god who is "not restful, silent, and still in its essence but constantly and restlessly moving in ecstatic play."[12] This image of God stands in sharp contrast to Greek philosophical concepts of a God who is an "unmoved mover," entirely removed from the world, and unaffected by the activities of creation. Instead, Krishna provides an image of God who is fully engaged with the world, thoroughly involved in the lives of God's creatures, and endlessly creative in God's activities. Because God is perfectly free, unconstrained, and ceaselessly generative, God's dynamism points to God's inherent creativity, through which God is continually doing a new thing in the world, continually bringing what is unique and original into being. This serves as a reminder that God is always present in the world in an active rather than a passive way, and that God always can be counted on to express Godself—to make the divine presence felt and known and to interact with God's creatures.

This dynamism is seen repeatedly in the stories of Krishna's youth as over and over Krishna engages the people of Vraj in endearing, surprising ways.

> The theophany of the child Krishna, then, expresses the nature of the divine as unconditioned...For the divine to become embodied as a child is eminently suitable, for they behave in similar ways. Each belongs to a joyous realm of energetic, aimless, erratic activity that is pointless, yet significant: pointless, but at the same time imaginative and rich, and therefore creative.[13]

Krishna's playfulness and energetic engagement with the world continue to be celebrated today among Hindus, particularly in the festival of Holi. This festival has its roots in a variety of different religious celebrations, but today it is primarily associated with Krishna.[14] The celebration, which can last up to sixteen days in some regions of India, occurs in the early spring. Three components of the festival are particularly relevant here. First is the overarching mode of rebellion and defiance of social norms. During Holi, a general mood of playfulness reigns, with more open flirting, mischievousness, and a loosening of social restrictions based on age, economic status, and gender. A second component involves throwing colored powder, paints, and water. Men and women both enjoy ambushing friends and strangers alike in the street and dousing them with a rainbow of colors. It is this practice that gives Holi the name, "the Festival of Colors." Third is the role of images of Krishna and his most beloved *gopi* lover, Radha. In some places, these images are swung together or paraded through the street while revelers dance around them, sing, and smear the images with colored powders. The celebration of Krishna's and Radha's love inspires a spirit of teasing and merrymaking that infects everyone around.[15]

Divine Beauty

A third divine attribute of play in Krishna's case is the link between God's playfulness and God's beauty. Krishna's beauty is legendary, and almost all descriptions of him emphasize his physical loveliness.[16] The connection between divine play and beauty concerns the non-utilitarian aspect of both—neither exists for some ulterior purpose or for some specific function or role. Instead, both beauty and play are ends in and of themselves. They exist for their own sake: "For beauty, like play, is an end in itself. It strives for nothing, achieves nothing. It is apart from the instrumental world of necessity. It belongs to that other world of abundance. It is part of a world of effortless grace, an ornamental thing that justifies itself by simply being, and so like play belongs appropriately to the divine sphere."[17]

The idea of beauty as a divine attribute is certainly not unknown to Christianity; indeed, the entire discipline of theological aesthetics is concerned with the connection between God and beauty. God has always been seen as both the source and the highest expression of the True, the Beautiful, and the Good.[18] What is different in the case of Krishna is the way in which Krishna's beauty is linked to his physical appearance: his body, his face, and his desirability. In other words, there is a blatantly erotic character to Krishna's beauty. Here is an example from the *Gopalavimshati*, a fourteenth-century South Indian poem written by Venkatanatha, commonly known as Deshika:

> On his ears hang rings of *langali* flowers;
> His dark hair shines with feathers of a peacock
> And thick red *bandhujiva* [hibiscus] blossoms;
> ...He holds the playful shepherd's crook
> In the tender sprout of his right hand;
> His other hand fondles the slender shoulders
> Of the lady who thrills at his touch—
> The hairs on her body shining stand erect.
> Lovely, dark as the monsoon cloud,
> His flute tucked into the folds of his yellow waist-cloth,
> And his hair shimmering with garlands of *gunja*-beads,
> Praise Him, tender lover of the *gopis*.[19]

To most Christians, this description might seem decidedly undivine, and more fitting for secular poetry than sacred text. However, Christians should remember the Song of Solomon before passing too censorial a judgment on these words. Many noted Christian theologians, particularly those in the Middle Ages such as Bernard of Clairvaux, believed that the erotic language of the Song of Solomon describes with deep meaning and insight the relationship between God and the soul. So, too, for Krishna, since his beauty is a means through which he expresses his playful nature, drawing his devotees to himself:

For of all the Hindu gods Krishna expresses most completely all that is beautiful, graceful, and enticing in the other world of the divine. He embodies all those things that are extra in life, all those luxuries and characteristics that are not necessary to life but without which life would not be worth living. He is witty, gay, careless, accomplished at dancing, singing, and playing the flute. He is loved with abandon and loves with abandon. He is surpassingly beautiful. He is irresistibly and bewitchingly charming. All that he does is executed with effortless grace and harmony.[20]

Play as Transcending Distance

The attractiveness of Krishna's beauty leads to the next important aspect of Krishna's *lila*, and that is the way he uses his playful antics to transcend the distance between the human and the Divine. Barbara Powell describes Krishna's behavior this way:

Naughty Krishna, though exasperating, brings supreme joy to His elders. Their anger never lasts long. He bats His lotus-like eyes, pouts His pretty lips, sheds a few counterfeit tears and before you know it the adult is overcome with love and sweeps the child up in her arms. The naughtiness is also partly a guise designed to obscure His Godhead from them. Were His contemporaries aware of His true identity, they would be too overawed to exchange the natural loving intimacies for which He incarnated Himself. They must mistake Him for an ordinary boy and so, like a regular boy, Krishna is sometimes a pest.[21]

Contrast this to the Christian tradition, even in the most loving and personal descriptions of Jesus Christ: the aspect of awe and majesty that Jesus evokes are never entirely absent. One simple example will suffice. Martin Luther wrote his Small Catechism as a teaching tool not only for pastors to use in churches and schools but particularly for ordinary people to use at home and with their children. Here, then, we can expect that the Christian faith will be presented in its simplest form, straightforward and clear, focusing only on what is absolutely necessary to know and remember. It is significant, then, that Luther begins every one of his very brief explanations of each of the Ten Commandments with the words, "We are to fear and love God." I find it striking that even when teaching young children about God, and presumably wanting to instill positive feelings for God,

Luther emphasizes that *fear* is a necessary and integral part of our relationship with God.

Of course, Christians know that they are not meant to interpret this religious type of fear in the same way that one might describe one's fear of strangers, of the dark, or of spiders. Instead, the reminder that Christians are to fear God serves to emphasize the awe and wonder one should maintain when coming before God. In his classic text, *The Idea of the Holy*, Rudoph Otto famously described the encounter with the Holy as an experience of the numinous—the aspect of the Divine that is a *mysterium tremendum*, a mystery that both draws one in and frightens one away. The response to such a God, described in one famous hymn as the "immortal, invisible, God only wise, in light inaccessible hid from our eyes," is dropping to one's knees and averting one's eyes, knowing that none can see God face to face and live.

There is nothing inherently wrong with this, of course, and it is quite a natural response to the God who is the Lord of the universe, Ruler of creation, King of kings, and so on—to use the imagery that has dominated the Christian tradition through the centuries. However, it should be clear that the relationship one has with such a God has its constraints, as it presupposes a certain distance, a certain respect, and a certain level of intimidation that precludes the possibility of intimacy. Incidentally, this is thought to be one reason why the Virgin Mary in particular and the saints in general have been so popular historically in the Catholic tradition—they are seen as more approachable, easier to relate to, and more sympathetic than either God the Father or Jesus Christ.

Juxtapose the image of a divine ruler, sitting enthroned in heaven, with a very different one: the baby Krishna, crawling around on all fours, stealing butter and teasing his mother and the other cowherd women. Obviously, the relationship Krishna inspires in those around him, particularly in the relationship he has with his mother, Yashoda, and his *gopi* lovers, is also very different. The intimacy here offers a very special sort of divine invitation: in Krishna's youthful exploits, the faithful see how "God, revealing himself as an infant, invites man [sic] to dispense with formality and undue respect and come to him openly, delighting in him intimately."[22]

Since we have no stories of Jesus' young childhood, it is impossible to know anything of the day-to-day relationship that his parents, and Mary in particular, had with him. Did she ever spank him? Put him in a "time-out"? Was he rebellious? The brief mention the Bible makes of Mary's explicit contemplation of her young son emphasizes the mystery and wonder with which she considers him. Both after the shepherds visit Jesus in the manger and after she and Joseph find the twelve-year-old in the temple in Jerusalem, Luke records that Mary "treasured" the words that were spoken about him, and kept them close in her heart. Beyond that, the Bible is silent.

By contrast, as was demonstrated in chapter 2, the Hindu scriptures are full of stories about Yashoda and Krishna, detailing the many ways he drove her to distraction, causing chaos not only in her household but in the households of others as well. In these stories Krishna seems no more than an ordinary little boy at play who encourages his mother, his cowherd friends, and the other women to respond to him accordingly. The tradition is clear, however, that this intimate, informal, up-close and personal relationship Krishna fosters is very intentionally and carefully managed by him, through the power of his *yogamaya*, or illusion.

It is instructive to revisit the story of the theophany of Krishna's universal form. Yashoda holds Krishna in her arms, scolding him because she has been told that Krishna was eating mud. He protests his innocence, and tells her she should look into his mouth for proof, and when she does, she sees the whole universe therein. She is completely bewildered and shocked, and the text says that she immediately offers homage to him as the omnipotent, supreme Lord. However, Krishna does not desire such awe-inspired veneration from Yashoda, and so the story concludes by telling how Krishna "cast his *yogamaya*" over his mother, erasing the memory of what she has just seen, and filling her heart with intense love and maternal affection. In this way, over and over, he appears and acts as a regular young boy— lifting the mask only when and where he chooses and quickly pulling it back down again in order to facilitate intimate relationships with his devotees. Steven Rosen explains it this way:

> After all, awareness of Krishna's Lordship evokes a sense of majesty and subservience before the Supreme. To enable his devotees to rise beyond this stage, with the ability to engage in intimate, loving exchange with him, he masks his divinity. Imagine the *gopis* getting angry at Krishna for stealing their yogurt and butter if they were aware of his supreme position in the cosmic scheme of things. Or consider mother Yashoda: Would she bother to chase after him or enjoy motherly affection if she were conscious that he is God?[23]

The kind of easy intimacy with and uninhibited love for Krishna that Yashoda and others are able to experience is believed by those who worship him to be superior to a relationship that consists primarily of philosophical reflection or dutiful worship. Thus, for devotees of Krishna through the succeeding centuries, this unique type of relationship that both Yashoda and the *gopis* have with Krishna is held as the highest standard and the goal for all Krishna's followers. Seen in this light, "Krishna's 'mischief' is far from ordinary. His life as an impetuous young boy is a gift to his devotees...Rather than evoking consternation, his rowdy pastimes ultimately serve a purifying function, healing and giving joy to all who take part in them. In short, these stories enable devotees to transcend the distance created by awe and reverence and situate them in a loving mood of divine intimacy."[24]

There is a lesson in all this for contemporary Hindus, as it points to the soteriological value of finding joy with God in the everyday activities of daily life, and meeting God just as one is, in the midst of mundane tasks and obligations. No extraordinary measures need to be taken; no special skills need to be developed. One need not leave one's home behind and go to the church or temple to seek God; instead, God is readily present while one is cooking dinner, or caring for children, or tending the garden.

> The story of Yashoda is charming, and it is also relevant for us. We need to respect the heroic quests which often characterize the path to spiritual wisdom, the great confrontations with life and death. But it would be a mistake to confine wisdom to heroic circumstances. Yashoda's example suggests that we do not need the extraordinary and the exotic; ordinary religious practice, persevering love in ordinary duties and relationships, can be the vehicle of divine presence and provide the opportunity for unexpected encounters with God. Life itself is infused with divine presence; the details of ordinary life can become the occasion for moments of vision.[25]

There may well be an infinite distance separating humanity from God, but in his infancy and youth, Krishna shows himself ready and eager to fully bridge it, inviting his devotees into a relationship characterized by simplicity, familial affection, and personal intimacy. For this reason, like no other divine figure in Hinduism, "[Krishna] most perfectly exemplifies the divine nearness, rare embodiment, extraordinary loveliness, and most astonishing acts of divine tenderness."[26] Unsurprisingly, then, as we have seen, in response to Krishna's activity in the world, he inspires the most tender expressions of love in his devotees. Let me conclude this section with an extended quote from Diana Eck, describing a store in India dedicated to the child Krishna:

In Vishvanath Gali, the most crowded of Banaras commercial lanes, there is one store that sells nothing but clothing and adornments for the child Krishna. It opens into the lane like a cupboard stocked with dazzling piles of color: blue, pink, and gold satin outfits, trimmed with silvery ribbon; tiny ornaments and necklaces; crowns and headdresses, tiny peacock feathers to top off the crowns; little silver flutes; little enameled eyes to add to an image at the time it is installed on the home altar. Visiting that shop with a friend and trying the little outfits on the brass image of the crawling Krishna, I had to admit that there is something in all of us that loves this sort of thing. There is a lightness and playfulness to it that is consonant with the spirit of Krishna devotion. No one imagines for a moment that Krishna needs the little blue satin outfit we have just slipped on around his arms or the tiny strand of beads we have put around his neck. Indeed, no one imagines that the world-spanning Krishna is confined to this little brass image at all. This acting out, this "playing house," has to do with us and the ability to bring our affections and sensibilities to the service of God.[27]

It is this last point Eck makes—Krishna's *lila* facilitating our "ability to bring our affections and sensibilities to the service of God"—that will be examined in the next section, which explores the soteriological efficacy of this loving relationship between Krishna and his devotees.

Saved in Relationship: Loving Devotion to Krishna

In *World Religions Today*, a popular college textbook, Hinduism is characterized with the phrase "myriad paths to salvation."[28] While chapter 2 here provides a taste of the diversity Hinduism contains, describing with any brevity the vast multiplicity of beliefs and practices that it encompasses would be impossible. However, when it comes to "paths to salvation," there are three particular "forms of Hindu religiosity" that dominate. The first, called *karma-marga* or *karma-yoga*, represents the path of duty and sacrifice; the second, *jñana-marga* or *jñana-yoga*, represents the path of knowledge; and the third, *bhatki-marga* or *bhakti-yoga*, represents the path of devotional participation.[29]

One path is not necessarily better than another—although practitioners within each camp might argue the superior virtues of their chosen path over and against the others. Instead, the particular way in which one chooses to live out one's faith often is determined by family, social status, personal disposition, and geographical location. The path that concerns us here is the third path, called *bhakti*, which encompasses the relationship of love and devotion that one cultivates with a specific deity.

The *bhakti* movement, which originated in South India, dates back to roughly the seventh century. A vast literature of songs and poetry written in vernacular languages developed along with this movement. In particular, the writings of the twelve poets called *alvars*, who lived between the sixth and tenth centuries CE and were believed to be deeply and fully devoted to Vishnu, are given pride of place in *bhakti* literature. They, along with the *Bhagavata Purana*, epitomize the true nature of the movement.[30] Thomas Hopkins writes that "in the *Bhagavata*, as for the Alvars, [*bhakti*] is a passionate devotion of one's whole self in complete surrender to the Lord, a total way of life that is not one way among many but the only way to true salvation."[31] Exclusive devotion to Krishna, however, really developed from the eleventh century onward, with such poems as the *Gita Govinda*, written by Jayadeva in the twelfth century and celebrating Krishna as the cowherd lover.[32] Since then, *bhakti* movements dedicated to Krishna have been a strong presence in the Hindu landscape and have spread into all of India and beyond.

What is probably still the most well-known Hindu tradition in North America is the "Hare Krishna" movement, or ISKON (International Society for Krisha Consciousness). This *bhakti* movement was launched by Swami Bhaktivedanta in New York City in 1965. Bhaktivedanta, who became a Krishna devotee in India, was challenged early on by his guru to "preach Krishna throughout the world." When he was sixty-nine, he finally got the opportunity to come to America, where he found a welcome in the hippie culture of the 1960s. Basically, he taught that chanting the god's name makes god present, and infuses the chanter with the bliss that is god's nature. In the United States, ISKON has lost much of its following, but in India it is still a growing religious presence.

Turning back to India, it is important to realize how strong a role the *bhakti* movements continue to play in contemporary Hinduism. Axel Michaels writes that "Devotionalism is currently the most popular form of religiosity in India,"[33] and there are good reasons for this. To be a *bhakta*, one does not have to have any particular level of education or special intellectual abilities, nor does one need to speak and/or read Sanskrit. One does not need to be a member of a certain caste, with certain privileges, nor does one need to have a certain level of wealth. This path is also freely open to women. In other words, anyone, in any condition of life, can live out the practice of devoting oneself in faithfulness and love to God—in fact, historically, tradition held that lower-caste Hindus, because of their "natural disposition" to service, are ideal candidates for this path, and actually are better *bhaktis* than high-caste Brahmins.[34]

Bhakti, then, is an equal-opportunity path and, in addition, it is a path with a high degree of emotional appeal, as it puts the believer in an intimate, personal relationship with a god who returns all the love she or he is given a hundredfold. Michaels writes that

> The Bhakti notion of god is extremely anthropomorphic and personal . . . the believers see themselves as the children of the god or as his servants (*dasa*) . . . The idea of god as a savior and redeemer, of the savior and "Descender" (*avatara*), who seeks the proximity of men [*sic*] to support them in their need, is also closely connected with Bhakti movements. On the other hand, the image of the united lovers, for whom there is no longer a painful, yearning separation, is a favorite metaphor for a successful or desired encounter with God.[35]

The gods most associated with the *bhakti* path are Shiva and Vishnu. As an *avatar* of Vishnu, Krishna is obviously included here as well. However, it is fair to say that because of who Krishna is and the kind of life he lived while on earth—especially the way he lived as an infant and young boy—Krishna is the deity above all who inspires devotees to follow the *bhakti* path. Indeed, one definition of *bhakti* says that "*Bhakti* is selfless dedication to the Bhagavat [supreme Lord], the *svarupa* [true form or essence] of which is Krishna."[36]

Some of the most fervent disciples of this path, including some of the most famous poets and songwriters, have favored Krishna with their love and devotion, even those who still consider themselves Vaishnavites. For example, the Vaishnava theologian Bhaktivinoda Thakur writes that "Krishna, among all manifestations of Vishnu, is an ocean of intimacy, and one can derive the highest bliss by becoming reestablished in one's eternal relationship with him, which is now dormant." He goes on to define the *bhakti* path this way:

> "Devotional service" (Bhakti-yoga) is the mystical path by which one can enter into a relationship with God—it supersedes all pious action, the cultivation of knowledge, and various mystical endeavors, such as yoga and meditation (though

in its practice it subsumes various forms of yogic mysticism). The science of this holy devotion is detailed in books such as the *Bhagavad-Gita* and the *Bhagavata-Purana*, but it is chiefly understood by associating with devotees who carry it in their hearts. The central practices of this path include singing the praises of God, chanting his names in regulated fashion, offering food to him as a sacrament of devotion, and worshiping his image in the temple or in one's home. Pure love of God is alone the ultimate fruit of the spiritual journey.[37]

Three characteristics of the *bhakti* path have special relevance to Krishna and his devotees: love, joy, and physicality.

Love and Eros

Far and away the most important aspect of the *bhakti* path is love—the love one feels for god, the deeply loving relationship one cultivates with god, and the love god returns to the disciple. For those on the *bhakti* path, this disposition and experience of love far outweigh any other type of relationship one might cultivate with the Divine, and Krishna, more than any other Hindu deity, embodies this passionate love: "Krishnaite Vaishnavas draw on the fact that Krishna is the embodiment of intimacy and love, qualities that, among all others, stand supreme."[38] There is no need to rehearse all the ways in which Krishna manifests love in the course of his young life; in particular, the love was embodied in Krishna's relationship with his mother and with the *gopis.*

What is particularly important to emphasize here, however, is the erotic quality of that love—and this certainly needs some explanation for Christian ears. Christians are used to a threefold distinction when it comes to love: *eros,* which refers to the kind of love partners and spouses have for each other and from which we get the word erotic (which leads to some unfortunate, and not entirely accurate, caricatures); *philia,* which refers to the kind of love we have for friends; and *agape,* referring to the kind of love that God has for God's people. *Agape* is not motivated by what one can get for oneself, but is instead moved by care and concern for the well-being of the other. It is this kind of love to which Christians have traditionally seen themselves called, and to which Christians have aspired, because it calls forth a response of charity, grace, and kindness toward poor and rich, weak and strong, friend and foe alike. It does not seek its own satisfaction, but only the good of the other. There is nothing inherently wrong with this focus on *agape* love, except that, over the course of time, the other two types of love, and particularly *eros*, were dramatically downplayed and even demonized in the church, so that *agape* became synonymous with the highest expression of Christian love, and every other form of love was seen as something less, something outside the church, and again, even something sinful.[39]

With Krishna, however, love is understood quite differently, and the erotic component of love is front and center. As we saw in Krishna's dance with the *gopis*, his physical passion and their amorous attentions toward him are a key part of the divine experience of love—and Krishna intentionally courts this physical, sexual response from the young women. In the *bhakti* tradition, the physical desire of the *gopis* for Krishna is a manifestation of the depth of their love for him, and it is this desire that later generations of devotees have sought to replicate. Indeed, this erotic love is even argued to be the highest form of love one can experience: "To be an intimate associate of God, particularly one with the intensity of love exhibited by the *gopis*, is the highest possible perfection of human existence in the Bhagavata."[40]

It should be noted that this type of love is not unknown to Christianity. In fact, the medieval mystics drew heavily upon the biblical imagery of bride and bridegroom as well as the language of ecstasy to describe their own profound, intimate experiences of union with Christ. Indeed, both male and female mystics described being penetrated by the arrows of God's love, ravished by Christ, and physically transported by divine rapture that left one weak, trembling, and feeling "inebriated"—sometimes for days. One needs only call to mind the image of Bernini's famous sculpture, "The Ecstasy of Saint Teresa," to remember the place such ecstatic—yes, even erotic—love has held in at least some expressions of Christianity.

This kind of rapture that Krishna invites points to the fact that such physical experiences of love are an integral part of the salvific relationship the devotee has with Krishna. It also points to the body as being a locus of salvation. In the *bhakti* relationship, the body is capable of receiving divine love, of expressing love for the Divine, and, indeed, the body is the place above all where the loving relationship with the Divine is experienced. Unlike the typical negative stereotype of sexual desire and physical affection, so prevalent in Christianity, that conflates love and lust, desire and domination, enjoyment and exploitation, Krishna invites his devotees into a deeply moving physical relationship that captivates all their senses and moves them at every level, inviting a full-body reply: "Krishna moves in a realm of love and lovemaking that invites (indeed, demands) a total, impassioned response. All those who enter this realm are freed from bondage to the ordinary and customary, freed to behave imaginatively and spontaneously. The erotic aspect of this other world is not degrading but life-affirming."[41]

This affirmation of the body and of the role of physical desire in the saving relationship one has with the Divine relates to another important theological and soteriological issue on which *bhaktis* express strong opinions. Arguing against those who would maintain that God cannot have a form, or that it is somehow higher or better—more spiritually advanced, if you will—to relate to a God without specific characteristics, Vaishnava philosophy posits that "if loving exchange is the highest activity, as most will admit, then God would most definitely deign to be a person—for loving exchange loses meaning without personhood; it can only exist between people."[42]

Note what is being argued here: love, which is unquestionably the highest expression of devotion and the most important aspect of the human-divine relationship, cannot truly exist without two partners— two players who can willfully and joyfully develop a connection that is personal, particular, and expressed and experienced in the material world. For *bhaktis*, the love of an abstract, transpersonal entity—even a divine entity—is decidedly inferior (and not really love at all). So, too, is the idea that the lover and the beloved are the same—the idea that while there appear to be two in an I/Thou relationship, in reality, there is only the divine I, and everything apart from the Divine is an illusion. Both of these two options for understanding and interpreting the divine/human relationship are thoroughly rejected by *bhaktis*:

> To describe the absolute as merely *nirvishesha*, or without quality and attributes, is to make Him imperfect by amputating, as it were, the auspicious limbs of His divine personality. Once the absolute, complete, and perfect nature of the Divine Being is recognized, the philosophy of impersonalism cannot consistently be maintained. The Bhagavad Gita clearly describes the Absolute as both personal and impersonal, or rather as possessing infinite attributes and forms, including an impersonal dimension. When this is properly understood, the conflicting statements of the Vedas and the Puranas can easily be reconciled. But according to the primary and general sense of the scriptures, the Absolute is essentially personal, because only in a personal Absolute, possessing infinite and inconceivable potencies, can the manifest forms of

Godhead, including the impersonal Brahman, have their place. In fact, complete monism, or Advaita Vedanta, would inadvertently obliterate the entire spiritual quest as we know it—for how can one worship oneself? On a practical level, it is simply not possible, leading to frustration and the abandonment of spirituality in general. But more to the point is this: If one is, in the ultimate sense, God, there is no need for submission to a superior spirit. There is no I and Thou, no relationship and no love.[43]

One certainly can say that in Hinduism, Krishna, more than any other god or goddess, creates, facilitates, and nurtures the I/Thou relationship with each and every one of his devotees, filling them with desire and bestowing upon them his abundant love. Two central aspects of this relationship, joy and physicality, which are reflections of this key characteristic of love, need also be briefly mentioned here.

Joy

Intimately related to the experience of love is the experience of joy. The love Krishna himself displays, and the love he calls forth from his devotees, is not the grave sort that demands austerity, somber reflection, or physical deprivation. Instead, as we have seen over and over in Krishna's biography, Krishna's kind of love is better described as reckless abandon, giddy excitement, and spontaneous outbursts of sheer glee. Krishna clearly takes delight in his playfulness, and he inspires delight in others, even as he exasperates them with his willfulness. It is clear, then, that a central part of what it means to be a devotee of Krishna is rejoicing in him, giving oneself over to the happiness of reading about him, thinking about him, and listening to the stories of his life. In short, a relationship with Krishna demands that one allow oneself to be carried away by the spirit of pleasure and play that permeates the whole of Krishna's young life.

It is this shared joyous play with the Divine, more than obedience, more than adoration, more than exultation, that characterizes the saving relationship a devotee has with Krishna: "According to the *Bhagavata* (10.47.58), to be an intimate associate of God able to play with him by participating in this *lila* is the highest possible perfection of human existence."[44] For it is in this shared play that the Divine and the human are joined in a union of absolute bliss—sheer joy and delight. All constraint is removed, all the boundaries that would separate god from humanity are bridged, and humanity's own inherent playful nature is set free to join with the Divine. As David Kinsley writes:

> *Bhakti*, like play, is nonutilitarian, transcending the barriers of pragmatic existence...It is superfluous activity that is undertaken as an end in itsel...Like play, it is also joyous, jubilant, and often merry, particularly when it is directed toward Krishna. *Bhakti*, then, seems to illustrate the fact that in his relationship to God man's nature as a player comes to the fore ...Or at least the implication is that the appropriate meeting ground [between God and humanity] is one of freedom and joy, where man is not bound by habit and necessity but is free to behave spontaneously.[45]

Physicality

Finally, it is important to note one of the key aspects of the Krishna/devotee relationship discussed above, and that is its corporeal character.

Francis Clooney offers the following description of Krishna: "When Hindus think of Krishna, they are thinking of a God who speaks to the human heart in a language we can understand, a God who appears with a face we can see. As the theologian Ramanuja put it in the eleventh century, Krishna is God—Lord Vishnu, Narayana—come down to this earth so that people can see and hear and touch God."[46] It is this seeing, this hearing, and, particularly, this touching that makes one's relationship to Krishna so powerful. There is a visceral character to this relationship that emphasizes its here-and-now aspect: one does not have to wait until death to experience Krishna's love and grace, nor does one have to reach a certain state of spiritual refinement or maturity. And, most certainly, one does not need to forget her body, deny her body, or be indifferent to her body to enter into relationship with Krishna. Instead, Krishna comes to his devotees right in the midst of their physical lives—their manual labors—right in the middle of their sweat, blood, and tears, incorporating all of it into the bond he creates with them. This is how he formed relationships when he was on earth, and this is how he continues to form relationships even now.

Contemporary devotees, then, look back to the *gopis* and to Yashoda herself to see how Krishna comes to those who worship him in the midst of their daily lives. This is one reason for the emphasis on telling and re-telling the stories of Krishna's infancy and youth and on the importance of imagining oneself as taking part in those stories. Imaginative play serves to make Krishna real for those who love him and make their experience of him more vivid:

> Traditionally, the deeds of the cowherd women are meant to be imitated by others, even those who have never actually seen Krishna. God can be approached and experienced if we remember, imagine, and allow ourselves to become actors in the drama of God's work on earth; as they play their parts devotees find, to their surprise and delight, that God comes and interacts with them too, in ways old and new. Such acts of remembering and imagining are very powerful, for they make it possible to experience anew God's mighty deeds from the past.[47]

The True Nature of Reality[48]

The most explicit aspect of Krishna's soteriological efficacy is what he teaches regarding the true nature of reality. This requires a brief explanation of a Hindu worldview. Like those in many Eastern religions, Hindus believe in reincarnation. That is, they believe that every soul goes through the cycle of birth, death, and rebirth (*samsara*) until that soul is released—which is called *moksha* or liberation—typically through right understanding, that is, the knowledge that the individual does not have permanent, enduring, discrete existence. Once this knowledge is achieved, upon death the person is completely obliterated—"de-individualized," if you will, and becomes one with the Absolute, ending the life cycle of that soul. In the meantime, however, one's karma determines one's rebirth: good karma produces good effects that are realized in one's next birth into a higher caste, for example; bad karma produces bad effects resulting in a lower birth as an animal, for example. This is a bare-bones description, of course, and Hindu belief and practice include many modifications and variations of these basic views.

Bhaktis comprise one such group that has adopted some variants in this soteriological schema. *Bhaktis* believe that God's grace ameliorates one's karma, and because God is all-powerful, God can at any time grant liberation to any person. Thus, *bhaktis* relate to God as their redeemer and savior, and they believe that the most important religious practice one can perform is wholehearted devotion and submission to God. This devotion results in liberation from the mundane world even in this life and guarantees that the individual will be able to continue his or her devotion after death: "The inner life of such a soul, then, allows one to be engaged in worldly affairs and, simultaneously, to be detached from such affairs, due to one's absorption in devotional love...For the devoted soul, death is conquered within this life through deep absorption in the beloved object."[49]

Not surprisingly, the end that is envisioned here is not perfect absorption into some impersonal Ultimate, but rather a kind of non-dualistic union with god that is eternal. In the case of Krishna, this often is envisioned as the everlasting joy of delighting in Krishna's presence and worshiping his "lotus feet" in his heavenly abode for eternity. In this view, if one speaks about "losing oneself," it is meant to carry more of a metaphorical connotation: "If there is any loss of the individualized self, it is not an ontological or metaphysical one, but a forgetfulness of one's own self through complete blissful absorption in meditation on God...the highest goal of life for the Bhagavata is to reside as an eternal individual in an eternal divine abode, rendering loving devotion to an eternal personal supreme being, Vishnu/Krishna."[50]

For his devotees, this is the end for which Krishna has come into the world, and thus his every move is geared toward their salvation as he pours on them grace upon grace in order to persuade them to give themselves over into his capable hands.

> [Krishna's] appearance in the world is seen as grace, pure and simple, a magic show, of sorts, performed for our benefit. In other words, his life in the material world has a soteriological function in that it is meant to cure us of our spiritual amnesia, reminding us of our real life in the spiritual realm—encouraging us to go back home, back to Godhead. His eternal pastimes are, ultimately, imported from the spiritual world, and he sometimes manifests them here, just to entice us.[51]

This is Krishna's whole reason for being, according to the *Bhagavata Purana*:

> Krishna is no longer regarded as having been born solely to kill a tyrant and rid the world of demons [an interpretation that we find in the *Bhagavad Gita*, for example]. His chief function now is to vindicate passion as the symbol of final union with God...The function of the new Krishna was to

defend these two premises—that romantic love was the most exalted experience in life and secondly, that of all the roads to salvation, the impassioned adoration of God was the one most valid. God must be adored.[52]

Krishna's particular playful character and loving, mischievous activities are one of the central ways in which he fulfills this function, drawing his devotees out of their preoccupation with transitory worldly matters into absolute devotion to himself. Through Krishna's irresistible attraction, beauty, and charm, he is able "to attract the souls lost in *samsara* [delusion and suffering] to the beauty of *lila* with God, and thus entice them to relinquish their attachment to the self-centered indulgences of this world of *samsara,* which simply perpetuate the cycle of *karma,* and thus of repeated birth and death."[53]

As might be imagined, given his surpassing popularity and his delightful character, Krishna has inspired a huge canon of devotional hymns and poetry in a wide variety of vernacular languages across the Indian subcontinent. One of the most important and well-known is the *Tiruvaymoli,* a central devotional poem for the Sri Vaishnava community in South India, written by the ninth-century poet Sathakopan (affectionately known as "Namalvar"). In this poem, he writes about "the salvific nature of thinking about Krishna's mischief" in the following words: "Leaving aside many kinds of knowledge that hit the mark, and penances performed over many ages, in this very birth, in a few days, I've attained their results, my heart follows my Lord who hid and ate in stealth the butter and milk in the hanging pot, ending the sorrows of being born."[54]

This poem points to one of the key beliefs of the *bhaktis*: devotion, particularly devotion to Krishna, is the superior soteriological aim, accomplishing in "a few days" what philosophical speculation, empty ritual, sacrifice, and physical austerities cannot accomplish in many lifetimes. This is also reflected in the *Bhagavata Purana,* where it is clear that those who relate to Krishna in love, yearning for a personal relationship with him, have a higher understanding of God than the *yogis* who have come to a more philosophical, de-personalized understanding of God.

The most significant incidents in Krishna's life are not the awe-inspiring demonstrations of power, but precisely the opposite. It is the quieter moments which strike a chord in the hearts of spiritual aspirants. Not so much what He does but what He *is* makes the difference. His gentleness, His playfulness, His sweetness and affection, His tender concerns for everyone, His bewitching smile, melting eyes and graceful movements, His genius and humor, everything together amounts to a Being ultimately worshipable as the Absolute Truth and yet infinitely lovable and approachable. His irresistible physical beauty and mesmerizing charm are far more indicative of His divinity than supernatural deeds because these are what grip the hearts of devotees and, in mystics, inspire ecstasy, *samadhi* and, eventually, God-realization.[55]

Devotion to Krishna is an unquestionably soteriological action—one that, by all accounts, is richly rewarding to all who undertake it.

Conclusion

Chapters 2 and 3 have introduced the reader to Krishna and also explained the soteriological significance of his infancy and youth. It should be clear that because an all-encompassing relationship of love with Krishna is viewed by his devotees as the superior path to salvation, the stories in which he is most approachable, most accessible, and most charming and attractive are of particular significance. It is during Krishna's boyhood, as in no other stage in his life, when Krishna is most willing and able to facilitate the type of relationship that is seen as salvific. Thus, it is that special relationship that Krishna had with his mother Yashoda and the *gopis* in particular that contemporary devotees most try to participate in and emulate in the course of their own daily lives. They do this by means of joyous celebration of Krishna in song and dance, single-minded meditation on his person and his actions, and recitation and reading of the stories of his life, particularly those of his youth. In all this, Krishna's devotees hope to receive his grace and the blessing of liberation both in this life and in eternity.

From this analysis of Krishna, then, Part 2 turns to Jesus Christ. Paralleling the methodology used in these two chapters, we will examine similar questions from the perspective of the Christian tradition.

PART II

Infant Christ

4

Immanuel

THE STORIES

Shifting now from Krishna to Jesus, it must be emphasized at the outset that the comparison of the stories of the two figures in their infancy and youth suffers from a grossly lopsided discrepancy between the raw data available for each. As noted in the previous chapters, a wealth of material is available about the young Krishna, while, as will be evidenced below, there is a paucity of information about the young Jesus—even when we look beyond the biblical canon and include the apocryphal gospels. As one commentator accurately observes, "The traditional Gospels provide sparse information about the infant years of Jesus. Apart from the birth stories in Matthew and Luke, and the Lukan story of the twelve-year-old Jesus in the Temple, these early 'hidden years' remain precisely that."[1] It is, then, at least to some degree, an unfair or weak comparison.

This fact in and of itself is important, and it pushes us to ask some key theological questions: Why isn't there more information about the young Jesus? Why is his role in the infancy narratives overwhelmingly passive, especially when compared to that of Krishna? And, finally, what do both the limited presence and the glaring absence of stories of Jesus' youth say about who Jesus is and how he saves? It is this final question that will be addressed briefly at the end of the chapter, after the stories themselves have been discussed, and then explored more fully in chapter 5.

While there is almost no information about Jesus prior to his baptism and the beginning of his public ministry in the canonical gospels, the primary story that does appear is almost universally known: the story of his birth, popularly branded as "the Christmas story." The "story" that most Christians know, the story that is depicted in nativity scenes of various configurations in yards, on mantels, and under Christmas trees across the globe every December, is typically an amalgam of two very different accounts of Jesus' birth, each having its own particular emphasis and context. The first step, then, is to look at each of these narratives independently, examining the unique picture each paints of Jesus, the specific circumstances of his birth, and their theological significance.

This delineation of the two stories is a critical step for several key reasons. While New Testament scholars agree that there is one historical figure, Jesus of Nazareth, who grounds all the various portraits of Jesus Christ painted by the authors of the different New Testament books, vigorous debate continues regarding the extent to which we can know this Jesus. The fact is that we simply do not have full access to the historical Jesus: all we have are portraits of him, and it is very clear that the authors were not neutral in their presentation of Jesus, nor were they concerned primarily with recording historical "facts" as defined today in a post-Enlightenment Western context.[2] Instead, the gospel writers described the one whom they had come to know and believe in as the Messiah, the Son of God. The point of their descriptions of Jesus was to convey this essential truth about his identity and to convince others of that identity so that they, too, might believe in him.

To that end, however, each writer took a slightly different tack, one emphasizing certain characteristics and aspects of Jesus' life and ministry and another emphasizing different facets—even telling different stories. Thus, as one New Testament scholar writes, it is helpful to think of the gospels as discrete "literary artworks":

> Each Gospel presents a portrait of Jesus that is distinctive from those of the other three. The temptation for Bible readers is to combine all four portraits in order to obtain as complete a picture of Jesus as possible. But doing that causes us to miss the particular image that each Gospel writer wanted to present. The goal of Gospel study should first be to recognize the four separate portraits that these individual books offer. When we focus on any one Gospel, and on that Gospel alone, what is the image of Jesus that emerges?[3]

What this means is that, in seeking to understand what the birth narratives reveal about who Jesus is and how he saves, it is important to distinguish between the pictures Matthew and Luke paint of the infant Jesus and the circumstances surrounding his birth.

After examining the accounts of Jesus' birth in Matthew and Luke, this chapter turns to the two most significant apocryphal gospels that treat Jesus' infancy and youth—the Infancy Gospel of James and the

Infancy Gospel of Thomas. These narratives are followed by a few theological hypotheses about what these various stories of Jesus' youth and infancy suggest about who Jesus is and how he saves.

A Tenuous Birth: The Birth Narrative according to Matthew

One important feature of Matthew's gospel that should be noted from the outset is that Matthew does not recount the specific details about Jesus' birth in the way Luke does. Instead of providing particulars, the writer of Matthew presents an overview, emphasizing only the events that further the gospel message he wants to convey, particularly those events that fulfill what was foretold of the Messiah by the Old Testament prophets.

In addition, particularly important in Matthew's story as a whole are those who rebuff Jesus. Barbara Reid observes that "each of the Gospels tells of those who not only reject Jesus but who actively seek to destroy him from the beginning of his ministry. Matthew begins this theme even earlier."[4] One way in which the theme of rejection plays out in Matthew is that at various key points in the birth narrative, Jesus' very existence is put at risk, and the dark specter of danger and peril hovers menacingly over the whole of his early life. Again and again Jesus' life hangs by a thread, and readers wonder how he is going to survive.

An Unheralded Pregnancy

Now the birth of Jesus the Messiah took place in this way.
When his mother Mary had been engaged to Joseph, but before they lived together, she was found to be with child from the Holy Spirit. Her husband Joseph, being a righteous man and unwilling to expose her to public disgrace, planned to dismiss her quietly. But just when he had resolved to do this, an angel of the Lord appeared to him in a dream and said, "Joseph, son of David, do not be afraid to take Mary as your wife, for the child conceived in her is from the Holy Spirit. She will bear a son, and you are to name him Jesus, for he will save his people from their sins." All this took place to fulfill what had been spoken by the Lord through the prophet: "Look, the virgin shall conceive and bear a son, and they shall name him Emmanuel," which means, "God is with us." When Joseph awoke from sleep, he did as the angel of

the Lord commanded him; he took her as his wife, but had
no marital relations with her until she had borne a son; and
he named him Jesus. (Mt 1:18–25)[5]

In Matthew's story of Jesus' birth, there is no cause for rejoicing—
indeed, no one at all seems happy that Mary is pregnant, least of all
Mary herself, and Joseph seems totally unsettled by the whole event.
Two things are of note in this account. First, Mary is completely ignored. It is Joseph who, with the help of an angel who comes to him
in dreams to reveal God's will, makes all the decisions in this account
of Jesus' birth. The account tells nothing of what Mary felt or thought;
there is no information about whether God came to her directly,
inviting her to participate in God's plan or communicating to her
what God intended to do in and through her. Similarly, there is no indication of what Mary felt toward Jesus. There is no record of what
she experienced during her pregnancy, what she felt toward the child
growing in her womb, nor is there any mention of her experience
during or after the birth—what, if anything, she thought when she
saw and held Jesus for the first time. For Matthew, Mary herself and
her relationship to her son appear to be entirely irrelevant, and he ig-
nores this key bond.
    Second, there is a tantalizing absence of adverbs in this account:
Did Joseph "take her" as his wife willingly or reluctantly? Did Mary
go into his household joyfully or resentfully? And, when Jesus was
born, was it an easy or difficult birth? Instead of presenting any elaboration of the experience of Jesus' parents, their reflections, their conversations, their day-to-day life as the child in Mary's womb grew, to
say nothing of the experience of the birth itself, Matthew provides a
bare-bones record of the simple facts: Mary was impregnated by the
Holy Spirit, Joseph kept her in his house, she bore the son promised
by the angel. Any indication that Jesus is in any way special or
unique comes only once, in the dream. Thus far, nothing in the real
world seems to verify what the angel has said.

Foreign Homage

In Matthew's gospel, the first event after Jesus is born is the arrival of visitors to honor him—foreign dignitaries of some sort,
"kings" in later Christian tradition.

In the time of King Herod, after Jesus was born in Bethlehem
of Judea, wise men from the East came to Jerusalem, asking,

"Where is the child who has been born king of the Jews? For we observed his star at its rising, and have come to pay him homage." Then Herod secretly called for the wise men and learned from them the exact time when the star had appeared. Then he sent them to Bethlehem, saying, "Go and search diligently for the child; and when you have found him, bring me word so that I may also go and pay him homage." ...When they had heard the king, they set out; and there, ahead of them, went the star that they had seen at its rising until it stopped over the place where the child was. When they saw that the star had stopped they were overwhelmed with joy. On entering the house, they saw the child with Mary his mother; and they knelt down and paid him homage. Then, opening their treasure-chests, they offered him gifts of gold, frankincense, and myrrh. And having been warned in a dream not to return to Herod, they left for their own country by another road. (Mt 2:1–2, 7–12)

What is important here is the recognition of who Jesus is—the rightful ruler of all nations—by representatives symbolizing every known corner of the earth. The homage of the wise men who have come from so very far away seems to signify the universal ramifications of Jesus' birth: it was significant not only for Jesus' own people, not only in Jesus' little corner of the world, but for everyone, in all places.

Here, finally, seems to be the verification of what the angel conveyed to Joseph, although there is no indication yet that Jesus is or will be a "savior." Instead, Jesus is treated as royalty; he is honored as though he will be king, born into a ruling family. He does nothing himself to warrant the homage, and the text does not tell us anything about whether or not Jesus is even aware of the presence of these wise men—although in many later artistic depictions of the event, Jesus is shown sitting up on his mother's lap, looking down at the kneeling wise men who are often dressed as kings, with one of his hands raised in a gesture of blessing, looking every bit the precocious ruler.[6] This will not be the only time that artists fill in what the gospel writers themselves leave out.[7]

Flight and Carnage

The scene quickly changes, however, to something much more sinister; and it is clear that not *all* the kings in the world honor and welcome Jesus.

Now after they had left, an angel of the Lord appeared to Joseph in a dream and said, "Get up, take the child and his mother, and flee to Egypt, and remain there until I tell you; for Herod is about to search for the child, to destroy him." Then Joseph got up, took the child and his mother by night, and went to Egypt, and remained there until the death of Herod. This was to fulfill what had been spoken by the Lord through the prophet, "Out of Egypt I have called my son." When Herod saw that he had been tricked by the wise men he was infuriated, and he sent and killed all the children in and around Bethlehem who were two years old or under, according to the time that he had learned from the wise men. (Mt 2:13-16)

Here again, the only member of the holy family who asserts any sort of agency is Joseph, and even Joseph does not seem to be able to act without first receiving instructions from a messenger of God. For a second time, without this divine intervention, Jesus well may have perished. Once again, for Matthew, the details seem unimportant: Did Mary doubt what Joseph told her (assuming he told her anything at all, a fact we have to infer from the story)? Did she resent the long trek into Egypt? Was Jesus fussy on the trip? What did they do while in Egypt? None of these questions are addressed as Matthew tells us only of the event itself, without any further explanation as to what was said or thought along the way.

Finally, it seems strange that Matthew's account of Jesus' birth closes with a terrible story of infanticide. After this tragedy occurs, what remains is a terse epilogue, telling the reader that once Herod dies, another angel comes to Joseph (again, always to Joseph!) to tell him it is safe to bring his family home, and thus they return to settle in Nazareth. End of story.

In Matthew's account, the very last act in the narrative of Jesus' birth is, ironically, a death—and not just one death, but a horrifying multitude of deaths that sets the whole village wailing. And where is Jesus when all this happens? He has fled the scene, assuredly not acting as the "savior" he was promised to be—in fact, quite the opposite. It can be argued that not only did Jesus not protect the children from slaughter, he himself was the cause of their deaths. The whole account leaves an unpleasant aftertaste. If Jesus himself has any divine power, there certainly is no evidence of it yet.

A World-Altering Event: The Birth Narrative According to Luke

Luke's telling of the birth of Jesus, while ostensibly an account of the same event, is radically different in almost every aspect. If one did not know better, one might well assume it was the story of an entirely different child, born under entirely different circumstances.

Mary as Prototype

One of the most noticeable and important differences between the accounts of Matthew and Luke is the role Mary plays. While in Matthew she is marginal at best, in Luke she takes center stage from the opening chapter.

> In the sixth month the angel Gabriel was sent by God to a town in Galilee called Nazareth, to a virgin engaged to a man whose name was Joseph, of the house of David. The virgin's name was Mary. And he came to her and said, "Greetings, favored one! The Lord is with you." But she was much perplexed by his words and pondered what sort of greeting this might be. The angel said to her, "Do not be afraid, Mary, for you have found favor with God. And now, you will conceive in your womb and bear a son, and you will name him Jesus. He will be great, and will be called the Son of the Most High, and the Lord God will give to him the throne of his ancestor David. He will reign over the house of Jacob forever, and of his kingdom there will be no end." Mary said to the angel, "How can this be, since I am a virgin?" The angel said to her, "The Holy Spirit will come upon you, and the power of the Most High will overshadow you; therefore the child to be born will be holy; he will be called Son of God. And now, your relative Elizabeth in her old age has also conceived a son; and this is the sixth month for her who was said to be barren. For nothing will be impossible with God." Then Mary said, "Here am I, the servant of the Lord; let it be with me according to your word." Then the angel departed from her ...And Mary said, "My soul magnifies the Lord, and my spirit rejoices in God my Savior, for he has looked with favor on the lowliness of his servant. Surely, from now on all generations will call me blessed; for the Mighty One has done great

things for me, and holy is his name. His mercy is for those
who fear him from generation to generation. He has shown
strength with his arm; he has scattered the proud in the
thoughts of their hearts. He has brought down the powerful
from their thrones, and lifted up the lowly; he has filled the
hungry with good things, and sent the rich away empty. He
has helped his servant Israel, in remembrance of his mercy,
according to the promise he made to our ancestors, to Abraham and to his descendants forever." (Lk 1:26–38, 46–55)

In some ways, it seems that in Luke Mary plays the role that
Joseph played in Matthew—Mary is the primary agent and recipient
of God's revealed wisdom. The angel seems to wait for Mary's acqui-
escence to put God's plan into action, and Mary herself becomes not
only the first sign of what God is going to do for the whole creation
in Jesus Christ but also the first "evangelist" of this divine plan. We
see this writ large in the Magnificat, where Mary narrates a vivid
image of what Jesus inaugurates for the world: a great reversal of status, expectations, and rewards; good news for the poor and lowly, but
judgment for the rich and powerful. This is the first concrete depiction of what "salvation" in Jesus might look like, indicating the purpose for which he is coming into the world.

This account makes it clear that the miraculous birth of Jesus
Christ is not simply a matter of spiritual importance but also has
ramifications in the concrete, material existence of human beings.
Luke's gospel plainly links the whole concept of salvation (God is described as Mary's "savior," but the reader will see shortly that title applied explicitly to Jesus) with one's economic status. As the gospel
unfolds, there is more and more evidence of Luke's heightened awareness of the unjust differences between the poor and the rich, and the
way in which love of money and material goods can get in the way of
one's relationship to God.

Coming to the Last as the Least

Again in contrast to Matthew, Luke provides much more detail
about the conditions surrounding the actual birth of Jesus, which occurs in a way quite congruous with what God has revealed in the circumstances of Mary's pregnancy.

In those days a decree went out from Emperor Augustus that
all the world should be registered. This was the first registra-

tion and was taken while Quirinius was governor of Syria. All
went to their own towns to be registered. Joseph also went
from the town of Nazareth in Galilee to Judea, to the city of
David called Bethlehem, because he was descended from the
house and family of David. He went to be registered with
Mary, to whom he was engaged and who was expecting a
child. While they were there, the time came for her to deliver
her child. And she gave birth to her firstborn son and
wrapped him in bands of cloth, and laid him in a manger, because there was no place for them in the inn.

In that region there were shepherds living in the fields,
keeping watch over their flock by night. Then an angel of the
Lord stood before them, and the glory of the Lord shone
around them, and they were terrified. But the angel said to
them, "Do not be afraid; for see—I am bringing you good
news of great joy for all the people: to you is born this day in
the city of David a Savior, who is the Messiah, the Lord. This
will be a sign for you: you will find a child wrapped in bands
of cloth and lying in a manger." And suddenly there was with
the angel a multitude of the heavenly host, praising God and
saying, "Glory to God in the highest heaven, and on earth
peace among those whom he favors!"

When the angels had left them and gone into heaven, the
shepherds said to one another, "Let us go now to Bethlehem
and see this thing that has taken place, which the Lord has
made known to us." So they went with haste and found Mary
and Joseph, and the child lying in the manger. When they
saw this, they made known what had been told them about
this child; and all who heard it were amazed at what the
shepherds told them. But Mary treasured all these words and
pondered them in her heart. The shepherds returned, glorify-
ing and praising God for all they had heard and seen, as it
had been told them. (Lk 2:1-20)

Shepherds, not wise men; a manger in a stable, not a bed in a
house: this is an account not of an honored prince but rather a non-
descript person coming into the world, an insignificant son of a poor
family. However, there is immediate and dramatic confirmation that
something extraordinary has happened, and the angels proclaim it
plainly: the promised savior has been born.

Joseph Fitzmyer comments that out of the three synoptic gospels,
only Luke uses the specific title of *soter* (savior) for Jesus, and this

particular story is the only place in Luke's gospel where the term is used to describe him (the writer of Luke-Acts uses it again in Acts 5:31).[8] The use is somewhat ironic—at the particular moment when Jesus is given this profoundly significant title, he is not actively engaged in saving. If it weren't for the angels' emphatic insistence that it is so, no one would assume that this baby could be capable of saving anyone. This illustrates an important theme: What role, if any, do these infancy narratives play in understanding what it means to call Jesus savior?

Fitzmyer describes salvation in the following way:

> "Salvation" denotes the deliverance of human beings from evil, physical, moral, political, or cataclysmic. It connotes a victory, a rescue of them from a state of negation and a restoration to wholeness or integrity. As applied to the Christ-event, the wholeness to which human beings are restored is a sound relation to God himself. That would imply a rescue from sin, the state of alienation from God and, in terms of a post-NT theology, a deliverance from eternal damnation.[9]

Do the stories of Jesus' infancy provide in any way an understanding of Jesus as the one who brings this vision of salvation to the world?

Jesus Acting "Womanish": Luke's Story of the Boy Jesus in the Temple

In all four gospels, only one story interrupts the leap from Jesus' birth to his baptism and the announcement of his public ministry. It is the only evidence that Jesus did have a childhood, one in which he apparently was given a traditional religious upbringing by his parents.

> The child grew and became strong, filled with wisdom; and the favor of God was upon him. Now every year his parents went to Jerusalem for the festival of the Passover. And when he was twelve years old, they went up as usual for the festival. When the festival was ended and they started to return, the boy Jesus stayed behind in Jerusalem, but his parents did not know it. Assuming that he was in the group of travelers, they went a day's journey. Then they started to look for him among their relatives and friends. When they did not find him, they returned to Jerusalem to search for him. After three days they found him in the temple, sitting among the teachers, listening to them and asking them questions. And all who heard him

were amazed at his understanding and his answers. When his parents saw him they were astonished; and his mother said to him, "Child, why have you treated us like this? Look, your father and I have been searching for you in great anxiety." He said to them, "Why were you searching for me? Did you not know that I must be in my Father's house?" But they did not understand what he said to them. Then he went down with them and came to Nazareth, and was obedient to them. His mother treasured all these things in her heart.

And Jesus increased in wisdom and in years, and in divine and human favor. (Lk 2:40–52)

"Womanish" is a term described by Alice Walker in her book *In Search of Our Mothers' Gardens*. According to Walker, this adjective was used by African-American women to describe their daughters when they were engaged in "willful behavior." For Walker, it indicates a woman responsible, in charge, serious, and wise beyond her years.[10] As such, it seems a fitting descriptor of Jesus' behavior in this account. Although still a boy, he is confident enough to stay behind, all by himself, in the big city of Jerusalem; not only that, he has the courage and the confidence to debate with the rabbis as their equal. (Note that Luke emphasizes twice in this short passage that Jesus is growing in wisdom.) This is an astounding event, and everyone listening to Jesus recognizes that he is exceptional. Here, finally, seems to be an indication from Jesus himself that he is more than what he seems, and here, finally, he is living up to the "hype" present at his birth.

Yet the event passes quickly. When his parents come and chastise him, he offers only the mildest of rebukes and reverts back to being an ordinary young boy who has been justly scolded by his parents. He immediately leaves with them, and the text emphasizes the "obedience" that characterizes his behavior from then on. The story closes with the report that Jesus continues to grow, both in size and in understanding, and that divine favor continues to rest upon him. It is a tantalizing peek behind the heavy curtain that veils the life of the young Jesus, but it offers only the briefest of glances.

Stories from the Non-Canonical Gospels: Why Bother?

This single story of Jesus' adolescence in Luke leads into the treatment of the child Jesus in non-canonical gospels such as the Infancy

Gospel of Thomas, which concludes with a similar account of this
episode in Jesus' life. As Edwin Freed notes,

> The behavior of young Jesus in the temple resembles the sto-
> ries of so-called "hidden years," an expression often used to
> designate the time Jesus spent at home before he began his
> public life. The years are "hidden" because the Gospels in
> the New Testament report nothing about Jesus during that
> time. However, those years became a biographical concern of
> the authors of certain apocryphal gospels from the second
> century.[11]

An obvious question to ask is why readers should turn to stories
from these non-canonical gospels. Why not simply stick to the biblical material? A partial answer lies in a story that appeared in the August 3, 2009 issue of *The New Yorker* magazine about the discovery of
what is called the "Codex Tchacos," which includes a twenty-six line
text entitled "The Gospel of Judas." This particular text is considered
a Gnostic gospel, and it reveals Gnostic biases in its pages. According
to "The Gospel of Judas," Judas is the only one who truly understood
Jesus and saw clearly his divine nature; Jesus and Judas were thus co-
conspirators in all the events leading up to and including Jesus' apparent death.

The author of the article draws an interesting conclusion for contemporary Christianity. She writes, "What use could this bizarre document be to modern Christians? Plenty. Many American religious
thinkers are more liberal than their churches. They wish that Christianity were more open—not a stone wall of doctrine. To these
people, the Gospel of Judas was a gift. As with the other Gnostic
gospels, its mere existence showed that there was no such thing as
fixed doctrine, or that there wasn't at the beginning."[12]

This author points to a fact that what most Christians today take
for granted—a clearly defined collection of sacred texts known as the
Bible—is something early Christians did not have. In the fertile mi-
lieu in which Christianity was taking shape, a large number of texts
circulated that claimed both authoritative apostolic authorship and
normative knowledge about Jesus and Christian discipleship. Thus,
even though today Christians begin with the starting point of a
closed canon—in other words, a very clear definition of what counts
as scripture, particularly when it comes to the New Testament—this
was not always the case in the early church. Consequently, while
Christians today overwhelmingly make crystal-clear and iron-clad

distinctions between those books that are "orthodox" (inspired revelation of reliable, true information about God and the Christian faith)
and those books that are "heterodox" (non-inspired, fictional accounts of Jesus' life and the early apostolic community that have no
relevance for one's understanding of the faith), our foremothers and
fathers in the faith simply did not always make those kinds of distinctions. By contrast, many early Christians had much more fluid, much
looser definitions of what constituted "gospel" and "orthodox belief."
Many of the "apocryphal" texts, of which most contemporary Christians are entirely ignorant, were actually quite influential in the developing church's views on doctrine and practice.

What might these texts mean for Christians today? I maintain that
there is value in gaining familiarity with the non-canonical texts themselves and being open to lessons one might learn about the Christian
faith from them. In the context of this particular study, that specifically means being open to what these texts might teach us about who
Jesus is and how he saves. It can be argued that such openness is a
way of being faithful to the genuine diversity that existed in early
Christianity. It also allows Christians to be positively influenced by a
wider range of voices in the tradition, voices that also sought to present a faithful witness to the person they understood Jesus to be.

As Paul Foster writes,

> It is in the recognition of this very diversity that the true
> value of the non-canonical gospels can be found. They repre-
> sent the varied currents that flowed in the formative cen-
> turies of the Jesus movement. They challenge any idea that
> there existed a pure source of "orthodoxy" from which other
> perspectives deviated. Rather these documents reveal that
> there was a plurality of understandings, and these became
> highly contested.[13]

Such openness is particularly helpful in today's context, where
such bitter, church-dividing battles are being fought over "right doctrine." It reminds us that Christianity has a colorful, multivalent history, and that the early church contained a vast choir of diverse voices
in which different interpretations of Jesus' life and ministry both
competed and coexisted, enriching the faith life of the church as a
whole. In other words:

> Perhaps the fundamental contributions of the non-canonical
> gospels to modern understandings of formative Christianity

are twofold. First, they allow direct access to the thought and theology of various groups that had alternative understandings of Christianity... Secondly, such a range of texts correct false understandings of a monolithic view Christianity existing from the second century onwards... The non-canonical gospels should be read and appreciated as being some of the earliest literary remains of the vibrant and diverse movements that linked their spiritual understandings to the person of Jesus.[14]

What Are Apocryphal Gospels?

Before looking specifically at the texts themselves, a word of introduction is in order. What are non-canonical, or apocryphal, gospels anyway? What does that term signify? To begin, the four canonical gospels date from roughly four to five decades after Jesus' crucifixion. The Gospel of Mark is widely regarded to be the oldest, dating from around 70 CE. It is worth noting that the oldest gospel is also the only one of the synoptic gospels that begins with Jesus' baptism, and contains no infancy narrative. The Gospels of Matthew and Luke are next, coming around ten to twenty years later, and the Gospel of John is the latest, having been written around the turn of the first century. This chronology is widely accepted primarily because so much of the material found in Mark (95 percent, according to at least one source)[15]] is also found in Matthew and Luke. Similarly, while it is clear that the author of John was familiar with the other three gospels, he did not use them as sources, given that there is a less than a 10 percent overlap between the content of the synoptic gospels and the Gospel of John.[16]

The canon of the New Testament, that is, the collection of writings regarded by the church as having "unique and normative significance for its life and thought,"[17] developed slowly over time. Not surprisingly, however, the first writings given normative status were the gospels. By the end of the first century, in fact, the authority of the four gospels—Matthew, Mark, Luke, and John—was well-attested. It has been suggested that the driving question for the early Christians concerned not the validity of these four, but rather whether any other circulating gospels should be added to their company.[18] By the end of the second century, the four canonical gospels, as they had come to be known, were well-established as a closed set, even though the Gospel of John did continue to garner some doubters even into the third century.[19]

As evidence of this, in his book, *The Non-Canonical Gospels*, editor Paul Foster quotes the second-century bishop Irenaeus, who affirmed:

> It is not possible that the Gospels can be either more or fewer in number than they are. For, since there are four zones of the world in which we live, and four principal winds, while the Church is scattered throughout all the world, and the pillar and ground of the Church is the Gospel and the spirit of life; it is fitting that she should have four pillars, breathing out immortality on every side, and vivifying men afresh…He who was manifested to men, has given us the Gospel under four aspects, but bound together by one Spirit.[20]

Nevertheless, even as the authority and status of the four gospels as we know them today were being solidified, "a larger and more diverse range of gospel-like writings circulated in antiquity and into the Middle Ages."[21] This collection of texts is called the "Apocryphal New Testament."

It was in the face of this large body of writings that the early Christian communities engaged in a protracted process of deciding which texts would be given authoritative status and which texts would not.[22] While some apocryphal texts had more standing in the early church than others, all the writings had to be evaluated. The canon of New Testament writings as we know them today was first articulated by Origen, who, in the early third century, organized Christian writings of the time into three categories: the "surely" authentic, the "surely not" authentic, and those about which opinion differed.[23] It was not until 367 CE that a list of authentic Christian texts that matches today's index of New Testament books was circulated by Athanasius; in his thirty-ninth festal letter, he referred to the current twenty-seven books of the contemporary New Testament as "springs of salvation."[24]

Nonetheless, even these continued steps toward solidifying the canon did not fully quash reading of the apocryphal writings. Especially when it came to the life of Jesus, the canonical gospels left unanswered many questions that were of great concern to the early Christians, questions having to do with, for example, the details of Jesus' origins, information about Mary, and matters relating to Jesus' youth. In fact, as one scholar notes, "It seems evident that folk-stories and legends about the childhood of Jesus circulated freely in every region during the early centuries."[25] The so-called infancy gospels sought to address these sorts of questions, and this is one reason why, even though the dating of these gospels is not precise, most scholars are confident that they all were written later than the four canonical gospels. They were written, at least in part, to answer questions on which the four canonical gospels were silent.

Two primary apocryphal gospels treat Jesus' infancy and youth, the Infancy Gospel of James and the Infancy Gospel of Thomas.[26] While there are other examples of this genre, including the *Arabic Infancy Gospel* and the *Gospel of Pseudo-Matthew*,[27] these two texts are "the earliest surviving examples of the burgeoning interest in the early church that continued into the medieval period concerning the childhood and the prehistory of Jesus."[28] The Infancy Gospel of Thomas focuses most specifically and with the most detail on Jesus' young life. By contrast, the Infancy Gospel of James deals primarily with Mary, and the theological assertions and insights of that gospel are almost exclusively concerned with her. However, the Infancy Gospel of James also contains an account of Jesus' birth, with several interesting deviations from and modifications of the birth narratives found in Matthew and Luke.

The Infancy Gospel of James

The Infancy Gospel of James, or *Protoevangelium of James*, as it is typically called, includes and elaborates upon material in both Matthew and Luke, but with its own particular focus. As noted above, it presents Mary in the most favorable light, explaining her own unique origins and upbringing. More specifically, Paul Foster argues that advocating for the "perpetual virginity" of Mary was its primary goal.[29] Therefore, Jesus actually plays a fairly minimal role.

About the Text

Both the dating and authorship of this gospel are uncertain. However, it can be stated definitively that it was *not* authored by James, the brother of Jesus, nor was it written, as it claims, "at the time when an uproar arose in Jerusalem at the death of Herod" (25:1). Given that Herod the Great died in 4 BCE, that would make this gospel the earliest of all known writings of the New Testament, and such a claim is not credible. While there has been a wide range of dates assigned to this gospel, most contemporary scholars put it somewhere in the mid-second century, as it was known to many early church fathers who were writing in the third century, such as Origen and Clement of Alexandria.[30]

The Narrative[31]

As stated above, the writer of this gospel is particularly concerned to portray Mary's purity, her own supernatural origins, and the miracle of her perpetual virginity, maintained even after Jesus' birth. Thus, the text tells us that Mary's parents, Anna and Joachim, were unable to have children until Anna prayed to God. She was then visited by an angel who told her that God had heard her prayer and promised that she would conceive: "And your child will be talked about all over the world" (4:1). Anna then promised to dedicate the child, whether a boy or a girl, to God. After Mary was born, Anna and Joachim kept her at home until she was three years old. At that point, they took her to the temple to leave her there, dedicated to God. The text records that "Mary lived in the temple of the Lord. She was fed there like a dove, receiving her food from the hand of a heavenly messenger" (8:2).

When she turned twelve, however, the priests became concerned, because if she began menstruating she would defile the temple. At that point, it was decided that she needed to marry. Word came from the Lord that Zechariah, the high priest, was to call all the village widowers to the temple and have each bring a staff: "She will become the wife of the one to whom the Lord God shows a sign" (8:8). All the widowers, including Joseph, ran to the temple at the sound of the trumpet, and it was to Joseph that the promised sign appeared—a dove flew out of his staff and perched upon his head. Joseph protested, saying that he was too old and that he already had sons, but out of fear of the Lord, he obeyed and took Mary into his house.

While Mary was in Joseph's house, a messenger from the Lord came to Mary and delivered roughly the same message recorded in Luke: "Greetings, favoured one! The Lord is with you. Blessed are you among women...Don't be afraid, Mary. You see, you've found favor in the sight of the Lord of all. You will conceive by means of his word" (11:2, 5). Mary, again in a manner accordant with Luke, replied, "Here I am, the Lord's slave before him. I pray that all you've told me comes true" (11:9). The gospel then recounts that Mary was sixteen years old when these events occurred.

Chapter 13 begins with Joseph returning home (back in chapter 9 we were told that as soon as Joseph brought Mary home, he left again to go build houses). By the time he returned home again, Mary was six months pregnant and most definitely showing her pregnancy. Understandably, Joseph was shocked and dismayed—he felt guilty because he had not protected her, but he was also angry with Mary for what he naturally interpreted as her sin and infidelity. Mary protested her innocence: "As the Lord my God lives, I don't know where [the child I am carrying] came from" (13:10)—but no one believed her. Then, as in Matthew's account, Joseph consequently decides to divorce her, but an angel of the Lord comes to him in a dream and confirms that Mary is pregnant by the Holy Spirit. She will bear a son and they are to name him Jesus.

What happens next is quite different from what is found in the canonical accounts. Mary and Joseph are summoned by the high priest, who gives them a test to see if they are telling the truth, what the text calls "the Lord's drink test." Both pass the test, of course, and the high priest sends them home. Shortly afterward, Emperor Augustus announces a census and the family begins the trip to Bethlehem. Soon after starting out, Mary is ready to give birth. Joseph finds a cave for her and goes out looking for a Hebrew midwife. The narrative is interrupted at this point with an interesting bit of commentary:

> Now I, Joseph, was walking along and yet not going anywhere. I looked up at the vault of the sky and saw it standing still, and then the clouds and saw them paused in amazement, and at the birds of the sky suspended in midair. As I looked on the earth, I saw a bowl lying there and workers reclining around it with their hands in the bowl; some were chewing and yet did not chew; some were picking up something to eat and yet did not pick it up; and some were putting food in their mouths and yet did not do so. Instead, they were all looking upward. I saw sheep being driven along and yet the sheep stood still; the shepherd was lifting his hand to strike them, and yet his hand remained raised. And I observed the current of the river and saw goats with their mouths in the water and yet they were not drinking. Then all of a sudden everything and everybody went on with what they had been doing. (18:3–11)

As Paul Foster notes, "Such a catalepsis of the natural realm, visible to Joseph alone, reflects the cosmological significance of the events that are transpiring in the cave."[32] It is a clear indication of the miraculous birth that is about to occur and the uniqueness of the child being born. However, this event is not commented upon or lingered on; it is simply recorded and then the narration continues.

Joseph finds a midwife and brings her back to the cave. As they are standing at the mouth of the cave, it is overshadowed by a dark cloud, prompting the midwife to say "I've been really privileged, because today my eyes have seen a miracle in that salvation has come to Israel" (19:14). The dark cloud immediately is banished by a blinding light, which fades after a bit to reveal the infant Jesus—one wonders if this is intended to be a sign that Jesus is "the light of the world." The midwife goes out of the cave proclaiming the miracle she has seen, and she runs into Salome, whom she tells about the virgin birth. Salome refuses to believe it until she personally gives Mary a thorough gynecological exam. For her lack of faith, her hand immediately catches on fire, but the fire is extinguished when she picks up the infant Jesus. Touching Jesus heals her immediately.

After she leaves, the "astrologers" come to pay Jesus homage. As in Matthew's account, they have seen a star, they have a similar exchange with Herod, and they also avoid him on their way home. Consequently, Herod orders the slaughter of all children two years and younger. In this gospel, however, there is no flight to Egypt. Instead, Mary hides Jesus in a cattle trough and Elizabeth flees with John up into the hills. The gospel concludes with the account of its authorship: "Now I, James, am the one who wrote this account at the time when an uproar arose in Jerusalem at the death of Herod. I took myself off to the wilderness until the uproar in Jerusalem died down. There I praised the Lord God, who gave me the wisdom to write this account" (25:1–3).

It should be clear even from this short narration of the gospel's content that the author of this text has a theological rather than historical purpose, one that centers on Mary instead of Jesus. The author is concerned first and foremost to provide justification for elevating Mary to supra-human status; Mary is less similar to and more distinct from the rest of humanity. To one degree or another, depending on both one's opinion and one's sources, such an elevation does occur in both the Eastern and Western churches in the centuries to come. In his evaluation of this text, Foster writes the following: "Thus, while the text may be of little or no historical value, apart from being a literary artifact that reflects a certain strand of Christian spirituality in the late second century, it proved to be of major theological significance in more than one branch of Christianity."[33] Unfortunately, for the purposes of this book, that theological significance was focused squarely on Mary, with Jesus almost an afterthought.

The Infancy Gospel of Thomas

The Infancy Gospel of Thomas is the most important document extant that records stories of Jesus' youth. Up until the now-famous Gospel of Thomas was discovered in Nag Hammadi, Egypt in 1945, this text bore that name; since that time it has been called by the more specific title of "Infancy Gospel" to distinguish it from the Gnostic text. This short infancy gospel is a compendium of stories of Jesus between the ages of five and twelve, "all of them illustrating in one way or another the extraordinary power and knowledge that Jesus possessed even as a youngster."[34] It is less a full-blown narrative of Jesus' life and more "a collection of largely self-contained stories that are only loosely held together by a series of indications of Jesus' age—five years (2:1), six (11:1), eight (12:4), nine (18:1), and finally twelve (19:1)."[35] However, Tony Chartrand-Burke, one of the foremost experts on this particular text, argues that even in spite of its fragmentary nature, "this gospel likely is one of the earliest pieces of Christian writing outside of the New Testament and its stories had a tremendous impact on art, literature and piety throughout the medieval period."[36]

About the Text

What is most striking to someone reading this text for the first time is the way in which Jesus acts. Far from being the "obedient" son of Luke's gospel, Jesus is defiant and haughty toward everyone with whom he comes in contact, including his parents—particularly poor Joseph, who seems to have the primary responsibility for keeping Jesus out of trouble. This is a futile and thankless task, to say the least. As one scholar says about this text, "The story at times recalls incidents and language from the canonical stories, but what is most noticeable is a strikingly different Jesus from the one in the canonical portraits—a vindictive, arrogant, unruly child who . . . 'seldom acts in a Christian way.'"[37]

As with the Infancy Gospel of James, dating and authorship are again indefinite: "No precision regarding the date of the Infancy Gospel of Thomas is possible, and even the range of possible dates is unusually large, extending from the first to the sixth centuries."[38] However, most scholars tend to put this gospel in the lower end of that range, not least because one story in particular—the exchange Jesus has with one of his teachers around the letters alpha and beta (described below)—was described in a mid-second century text called the *Epistula Apostolorum*, which, according to Irenaeus, was also known to a second-century Gnostic group called the Marcosians.[39]

As noted above, even though this gospel was never afforded canonical status, it continued to be circulated and read centuries after it was written. It is worthwhile asking, then, how this gospel served the nascent Christian communities. Why did people read this gospel? What did they hope to find here? One scholar suggests that "people would expect to read stories that anticipate the qualities of Jesus as an adult, of him as the powerful miracle worker and divine teacher that was so familiar from the canonical gospels."[40]

Similarly, Chartrand-Burke notes that this genre of childhood tales of a hero, god, great leader, and so on was well-known in the ancient world; he notes that "the primary purpose behind the tales is to foreshadow the adult career of their protagonist."[41] Thus, it is reasonable to conclude that "the sole purpose of the author [of this gospel] was to demonstrate the miraculous power of Jesus from his birth, and that he possessed the same extraordinary wisdom and insight in infancy that he exhibited in later years."[42]

The value of this particular gospel, then, is to show that Jesus was truly and definitively divine, even from his earliest years, that from his first engagement with other boys his age, his parents, and even his teachers, he demonstrated that he was unmistakably superior to them in every way. He knew things they didn't know, he had abilities they didn't have, and he had power over life and death. Simply put, Jesus is God, and he is above being questioned or disciplined by anyone. Just as the canonical gospels point to the fact that the adult Jesus is to be obeyed, worshiped, and honored, so too this gospel reminds us that such deference must be accorded to even the boy Jesus, as he is from the earliest time in his life already everything he will become as an adult. "In short, the Infancy Gospel of Thomas confirms what Christian readers already assumed, not just from the Lukan account of him at twelve but also from cultural expectations, that the παιδικὰ πράγματα [childhood things] of their Lord and Savior anticipated his adult achievements as miracle worker and divine teacher."[43]

Selected Stories: Jesus at the Age of Five

The bulk of the stories in this gospel and those that make up the longest section of the text relate to the time when Jesus was five years old. Most of the stories are short, with very little commentary and very little extraneous detail. Here, then, are the most significant.

After introducing the author of this gospel as "Thomas the Is-
raelite" and explaining his purpose for writing—"to make known the
extraordinary childhood deeds of our Lord Jesus Christ"—the narrative continues with the phrase, "This is how it all started." Chapter 2
opens with the first wondrous acts of Jesus' youth, which occurred as
Jesus was sitting and playing by a stream. As quoted in full in the introduction to this book, the story continues with Jesus making clay
from flowing water and molding the clay into twelve sparrows. When
he is criticized for creating on the Sabbath, he claps his hands, bringing the clay sparrows to life, and commands them to fly away and remember him.

This lovely story is something Christians may well hope that
Jesus did as a child: creating life is a pastime well-suited to a divine
young boy. However, in this account Jesus is not only creative and
playful, he is also short-tempered and prone to tantrums, like any
other five-year-old child. This unpleasant behavior of Jesus is on full
display as the story continues in chapter 3.

> The son of Annas the scholar, standing there with Jesus, took a
> willow branch and drained the water Jesus had collected.
> Jesus, however, saw what had happened and became angry,
> saying to him, "Damn you, you irreverent fool! What harm did
> the ponds of water do to you? From this moment you, too, will
> dry up like a tree, and you'll never produce leaves or root or
> bear fruit." In an instant the boy had completely withered
> away. (3:1–3)

This appalling behavior continues in chapter 4, where Jesus
causes a boy to drop dead simply because the boy bumped him on
the shoulder as he was walking through the village. As can well be
imagined, these acts of Jesus do not go unnoticed. The villagers are
losing their patience with Jesus and fearing for the lives of their children. They complain to Joseph, who in turn speaks to Jesus and tries
to discipline him, with little success. This is how that encounter goes:

> Joseph summoned his child and admonished him in private,
> saying, "Why are you doing all this? These people are suffer-
> ing and so they hate and harass us." Jesus said, "I know that
> the words I spoke are not my words. Still, I'll keep quiet for
> your sake. But those people must take their punishment."
> There and then his accusers became blind. Those who saw

this became very fearful and at a loss. All they could say was, "Every word he says, whether good or bad, has become a deed—a miracle, even!" When Joseph saw that Jesus had done such a thing, he got angry and grabbed his ear and pulled it very hard. The boy became infuriated with him and replied, "It's one thing for you to seek and not find; it's quite another for you to act this unwisely. Don't you know that I don't really belong to you? Don't make me upset." (5:1–3)

Clearly, Joseph is not getting anywhere with his son. At this point, another important character enters the story. At the beginning of chapter 6, we read that the teacher Zacchaeus had been standing there the whole time and listening to everything Joseph had been saying. Zacchaeus was amazed at Jesus' wisdom and could tell that he was exceptional. So, he asked Joseph to turn Jesus over to his own care, that he might teach him and in that way calm his behavior. Joseph responds by saying that "no one is able to rule this child except God alone," and he warns Zacchaeus that Jesus will be no "small cross."

Jesus, hearing Joseph speak this way, affirms the point:

Believe me, teacher, what my father told you is true. I am Lord of these people and I'm present with you and have been born among you and am with you. I know where you've come from and how many years you'll live. I swear to you, teacher, I existed when you were born. If you wish to be a perfect teacher, listen to me and I'll teach you a wisdom that no one else knows except for me and the one who sent me to you. It's you who happen to be my student, and I know how old you are and how long you have to live. When you see the cross that my father mentioned then you'll believe that everything I've told you is true. (6:4–8)

When the other villagers who were standing there express amazement at what Jesus has said, Jesus replies, "Are you really so amazed? Rather, consider what I've said to you. The truth is that I also know when you were born, and your parents, and I announce this paradox to you: when the world was created, I existed along with the one who sent me to you" (6:10).

In spite of all this, Zacchaeus still desires to teach Jesus, and so Joseph leads Jesus into his classroom. They start with the alphabet, and Zacchaeus repeats the letter "alpha," asking Jesus to repeat it back to him, but Jesus refuses to say anything for a long time. Zacchaeus grows angry and finishes by hitting Jesus on the head. Somewhat uncharacteristically, given what we have seen thus far, Jesus responds calmly, telling Zacchaeus that Zacchaeus knows nothing about the true meaning of these letters, while Jesus knows them all already—and he quickly recites the whole alphabet. Jesus looks at Zacchaeus and asks him to explain the true meaning of "alpha"—but Zacchaeus, humiliated, isn't able to say anything in response. Then Zacchaeus turns to the adults present and says,

> Poor me, I'm utterly bewildered, wretch that I am. I've heaped shame upon myself because I took on this child. So take him away, I beg you, brother Joseph. I can't endure the severity of his look or his lucid speech. This child is no ordinary mortal; he can tame fire! Perhaps he was born before the creation of the world. What sort of womb bore him, what sort of mother nourished him?—I don't know…What great thing he is— god or angel or whatever else I might call him—I don't know. (7:2-5, 11)

Jesus' encounter with Zacchaeus ends in chapter 8 as Jesus laughs and says, "Now let the infertile bear fruit and the blind see and the deaf in the understanding of their heart hear: I've come from above so that I might save those who are below and summon them to higher things, just as the one who sent me to you commanded me" (8:1–2). At this point, we are told that "when the child stopped speaking, all those who had fallen under the curse were instantly saved. And from then on no one dared to anger him for fear of being cursed and maimed for life" (8:3–4).

Also at five years of age, Jesus raises the dead for the first time. He is playing on the roof of a house with several other boys when one of them falls from the roof and dies. The other children are afraid and run away, leaving Jesus standing there by himself. The parents of the dead boy then accuse Jesus—who, with apparent good reason, is considered to be something of troublemaker—of throwing the boy off the roof. Jesus denies the charge, and then leaps down from the roof himself and shouts to the dead boy, "Zeno! Get up and tell me: Did I push you?" The text then records that "[Zeno] got up immediately and said, 'No, Lord, you didn't push me, you raised me up'" (9:4–5). At this point, Zeno's parents "praised God for the miracle that had happened and worshiped Jesus" (9:6). Jesus' activities as a five-year-old conclude with the healing of a young man who had cut his foot with an axe while chopping wood. After he performs this miracle, the crowd says, "Truly the spirit of God dwells in this child" (10:4).

Selected Stories: Jesus at the Age of Eight

Chapter 12 includes stories about Jesus as an eight-year-old boy, and the first is a "feeding miracle." After sowing one measure of grain that after the harvest and threshing yielded one hundred measures, Jesus calls the poor of the village to the threshing floor and gives them the grain. Yet, not all Jesus' miracles are so miraculous, as he performs several of what might be called "prosaic" miracles as well. In chapter 13, for example, Joseph, a carpenter, is at work on a bed that a rich man has ordered. As Joseph is working, he discovers that one crossbeam is shorter than the other. In a context in which wood is neither easily accessible nor cheap, this is a serious problem. As Joseph sits wondering what he should do, Jesus tells him to put the two boards next to each other, lining them up at one end. Once Joseph does this, Jesus "stood at the other end and grabbed hold of the shorter board, and, by stretching it, made it the same length as the other." Joseph responds by hugging and kissing Jesus and saying "How fortunate I am that God has given this child to me" (13:4).

This section also includes two separate stories of different teachers trying to teach Jesus his letters; unfortunately, both have the same experience as Zacchaeus. In the second story, however, the teacher demonstrates more wisdom than the others. In this particular episode, Jesus opens his book and begins speaking "by [the power of] the holy spirit and taught the law to those standing there." At that, the crowd marveled at his maturity—"a mere child able to say such things" (15:4). Joseph, however, knowing how Jesus has treated his teachers in the past, "feared the worst and ran to the schoolroom, imagining that this teacher was having trouble with Jesus" (15:5). However, such was not the case. Instead, the teacher replied "Brother, please know that I accepted this child as a student, but already he's full of grace and wisdom. So I'm asking you, brother, to take him back home" (15:6).

The last story in this section tells of an infant in Jesus' neighborhood who has died. When Jesus hears the wailing from the household, he runs there to see for himself what has happened. The story goes on: "When [Jesus] found the child dead, he touched its chest and said, 'I say to you, infant, don't die but live, and be with your mother.' And immediately the infant looked up and laughed. Jesus then said to the woman, 'Take it, give it your breast, and remember me.' The crowd of onlookers marveled at this: 'Truly this child was a god or a heavenly messenger of God—whatever he says instantly happens.' But Jesus left and went on playing with the other children" (17:2–4).

Jesus at the Age of Twelve

Jesus' activities at nine are also passed over with only one event of note, one final story in which Jesus raises the dead. It prompts the crowd to say, "This child's from heaven—he must be, because he has saved many souls from death, and he can go on saving all his life" (18:3).

The Infancy Gospel of Thomas then concludes with a slightly different version of the story of Jesus in the temple, told also by Luke. In this account, Jesus also goes up to Jerusalem with his parents for Passover and also gets left behind when they begin to travel back home. It takes them three days, but they finally find him sitting among the teachers in the temple, "listening to the law and asking them questions." The text notes that "All eyes were on him, and everyone was astounded that he, a mere child, could interrogate the elders and teachers of the people and explain the main points of the law and the parables of the prophets" (19:5).

The main difference in this version of the story is that after Mary scolds Jesus for worrying them and after Jesus responds that he is in his father's house, the scribes and the Pharisees turn to Mary and ask, "Are you the mother of this child?" When she answers affirmatively, they tell her, "You more than any woman are to be congratulated, for God has blessed the fruit of your womb! For we've never seen nor heard such glory and such virtue and wisdom" (19:10). Then the gospel concludes with the following words: "Jesus got up and went with his mother, and was obedient to his parents. His mother took careful note of all that had happened. And Jesus continued to excel in learning and gain respect. To him be glory for ever and ever. Amen."

Theological Ramifications of the Birth Narratives

Although the following chapter will take up in greater depth the issue of what significance these stories have for our understanding of

Jesus, a few initial observations are in order about how and why the stories might be important. Unquestionably, the central Christian assertion about the identity of Jesus Christ has been that he is both fully human and fully divine. This characterization is unique among world religions, and it is the *sine qua non* of Christian soteriological and Christological claims.

A key question, then, to be explored in the following chapter is how the birth narratives in Matthew and Luke, as well as the story of Jesus in the temple, serve to support this assertion, and whether or not they offer any special insight into that doctrinal claim. Certainly, the emphasis on the role of the Holy Spirit in Jesus' conception points to his divine origins, as do the objective signs present in the world at his birth, "heralds" that proclaim that something new and unique has happened in this moment: angels, wise men, shepherds, and stars. However, his humanity is also upheld in these accounts, particularly in the lack of agency Jesus has when readers might have expected a god to act. As noted above, this is particularly the case in Herod's slaughter of the innocents. Both Matthew and Luke seem to be intentionally balancing Jesus' divinity and humanity.

A further question is how the picture of Jesus in the non-canonical gospels either supports or endangers this delicate balance. Part of the problem with these stories is that they seem to call into question the true humanity of Jesus. Instead, as one scholar notes, when we read the Infancy Gospel of Thomas in particular, "Throughout, we are presented with a picture of one who is essentially not of this world, a Docetic Christ in whom, from the start, the Spirit of God fully dwelt."[44]

Yet, at the same time, it is important to ask how a contemporary understanding of Jesus might be enhanced by the new information available in the Infancy Gospel of Thomas. One might well argue that while the precocious young Jesus seems fully divine in his many demonstrations of power and wisdom, given his short temper and fits of pique he seems quite the typical young boy. How might his behavior in this gospel positively augment Christological statements today, if at all?

A second point to be discussed in the coming chapter is the fact that the particulars of Jesus' birth did not meet the standards that the Jews of his time had for a Messiah—a savior—nor do they meet many of our expectations of the Divine today. Yet, the fact that God becomes incarnate in the form of a baby, a vulnerable baby at that, says something important about who God is, how God exercises God's power, and how God has chosen to be in relationship to the world. Perhaps there is more going on here, theologically, than simply a touching story that warms our hearts at Christmas-time. Indeed, there is something quite radical and subversive about Jesus' birth that is too often overlooked.

Finally, it is important to ask what sort of picture of salvation the stories in both canonical and non-canonical gospels suggest. What does it mean to call the infant Jesus savior and what kind of relationship to those around him does this Jesus inspire? In other words, who is this Jesus, and what difference do these stories make in how we understand both his person and his work? Or, asked in a different way, what difference would it make for our image of Jesus if we didn't have these canonical stories? Finally, we might also ask what difference it would make if we were to incorporate more explicitly the non-canonical stories into our picture of Jesus as savior.

5

Jesus and His Disciples

HOW HE SAVES

The Christian assertion that affirms Jesus' full divinity and full humanity has been the hallmark of Christian belief and practice across both time and space throughout the tradition. This chapter specifically examines what new insights the birth narratives in both Matthew and Luke, as well as Luke's singular account of Jesus as a young boy, might shed on that key Christological claim. It also considers the Infancy Gospel of Thomas, asking how that claim is both challenged and perhaps enhanced through an examination of Jesus' person and work in this non-canonical text. While there is much to be wary of in this apocryphal gospel, there also might be some unmined riches that can shed some positive light on traditional Christian Christological claims.

It is important to explain more directly and in some detail why the Christian church has argued so consistently since its inception that Jesus must be both fully human and fully divine in order to realize his identity as savior. Most Christians today take this statement for granted, as they confess it by rote every Sunday in the creeds without thinking too hard about what they are saying. However, in the early centuries of the church, this theological position was by no means obvious or generally assumed. Indeed, what hardly raises an eyebrow for contemporary Christians was hotly disputed in those early days. This should not be surprising, as some problems are evident in the creedal statements about Jesus' identity: "How could someone be both human and divine? Would the divine not overwhelm the human and render it inconsequential? Would the human not taint or corrupt the divine? How did the two mix—was Jesus divine when he performed a miracle and human when he wept for Lazarus?"[1] These sorts of questions caused deep divisions in the early church for centuries, with great theological minds on all sides.

A full history of the Christological arguments of the early church is beyond the scope of this book, as is a full explication of the subsequent trinitarian arguments to which the claims about Jesus' fully divine nature naturally led. Nonetheless, in order to better appreciate why the infancy narratives are actually "gospel"—good news about the person and work of Jesus Christ—and also to understand what is novel and insightful about them, it is necessary to have a basic understanding of the core soteriological claims Christians have made, and continue to make, about Jesus Christ. The most straightforward way to do this is to briefly review the two most critical ecumenical councils of the early church.

A Tale of Two Councils[2]

The key Christological and soteriological issues that drove the work of the first ecumenical councils in the fourth and fifth centuries focused on the question, "Who do you say that I am?" rather than on the question, "How does he make a difference?" While it was of paramount importance to the early Christians to establish one definitive articulation of a definition of Jesus' person, they were willing to leave undetermined a final, conclusive explanation of Jesus' work. This emphasis has continued, and the Christian church as a whole has never established one single specific theory of atonement, that is, one particular doctrine of how, exactly, Jesus saves us. Instead, the doctrine of salvation was and continues to be understood through a variety of different images and metaphors, such as sacrifice, a cosmic battle with the devil, the loss and restoration of the divine image, and reconciliation with God.

In spite of these different metaphors, however, the commitment that anchored, and continues to anchor, each of these diverse explanations is that salvation comes through Jesus Christ. Scripture attests to this conviction in various places (for example, "Jesus said to him, 'I am the way, and the truth, and the life. No one comes to the Father except through me" [Jn 14:6]; "There is salvation in no one else, for there is no other name under heaven given among mortals by which we must be saved" [Acts 4:12]), and there have never been any serious challengers for the central place Jesus Christ always has held in every Christian understanding of salvation.[3] What has been debated, though, is the precise definition and description of who Jesus is: particularly how Jesus is related to God the Father, and also how his humanity is both similar to and different from Adam and Eve's—in other words, that of the human person. These key questions drove the early church councils and the answers agreed upon continue to fundamentally shape Christological and soteriological thinking today.

Heterodox Christianities

It is important to remember that at this time in the church's formation many different Christian groups, sects, and sub-sects existed, and the boundaries between "orthodox" and "heterodox" were not only fluid but also varied from century to century.[4] In what follows, then, Bart Ehrman's use of the term "proto-orthodox" is relied on to indicate the stream of Christianity that would come to be the normative source for Christian teaching and practice in subsequent centuries, up to and including the present. As Ehrman describes it, this is the "victorious" stream of Christianity, the one form that "decided what was the 'correct' Christian perspective"... the "victorious party" that rewrote the history of the early church controversies, making it appear that its views always had dominated and always had been "right."[5] A few examples of some "heterodox" Christian views that were both popular and persuasive during these early centuries will illustrate the core issues debated at these formative early church councils.

Marcionite Christianity

Many lay Christians today struggle with what they perceive to be a troubling inconsistency between the God of the Old Testament and the God of the New Testament. The argument typically runs that in the Old Testament God is vengeful, violent, and destructive, while in the New Testament the God revealed in Jesus Christ is merciful, loving, and forgiving. Certainly, it is undeniable that the Hebrew scriptures at times present us with a discomfiting picture of a wrathful God. As Terence Fretheim writes, in the Hebrew scriptures "the patriarchal bias *is* pervasive, God *is* represented as an abuser and a killer of children, God is said to command the rape of women and wholesale destruction of cities, including children and animals. To shrink from making such statements is dishonest."[6] However, at the same time, it must be recognized that such rigid distinctions between the Old and New Testaments are an oversimplification of a far more complex theological picture. Under further scrutiny they simply collapse under the weight of the commonalities between how God responds to injustice, how God regards sin, and how protective God is of the vulnerable and the marginalized in both Testaments.[7]

This contemporary concern about God's true nature is nothing new. It was also a concern for some of the earliest Christians, most notably a Christian named Marcion, a second-century theologian who completely rejected the God of the Old Testament, whom he regarded as a "lesser God"; the term he used was "Demiurge."[8] Marcion believed that this God had created the world, but that he was exclusively a God of law who had nothing in common with the God of Jesus Christ, who was exclusively a God of love. The intent of this God of love was to overthrow and replace the God of law. This is why Jesus came: "For it was the purpose of the coming of Jesus to abolish all the works belonging to 'this world' and to its Creator, the 'ruler of the universe.'"[9]

As part of his theological explication of these two Gods, Marcion denied the humanity of Jesus. Since Jesus had nothing to do with the God who had created the world, Jesus also had nothing to do with creation itself—he dropped into it from heaven, as it were, but remained apart from it and untainted by it. This appears logical: since creation itself was corrupt and polluted, Jesus, being purely divine and perfect, could have no part in it. As Jaroslav Pelikan explains, "This authentic Christ could not have assumed a material body that participated in the created world, for such a body would have been 'stuffed with excrement.' A material body and a physical birth . . . were unworthy of the true Christ."[10] Obviously, then, Marcion taught that Jesus was fundamentally different from the material world, and every aspect of his life that suggested a true humanity—his birth, his hunger, his anger, his suffering, and, of course, his death—were illusory. This is the critical point: "[Jesus] only *appeared* to be a human with a material existence like everyone else."[11] An important corollary of Marcion's theology then was its Docetic underpinnings.

While Marcion's position may have solved the problem as to how to reconcile the differences between biblical understandings of law and gospel, as well as the apparent differences between God's self-revelation in the Old and New Testaments, it created an even bigger problem for Christians in the ramifications it had for salvation: "How could Jesus die for the sins of the world if he did not have a real body? How could his shed blood bring atonement if he did not have real blood?"[12] To this list one could add the theological problems of demonizing the physical creation, including human bodies, and excluding it from salvation altogether—that is, completely divorcing creation and salvation—and also the explicit anti-Jewish bias that permeates this theology. Nonetheless, versions of Marcion's Christology persisted into the fourth and fifth centuries, not least because many Christians continued to struggle with how to ascribe a genuine birth and genuine suffering on the cross and death to the divine Son of God. In this way, Marcion's alternative understanding of Christianity, and the rival church he founded, posed a legitimate threat to proto-orthodox Christian teachings for several centuries, particularly in its understanding of Jesus.

Gnostic Christianity

Even today some Christians make the theological mistake of separating the soul from the body, denigrating the inherent value and goodness of the body—and the physical creation as a whole—and implicitly rejecting the resurrection of the body in favor of some spiritualized form of an afterlife. These ideas have been around for millennia. In the early church, they were promoted and promulgated most effectively by the Gnostics, perhaps the most well-known of the early church heterodox Christians, and certainly by the most formidable promulgators of Docetism. The Gnostics were a dominant force in the first few centuries of the church's existence, and their teachings were widespread, persuasive, and persistent. There were different forms of Gnosticism, but perhaps the most notable and influential Gnostic figure is Valentinus, against whom both Irenaeus and Tertullian composed treatises. While there were some differences between the various teachers and sects, some generalizations about the movement as a whole can be made.

The Gnostics were primarily concerned with salvation, but they understood salvation to mean something quite different from how Christians describe salvation today. The Gnostics taught that matter was evil, and that salvation pointed to a human soul being freed from its physical confinement in the body. For the Gnostics, true human existence was exclusively spiritual, and this material world in which we found ourselves was not our true home; instead, it was a prison from which we needed to escape in order to be saved. As Pelikan describes it, "Gnosticism may be defined as a system which taught the cosmic redemption of the spirit through knowledge."[13] The primary impediment to our salvation is our lack of right knowledge —not "book smarts," but the secret wisdom of salvation. Humanity has forgotten its genuine spiritual nature, and thus we need a divine messenger to come and teach us the truth of our existence and the true path to salvation. For the Christian Gnostics, that messenger was Jesus Christ.

As should be immediately apparent, this body-denying theology had important ramifications for Christology. Since Christ was a heavenly messenger without any connection to the fallen world of matter, the Gnostics had to come up with an alternate explanation of Jesus' incarnation. They avoided the idea that the Divine truly had joined itself to the physical human creation by teaching that the divine Christ only *seemed* to take on a human body; in actuality, he was only inhabiting it for a time—wearing it like an easily discarded cloak. In this way, they posited a separation between the divine Christ and the human man Jesus, arguing that this divine Christ entered the man Jesus at baptism, and subsequently exited him on the cross, so that it was only the human Jesus who suffered death; the divinity remained immutable and passionless.

Gnostic soteriology focused on Jesus as a spiritual teacher. Jesus saves by teaching the divine knowledge necessary for liberation from the flesh. However, not everyone is able to be saved, that is, to hear and understand this knowledge. Instead, only some people are created with the possibility of receiving this divine knowledge; these are the "Gnostics," those "in the know, who have within them a spark of the Divine, who have learned who they really are, how they got here, and how they can return. These people [and only these people] will have a *fantastic* afterlife, in that they will return to the divine realm from which they came and live eternally in the presence of God."[14]

As with the theology of Marcion, this theology has severe limitations as it relates to Jesus' person and work. Again, salvation is divorced from creation, and the entire physical creation is cast outside of the realm of God's saving grace, being inherently evil. In this view, Jesus did not descend out of love for "the world," but only to enlighten the spiritually elite of humankind. Therefore, nothing in his earthly ministry matters except his esoteric teachings (the Gnostics had their own gospels, such as the Gospel of Thomas, in which these teachings were recorded), and Jesus' suffering and death were illusory, with no salvific import at all. He did not take on our human nature, he did not share the human condition, he did not and does not know us from the inside out. He is simply a divine messenger, standing over and above humanity—not beside and with us—who has come to teach the truth of escaping this world to those few with the capacity to hear that truth.

Finally, one additional problem with the rejection of Jesus' humanity was a much bigger concern for the early Christians than for most Christians today. Until the time of Constantine, persecution and martyrdom were very real possibilities for Christians. One of the main theological justifications for not only accepting the terrible physical suffering that such persecution entailed, but even welcoming and reveling in it, was the fact that it linked one to Christ and enabled one to share in his physical sufferings. If Christ did not really suffer, this argument falls flat.

Ignatius was one prominent Christian theologian who had such concerns. As Ehrman notes, "Some people have suggested that Ignatius may have been personally troubled by this christological issue because of how it related to his own situation. He himself was on the road to martyrdom. If Christ did not actually suffer in the flesh, there would be little reason for Ignatius himself to do so."[15]

Ebionite Christianity

The counter argument to the Marcionite and Gnostic teachings regarding Jesus Christ can be found in the doctrines of the Ebionites, a sect of Jewish Christians. Where both Marcion and the different Gnostic Christians all worked to protect Jesus' divinity at the expense of his true humanity, the Ebionites took the opposite approach. Their solution to the problem of how to understand Jesus as both human and divine was to deny his divinity entirely, and argue instead that he was only human, however "pre-eminently endowed"[16] he might have been. This is how Ehrman defines their position:

> For them, Jesus was the Son of God not because of his divine nature or virgin birth but because of his "adoption" by God to be [God's] son . . . The Ebionites believed that Jesus was a real flesh-and-blood human like the rest of us, born as the eldest son of the sexual union of his parents, Joseph and Mary. What set Jesus apart from all other people was that he kept God's law perfectly and so was the most righteous man on earth. As such, God chose him to be [God's] son and assigned to him a special mission, to sacrifice himself for the sake of others.[17]

It is clear that for the Ebionites Jesus was much more in line with the human Messiah awaited in the Jewish tradition. In their view, he was a great prophet like Moses, but in no way divine. Consequently, they rejected the virgin birth as well as the resurrection, and also the idea that Jesus saved humanity by his death. Instead, they emphasized the need to keep the Mosaic law for salvation.

The problems with these teachings are the inverse of those of the Gnostics. If Jesus was not truly divine and salvation was the province of God alone, how could Jesus be the savior? Further, if Jesus was only another human being, regardless of how exemplary, certainly he would not be deserving of worship and adoration; one would not pray to him, for example. Finally, if he were not divine, he could only show humanity the way to salvation, but he could not actually bring about that salvation—it would still be up to humanity to save itself. Indeed, it is difficult to imagine how one individual could be expected to effectively teach the entire human community at all times and in all places. In short, the notion of a human savior has serious theological shortcomings.

With so many rival Christologies prevalent at this time and competing for the faithful, church leaders felt the need to clarify acceptable Christian beliefs. While they didn't abolish once and for all the dissenting voices of heterodox Christianities, the church councils did establish a proto-orthodox theology that would come to define Christianity in subsequent centuries.

The Council of Nicaea

The Council of Nicaea, held in 325, was the first and arguably the most important of the early ecumenical church councils. This council established the full divinity of Jesus Christ. The council was convened by Emperor Constantine, under whom the face and role of the Christian Church in the Roman Empire had radically changed. While it was not Constantine who declared Christianity to be the official religion of the Roman Empire—that was Emperor Theodosius I—Constantine did make Christianity a legal, state-sanctioned religion, instantly removing the threat of persecution and martyrdom for the nascent Christian community. This law caused an enormous transformation in Roman society. Bart Ehrman notes that after Constantine's conversion to Christianity, the number of Christians in the population went from 5 to 7 percent in the early years of the fourth century to 50 percent by the end of that century.[18]

One of the primary reasons for calling the council, then, was to arbitrate between the competing doctrinal claims of different Christian groups, particularly regarding the nature of Jesus Christ. As J. N. D. Kelly describes it, the question about Jesus was the following: "Was He fully divine, in the precise sense of the term, and therefore really akin to the Father? Or was He after all a creature, superior no doubt to the rest of creation, even by courtesy designated divine, but all the same separated by an unbridgeable chasm from the Godhead?"[19]

As these claims concerned the true nature of Christ, this meant they also had to do with the true nature of his work. Thus, the concerns of all parties were fundamentally soteriological in nature. Stephen Need states it this way: "The key issue was salvation: if the pre-existent

Son were not one with the Father, how could he bring salvation to humanity even if he became incarnate in Jesus? And how could salvation depend upon someone who was not eternal and not fully divine?"[20]

The main players at the council were Arius, a fourth-century priest, and Alexander, the bishop of Alexandria. Arius played the role of "the villain in the piece."[21] Arius's primary theological commitment was to maintain the unity of God. For him, Jesus Christ, no matter how exalted he was above the rest of creation, simply could not be divine or share in the divine nature of God the Father. The oft-cited slogan of his theology is: "There was [a time] when he [Jesus] was not."

J. N. D. Kelly sums up exactly the meaning of this assertion for the person and work of Jesus Christ in four propositions.[22] First, Jesus Christ had to be a creature, not the creator—a perfect creature, true, but still a creature. Second, Jesus was not eternal, but came into being at a given time—again, before the rest of creation and, indeed, before time itself; however, he still was not co-eternal with God the Father. Third, Jesus Christ had no direct knowledge of or communication with God the Father. Finally, Jesus was subject both to change and to sin. Though Arius and his followers never claimed that Jesus actually sinned, they admitted that sin was a possibility. All this left Jesus as some middle-creature, a "demi-god" who was somehow in between God and humanity but fundamentally different from both. As should be obvious, this put the doctrine of salvation at grave risk.

By contrast, Alexander and his brilliant assistant Athanasius were more concerned with asserting the divinity of Christ, which, at least for Athanasius, was the central proviso of a coherent and convincing doctrine of salvation. The argument was simple and straightforward: only God can save, and if Jesus is not God, then he cannot save us. Divinity is required for him to be the savior of humankind.

What was needed, then, was a formula that upheld the delicate balance between God's oneness and God's threeness—the divinity possessed equally by the Father, the Son, and the Holy Spirit. The phraseology finally agreed upon stated that God existed as one being or essence (the Greek terms, used as synonyms, are *hypostasis* and *ousia*), but in three persons (*prosopon*) and, most important, that Jesus Christ was "of the same substance" (*homoousios*) of God the Father. In the resulting "Creed of Nicaea" (not to be confused with the creed popularly known today as the Nicene Creed, which received its final form only after the Council of Constantinople in 381), phrases such as "begotten, not made," "of one essence with the Father," and "came down and became man" were added to emphasize the argument against the Arian camp and Arius himself, who subsequently was exiled.[23]

Given the obvious tensions inherent in such a delicate balance, it should be no surprise that divisions and debates lingered for decades after Nicaea, requiring further councils to continue the difficult work of trying to unite the early Christians around specific doctrinal assertions to which assent was required. The reason for this is clear: "Many of the views espoused in these creeds are profoundly paradoxical. Is Christ God or Man? He is both. If he is both, is he two persons? No, he is the 'one Lord Jesus Christ.' If Christ is God and his Father is God, are there two Gods? No. 'We believe in *one* God.'"[24] What Nicaea left unresolved was exactly in what way Jesus was both God and human, and how this seemingly impossible paradox could be cogently and clearly argued.

Chalcedon

Christologically, the most important of the early councils was the Council of Chalcedon, which took place in 451 and was convened to settle lingering questions about Jesus Christ. Ehrman describes the pressing issues:

> Once proto-orthodoxy has established that Christ was both human and divine, the relationship between his humanity and divinity still needed to be resolved. How could Christ be both a man and a God? Was it that Christ had a human body but that his human soul was replaced by a soul that was divine? If so, then how was he "fully" human? Or was it that the incarnate Christ was two separate persons, one divine and one human? If that were the case, would that not mean he was *half* divine and *half* human, rather than fully both? Or was it that he was one solitary person, but that within that person he had two natures, one fully divine and one fully human? Or does he have just one nature, that is at one and the same time both fully divine and fully human? All of these options were proposed and hotly debated over the course of the fourth and fifth centuries.[25]

A variety of positions were put forth, all attempting to explain what was, at least for Greek philosophy, a near logical impossibility: true divinity uniting itself at an ontological level with true humanity—the impassible becoming passible, the Word becoming flesh, the infinite becoming finite. How could this possibly be true? In the centuries leading up to Chalcedon many solutions had been proposed, all of which "slid down one of two slippery slopes: they ended up either reducing Christ to an ordinary human being or turning him into some sort of demi-god or angel."[26] Even at Chalcedon, "the spectre of turning Christ into a figure that was neither divine nor human, a semi-divine creature, threatened the debate on all sides."[27] Nonetheless, the roughly six hundred bishops present were able to finally agree upon language that, while not satisfying all parties, created a rich, fertile seedbed in which the roots of later theological flourishing were to grow and be nourished.

The bishops at Chalcedon endorsed and reaffirmed the Nicene Creed and also availed themselves of the interpretation of it put forth in what was known as the "Tome of Leo," written by Pope Leo I to refute the heterodox teaching that Jesus had only one nature. It read, in part: "Jesus Christ was born from a virgin's womb, by a miraculous birth. And yet his nature is not on that account unlike to ours, for he that is true God is also true man...For just as the God [deity] is not changed by his compassion, so the man [manhood] is not swallowed up by the dignity [of the Godhead]."[28]

After much deliberation, the document that came out of the conference, the Chalcedonian Definition, was signed by 452 bishops. It is worth quoting extensively because in its particular detail and emphasis it reveals not only the positive position that was being argued, but also the negative positions that were being refuted:

> Therefore, following the holy fathers, we all with one accord teach men to acknowledge one and the same Son, our Lord Jesus Christ, at once complete in Godhead and complete in manhood, truly God and truly man, consisting also of a reasonable soul and body; of one substance with the Father as regards his Godhead, and at the same time of one substance with us as regards his manhood; like us in all respects, apart from sin; as regards his Godhead, begotten of the Father before the ages, but yet as regards his manhood begotten, for us men and for our salvation, of Mary the Virgin, the God-bearer; one and the same Christ, Son, Lord, Only-begotten, recognized IN TWO NATURES, WITHOUT CONFUSION, WITHOUT CHANGE, WITHOUT DIVISION, WITHOUT SEPARATION; the distinction of natures being in no way annulled by the union, but rather the characteristics of each nature being preserved and coming together to form one person

and subsistence, not as parted or separated into two persons, but one and the same Son and Only-begotten God the Word, Lord Jesus Christ.[29]

Note what is affirmed about Jesus: Is Jesus subordinate to the Father? No, he is not; he is just as divine as is God the Father. Is Jesus human like us in every way (except for the stain of sin)? Yes, he is; he truly and fully shares our human condition. Does he have some unique nature that is an inimitable combination of divine and human? No, he does not; instead, his divine nature shares identical "DNA" with God the Father, and his human nature shares the "DNA" we have.

This is the tradition that has come down to Christians today, and all orthodox Christian theology must make its peace with these specific conclusions, even while allowing for flexibility and novelty in language and imagery. Certainly, Chalcedon did not fully answer the question of *how* this delicate balance is maintained, but, at the very least, it did answer *what* the balance was: Jesus was truly, fully human, and to the same degree Jesus was truly, fully divine. The question now remains: What insights and challenges do the infancy narratives— both canonical and non-canonical—offer to this formulation?

Infancy Narratives in Matthew and Luke

In his seminal work, *The Birth of the Messiah*, Raymond Brown observes that "paradoxically, one may speak of the Gospels as developing backwards."[30] By this, he means that while Matthew and Luke trace the life of Jesus chronologically, from birth to death and resurrection, the proclamation of the gospel of Jesus Christ—his saving, redeeming work for the whole creation—began with his resurrection. One of the main ways in which we know this to be true is that the earliest Christian texts include hardly any mention of Jesus' birth (the Gospel of Mark, for example, and the Pauline letters). It is only in later texts that one begins to find such references. Indeed, Brown notes that "In the early Christian preaching the birth of Jesus had not yet been seen in the same salvific light as the death and resurrection."[31] Thus, we must ask the question of how the infancy narratives are "saving" at all, given that such an assumption was clearly not self-evident to the early church. That this is true is obvious even in the construction of the gospels themselves: "As was true also with Matthew's Gospel none of the Lucan infancy narrative has had a major influence on the body of the Gospel, so that, if the first two chapters had been lost, we could never have suspected their existence."[32]

Nonetheless, it is certainly significant that both Matthew and Luke chose to incorporate the stories of Jesus' origins and gave them theological significance when they could just as easily have left out that part of Jesus' biography. Instead, their inclusion leads us to conclude that "Matthew and Luke saw Christological implications in stories that were in circulation about Jesus' birth; or, at least, they saw the possibility of weaving such stories into a narrative of their own composition which could be made the vehicle of the message that Jesus was the Son of God acting for the salvation of mankind."[33] Indeed, one foundational assertion of this book is that these stories are indeed a "vehicle" of the salvific efficacy of Jesus' life and that, in fact, there is more going on here theologically than simply a charming narrative that provides a pleasant backdrop for Christmas festivities.

Several aspects of Jesus' person and work are uniquely present in these infancy narratives in that we can learn something important from them not easily found in the rest of the gospel stories, something that might otherwise not be accessible at all. First, the infancy narratives remind us that Jesus' humanity is real. Against all those who would spiritualize him, downplay the concrete tangibility of his physical body, and emphasize the categorical differences between "him" and "us," the infancy narratives describe Jesus developing in a human womb, being birthed in an ordinary human way, and, like any baby, utterly dependent upon his parents for his every need.

Second, the stories of Jesus' birth and infancy remind us that what it means to be human cannot simply be reduced to rationality, maturity, language capabilities, or a specific age of discernment. Instead, the fact that God became incarnate as an infant witnesses to the fact that every single human being, regardless of age, mental capabilities, race, or gender, bears equally the image of God, and is equally and fully united to the Divine by virtue of the common humanity we share with Jesus Christ.

Third, these narratives serve as a defense against adoptionism (the doctrine that Jesus became divine at his baptism, rather than being born divine), the first line in the attack on Jesus' full divinity, in that they demonstrate the work of the Holy Spirit present in every aspect, every moment of Jesus' life.

Fourth, the fact that God chose to come into creation as a helpless, vulnerable infant says something about who God is and how God chooses to exercise God's power.

Finally, the one story of Jesus' youth in Luke emphasizes that Jesus the Christ grew, developed, and matured, which opens up the possibility of understanding God as changing, growing, and being transformed by God's relationship to creation, as Jesus was by his relationships to his disciples and others with whom he came in contact.

Fully Human

One of the most obvious confessional statements about Jesus reinforced by the infancy narratives is his true humanity, which is an indispensible component of his identity as savior. As mentioned in the introduction, the great Cappadocian theologian Gregory Nazianzus coined the well-known phrase that tersely and plainly describes the necessity for Jesus' true humanity: "That which has not been assumed cannot be redeemed." In other words, if Jesus had not taken on a fully human nature, he could not have saved our human nature.[34] Gregory understood that if Jesus was only 80 percent human, for example, then the salvation of our 100 percent humanity would be at risk. If Jesus had, say, a true human soul, but a divine mind, then how could our human minds be redeemed? Or, if he had a true human mind, but a divine will, then how could our human wills be redeemed? No, to save all of who we are, Jesus had to become all of who we are: "Adam and Eve sinned by using their reason and will to make a decision; how can Jesus redeem us unless he too has a human mind and will? And how could Jesus save our immortal souls if he did not have one himself?"[35]

Irenaeus used different language to assert the same theological principle.

> Had it not been God who bestowed salvation we should not have it as a secure possession. And if man had not been united to God, man could not have become a partaker of immortality. For the mediator between God and man had to bring both parties into friendship and concord through his kinship with both; and to present man to God, and make God known to man. In what way could we share in the adoption of the sons of God unless through the Son we had received the fellowship with the Father, unless the Word of God made flesh had entered into communion with us? Therefore he passed through every stage of life, restoring to each age fellowship with God.[36]

Note the final sentence in that citation: "[Jesus] passed through every stage of life, restoring to each age fellowship with God." Irenaeus thus included even the infancy of Jesus: "It was not enough simply that the Word should become a human being: it was necessary that he should pass through every age of life, from infancy to mature years, sanctifying infants, children, youths and elders and offering to each age an appropriate example of holiness, justice, obedience and authority."[37]

Jesus' true humanity was a sticking point for his followers in the early church as many early Christians found it very difficult to reconcile the human with the divine. This is easily seen in the theological debates of the early church, many of which were designed to safeguard the purity of his divinity and to "preserve his divinity from corruption or compromise with his humanity."[38] As was noted earlier, however, without such a reconciliation the whole Christian doctrine of salvation falls apart, and it is thus essential that Christians be able to harmonize their understanding of Jesus' divinity with his true humanity.

Reconciling Jesus' divinity and humanity continues to be a struggle today. Many Christians who have never heard of Arius operate with a theology in which Jesus is not quite divine in the way God the Father is—some going so far as to consider him a "son" of God no different from the way in which we are sons and daughters of God. On the other hand, others tend not to think of Jesus as a "real" human being who shares their nature, but more like one manifestation among others of divine love and grace. In a May 2010 *New Yorker* article that reviewed a selection of newly released books on Jesus, the author puts the central problem at the heart of Jesus' existence clearly and vividly:

> If Jesus is truly one with God, in what sense could he suffer doubt, fear, exasperation, pain, horror, and so on? So we get the Jesus rendered in the Book of John, who doesn't. But if he doesn't suffer doubt, fear, exasperation, pain, and horror, in what sense is his death a sacrifice rather than just a theatrical enactment? A lamb whose throat is not cut and does not bleed is not really much of an offering. None of this is very troubling if one has a pagan idea of divinity: the Son of God might then be half human and half divine, suffering and triumphing and working out his heroic destiny in the half-mortal way of Hercules, for instance. But that's ruled out by the full weight of the Jewish idea of divinity—omnipresent and omniscient, knowing all and seeing all. If God he was—not some Hindu-ish avatar or offspring of God, but actually one with God—then God once was born and had dirty diapers

and took naps. The longer you think about it, the more astounding, or absurd, it becomes.[39]

The birth narratives are precisely the place where this theological "absurdity" comes to view in full force, which is one important reason why they continue to play such a critical role in our understanding of Jesus' person and work today. In the birth narratives, one cannot escape the earthiness, the fleshliness of Jesus' existence—not only with the image of naps and dirty diapers, but also of being burped and spitting up, none of which are "god-like" activities.

Another important activity of the infant Jesus that certainly warrants mention here is breast-feeding. As Margaret Miles notes in her book, *A Complex Delight*, images of Mary with one breast exposed, breast-feeding Jesus, gained popularity in the fourteenth century and actually had profound theological significance.[40] These images made a strong statement about the full humanity of Jesus Christ: "A human body's best show of power, and the evidence of Christ's fully human incarnation, was the Virgin's presentation of Christ *from her own body*."[41] Mary's true humanity testified to Christ's true humanity. Indeed, the images of Mary nursing Jesus, particularly those images in which the infant Jesus' gaze is twisted "to engage the viewer's eye . . . inviting the viewer to participate in the pictured scene,"[42] were seen as images of salvation. Writing of the symbolic power of the breast, Miles argues, "in early modern Western societies in which Christianity was the dominant religion, [Mary's] bared breast, appearing in paintings and sculptures, signified nourishment and loving care—God's provision for the Christian, ever in need of God's grace."[43]

This is another way in which the infancy narratives open us to a new way of thinking about God and understanding our own humanity in relationship to God. Although in the twenty-first century most Christians do not model their relationship to God after Jesus' relationship with his mother, earlier generations of Christians saw the image of Jesus nursing at Mary's breast as a metaphor for their own reliance upon God for their very existence. For example, Miles quotes Augustine, who, in her words, "made the infant's experience of delight the prototype for his experience of God," writing, "What am I at my best but suckling the milk you give and feeding on you, the food that is incorruptible?"[44]

What the birth narratives make clear is that Jesus lived a full human life from start to finish—he did not spring full grown, like Athena, from the head of his father. Instead, the Son of God was born into the world as a baby, showing no special intelligence, no unusual gifts, and certainly no miraculous power. In the infancy narratives, Jesus' humanity was ordinary, conventional, typical, and in that way these stories forcefully press upon us the reality of Jesus' true humanity.

While the gospels do not include such details, we can be sure that Jesus cried when he was hungry and got angry at his mother when she did not pick him up as quickly as he would have liked. Certainly, he would have been fussy, even irritable, and he probably fought nap time tooth and nail like all children do at one time or another. Imagine him teething, being potty-trained, being spanked. Imagine him learning to speak, learning to walk, learning to read and write. We usually do not consider these things when we think about God, but the infancy narratives in scripture encourage us to do so. Jesus' humanity is not *sui generis*, it is *our* humanity, and the infancy narratives are the most vivid reminders of the common human nature we share with Christ.

Humanity Is More Than Rationality

Another unique contribution of the infancy narratives is to remind us that "humanity" does not equal "rationality," and that, theologically, every single human being, regardless of age or intellectual capacity, is capable of bearing the Divine—and indeed, in the incarnation of Jesus Christ, has been united to the Divine.

In the Christian tradition, one dominant strain of theological explication of the concept of the *imago Dei*—humanity as created in the image of God—has emphasized the role of human reason. This is not surprising. It has long been thought that what separates *homo sapiens* from the rest of the animal kingdom is our brains—the capacity for language, complex reasoning, imagination, creativity, and so on. It is only natural, then, to associate such skills and abilities with the Divine and to consider them analogous to divine wisdom and a point of connection between humanity and God. From this vein of theological interpretation, then, human intellect came to be seen as the locus for our true humanity, the defining mark of what it means to be human. It is not insignificant that both the theology and practice of a wide variety of denominations and individual congregations continue to support this interpretation of humanity, both explicitly and implicitly, in that many church bodies do not offer communon to and/or baptize infants and young children, instead waiting until they have a certain level of reason or understanding of the sacrament.

Such a conclusion may seem quite sensible and fully benign, until its ramifications are followed through to their logical ends. If rationality and intellect are the mark of what it means to be human, what does that say about the full humanity of children, for example, or the mentally ill, or those with diminished mental capabilities? Surely, then, a theological justification has been laid for seeing them as somehow "less." Even if no one ever explicitly denies their full humanity, the fact is that such a bifurcating of the human population into "fully human" and "lesser human" happens all the time and in contexts all over the globe. There is not enough space here to list all the examples of such dehumanizing treatment that occurs even today, let alone the examples from history, such as the eugenics movement in Nazi Germany, the witchcraft trials in the Middle Ages, and the enslavement both of Africans and other indigenous populations. They all illustrate what can happen when certain standards of "reason" (typically decided upon and applied by men in positions of power) are the criteria used to judge one's full humanity. However, a few contemporary examples illustrate this point.

The Commodification of Being Human

Children all over the world are bought and sold as slave labor, child prostitutes, and mercenary soldiers. They are sold by parents desperate for money; they are discarded when they evince a disability, including the "wrong" gender, and left to fend for themselves; and they are kidnapped by those who see them not as human beings but as commodities. Children constitute fully half of all victims of human trafficking, which itself manifests the belief that all people are *not* equal—some are worth only the market price. For this reason, this sinful epidemic merits elaboration.

It is difficult to find accurate statistics on trafficking due to the secrecy and covert nature of trafficking activities. However, some estimates can be made. According to the U.S. State Department *Trafficking in Persons* report from 2004,

> Each year, an estimated 600,000 to 800,000 men, women, and children are trafficked across international borders (some international and non-governmental organizations place the number far higher), and the trade is growing. Of the 600,000–800,000 people trafficked across international borders each year, 70 percent are female and 50 percent are children. The majority of these victims are forced into the commercial sex trade.[45]

It is widely believed that the enslavement and commodification of human beings that are at the heart of human trafficking constitute the third most profitable criminal activity in the world, behind only drug dealing and illegal weapons sales. It is estimated that 9.5 billion dollars are generated in annual revenue from all trafficking activities.[46]

Human trafficking is a direct result of the economic climate in which we live, and particularly the dire economic conditions faced by so many people around the world. However, human trafficking is not the only reprehensible consequence of sinful economic structures that perpetuate a denial of the full humanity of every individual. In *Consuming Religion*, Vincent Miller describes in detail the harrowing conditions of young workers in China who participate in the production of an uncomfortable number of items we all most likely have in our homes right now. One of them, Li Chunmei, collapsed and died due to overwork in her position as a "runner" in a Chinese factory that makes stuffed animals. Her job was to run the partially completed animals from work station to work station, which she had been doing from 8:00 AM to midnight for sixty days straight before her death. Vincent J. Miller puts it bluntly: "She was worked to death making things that we try not to call shit."[47] As much as we would like to pretend otherwise, the full humanity of men, women, and children cannot be taken for granted. There are myriad examples that demonstrate the multiple ways in which the fundamental humanity of certain sectors of the population is systematically denied and violated.

An obvious case is the treatment of the mentally ill. The facilities used to house and care for the mentally ill in the nineteenth and early twentieth centuries in Britain and the United States were shocking in both their wanton cruelty and absolute lack of sympathy for patients. Basic living conditions were appalling: chains, beds of straw, lack of heat in the winter, and poor nutrition, to say nothing of the terrible physical experiments that were carried out on them, such as shock treatments, lobotomies, and dangerous experimental drug regiments.

In her account of her family's struggle with her son David's schizophrenia, Rosemary Radford Ruether offers a brief history of these conditions, describing how the responsibility for care for the mentally ill fell first on families exclusively, with government authorities stepping in only when absolutely necessary. She notes that family care was not always good care, however; some families were ashamed of their children, so parents and siblings hid them away, even locking them in attics or basements.[48] This was not the only option, however. In colonial times, she notes, the mentally ill could be "boarded out," which could include being auctioned off to those who were free to use them in any way they chose. "Farmers particularly were on the lookout for able-bodied poor people, including the more docile among 'the retarded' or 'mentally ill,' who could be used for farm labor."[49] Sometimes the mentally ill were simply "dumped"—forced out of whatever home they were living in and left to wander the streets and fend for themselves. Poorhouses and mental hospitals, some of them providing horrific living conditions, rounded out the options for the mentally ill in the seventeenth, eighteenth, and nineteenth centuries and continuing into the twentieth century.

While the most egregious care options have been reformed, many would argue that in the United States even today the mentally ill continue to be discriminated against and left to get by with substandard medical care, a lack of adequate housing, and unaffordable medication. This kind of treatment demonstrates clearly that the mentally ill have not always been considered "fully human," and indeed, in some situations, still are not.

The infancy narratives provide a strong, compelling argument against any and all such forms of human degradation, exploitation, and commodification, as they demonstrate clearly that Jesus was fully human himself from birth. Even as an infant, he was not less than the savior of the world, not less than God's only begotten son, not less than fully divine, and certainly not less than fully human. He did not "become" the Son of God at some time in his early adulthood, nor did he "develop" his identity as savior, realizing it gradually over the years. Instead, from the moment he was born, he was completely and totally the one whom the disciples proclaimed him to be after the resurrection, the one whom Paul wrote and preached about all through Asia Minor, the one in whom countless Christians have professed their faith for millennia. Thus, we might well say that at the moment of his incarnation the world was changed forever, and the chasm between the Divine and the human was overcome.

Some would even argue that it is the incarnation, rather than the resurrection, where we see our salvation most clearly. For example, Rita Nakashima Brock and Rebecca Parker, in their book *Saving Paradise*, discuss in detail the concept of *theosis*, in which the power of God forms humans into the image of Christ, and humans then evidence a likeness to the Divine in their own lives. They argue that at his birth Jesus "incarnated God in human flesh and infused humanity with divinity."[50] What that meant for humanity was that "Doing the work of Christ and sharing his Spirit, Christians manifested divinity... This understanding of salvation permeated many regions and branches of the first millennium of Christianity."[51] Certainly, Brock and Parker note that this was particularly visible as Christians modeled the work of Christ during his earthly ministry, tending to the sick and loving the neighbor. However, it certainly can be argued that if salvation is understood, at least in part, to be a sharing in the nature of the Divine and in union with God in Christ, this happens first and foremost with the incarnation and not in Jesus' adult ministry.

The infancy narratives, with their emphasis on both Jesus' full divinity and full humanity, continue to remind us of the full, equal worth of every single human being and the inadequacy of relying solely on human reason to measure a person's true humanity. The wiser are no closer to God, and conversely the weak, the infirm, the young, and the challenged are no further from God and thus disposable or expendable. As the fullness of God chose to dwell in the infant Christ, so too does God dwell in every single human being. Jesus' infancy thus stands against any who would exploit, abuse, or mistreat any child of God, regardless of age, gender, social status, or ability.

Fully Divine

In *The Odyssey*, Homer's great epic of Odysseus's ten years of wandering as he tries to get home after the fall of Troy and the end of the Trojan War, a point comes when Odysseus and his crew must cross a particularly dangerous straight of water that separates mainland Italy from Sicily. There is no room for error as they must navigate away from Scylla—a monster with six heads on long necks and a penchant for devouring sailors—on the one side, and, on the other, from Charybdis—a monster with an enormous gaping mouth that continually sucks in and spits out great quantities of water, creating giant whirlpools.

The task of navigating between two equally dangerous poles is a fitting metaphor for what the early church fathers faced in their theological descriptions of Jesus Christ. The loss of Jesus' full humanity was not the only danger the early church fathers had to circumvent. The other "monster" that had to be avoided at all costs was the ever-present danger of seeing Jesus as a creature—not fully divine as is God the Father, but divine in only a derivative way. Here, too, the infancy narratives are of great significance. A primary facet of the soteriological significance of the birth narratives is the way in which they "press back"[52] Jesus' divine identity from his baptism to his conception.

Historically, the most significant form that embodied this danger was the doctrine of adoptionism, which was primarily associated with

Arius, discussed above. This doctrine articulated a position in which Jesus was not born fully divine, but became fully divine at his baptism when the Holy Spirit descended upon him in the form of a dove, and he was "adopted" by God. In the words of Mark's gospel, "You are my Son, the Beloved; with you I am well pleased." These words inaugurated Jesus' public ministry, seemingly endowing him with divine power and wisdom, effectively making him the Son of God in a way in which he was not before.

However, the infancy narratives provide a strong rebuttal to the argument that Jesus was not fully divine from his birth. They do this most clearly through their description of the virgin birth, specifically in their emphasis on Mary's being overshadowed by the Holy Spirit and conceiving through the power of that Spirit. The presence and action of the Spirit is particularly significant in that it demonstrates that Mary's virginity does not grant her special status in and of herself, but rather emphasizes that the virgin birth is first and foremost a theological statement about Jesus and the full divinity with which he is endowed from the moment of his spiritual conception.

Raymond Brown's description of the significance of this insight is especially apt. He points out that "the christological moment (i.e., the moment of the revelation of who Jesus is—the Messiah—the Son of God in power through the Holy Spirit), which was once attached to the resurrection and then to baptism, has in the infancy narratives been moved to the conception: it is the virginal conception that serves now as the begetting of God's Son."[53] This is of critical importance—it unequivocally refutes the notion that Jesus was anything less than fully divine from his birth.

Matthew and Luke both emphasize this fact, albeit in different ways. After noting that Mary was "found to be with child from the Holy Spirit," Matthew describes the visit from an angel of the Lord who watches over Jesus protectively, clarifying to Joseph why there is no shame in taking Mary as his wife and reiterating that Jesus is fully divine, explaining that he is God in the flesh, "God with us." Further, this angel continues to appear at regular intervals, guiding Joseph to take the actions needful to safeguard Jesus from danger. In addition, Matthew describes a visit from "the wise men," who recognize that Jesus is a king and pay him homage, prompting Herod's realization that Jesus is the Messiah.

In Luke, however, this christological insight is most richly developed. God enters onto the scene in spectacular form, in the manner of an angel who delivers shocking news to Mary:

"Greetings, favored one! The Lord is with you...Do not be afraid, Mary, for you have found favor with God. And now, you will conceive in your womb and bear a son..." Mary said to the angel, "How can this be, since I am a virgin?" The angel said to her, "The Holy Spirit will come upon you, and the power of the Most High will overshadow you; therefore the child to be born will be holy; he will be called Son of God." (Lk 1:28–35)

As proof, the angel points to what God has already done for Elizabeth, Mary's barren relative, whom God has caused to conceive in her old age.

The text makes clear, however, that what God has done for Mary is not the same as what God does for many women in scripture, that is, removing their barrenness and allowing them to conceive a child after intercourse with their husbands. Instead, this action of God is radical and unique. As Mary's Magnificat makes clear, it has drastic ramifications for all of creation.

In this context, Raymond Brown makes a particular rich and fascinating connection between the activity of the Holy Spirit in Jesus' virgin birth and the Spirit's activity in creation:

The begetting [of Jesus] is not quasi-sexual as if God takes the place of a male principle in mating with Mary. There is more of a connotation of creativity. Mary is not barren, and in her case the child does not come into existence because God co-operates with the husband's generative action and removes the sterility. Rather, Mary is a virgin who has not known man, and therefore the child is totally God's work—a new creation ...The Spirit that comes upon Mary is closer to the Spirit of God that hovered over the waters before creation in Gen 1:2. The earth was void and without form when that Spirit appeared; just so Mary's womb was a void until through the Spirit God filled it with a child who was His Son...Since Mary is a virgin who has not yet lived with her husband, there is no yearning for or human expectation of a child—it is the surprise of creation. No longer are we dealing with human request and God's generous fulfillment; this is God's initiative going beyond anything man or woman has dreamed of.[54]

It could well be argued that another way in which Luke emphasizes Jesus' true and full divinity is the way in which he depicts Mary as the first disciple, that is, one who professes faith in Jesus as the savior and believes in him. In light of Mary's declaration in the Magnificat of what God has done in her and the salvific import of Jesus' conception, as well as her willing "yes" to the work of the Holy Spirit, Brown confidently asserts that Luke "esteems Mary as the first Christian disciple."[55] He notes that because she is the first to proclaim the news of salvation that Jesus Christ inaugurates, Luke has linked the salvation that was previously tied exclusively to Jesus' death and resurrection to Jesus' birth.[56] Thus, we can say with confidence that not only do the infancy narratives assert Jesus' full divinity, they also make the radical claim that salvation has come to the world in the form of an infant—another rich theological proclamation that warrants examination.

God as a Baby

It goes without saying that the conditions of Jesus' birth do not fit the expectations one might justifiably have for the incarnation of the Divine. Obviously, this is no accident. The fact that God takes flesh in the form of a baby—a vulnerable baby at that—says something important about who God is, how God chooses to exercise God's power, how God has chosen to be in relationship to the world, and, in addition, how the followers of God are supposed to act.

Diana Eck describes the significance of the incarnation in this way: "God did not first show his human face as the young and fearless prophet, but as a child. A world in which children are the most vulnerable victims of poverty, malnutrition, and violence is surely in need of the refinement and enlargement of our capacity to see Christ as a child."[57]

Certainly, the infancy narratives remind us of the immeasurable worth of children. More to the point, however, is the fact that the infancy narratives set a specific tone from the very beginning of God's incarnation on earth. Taking our lead from the stories of Jesus' birth, we can say with confidence that Jesus' ministry is not going to be about destroying his enemies, punishing those who doubt him, or raising a mighty army to overturn the Roman Empire. Instead, given the way God has chosen to enter into the world, God's plan for salvation is going to take a very different shape. Jesus is going to reveal his identity as savior not by installing himself as the head of the Pharisees or supplanting Herod as king. Instead, his identity, that of an itinerant person, will be carried out in poverty and consist of such activities as healing lepers, feeding the hungry, dining with prostitutes, and singling out tax collectors for special attention.

It is no surprise that both the Roman officials and the religious leaders fear and mistrust Jesus and, in the end, want him dead. He is not acting in the way that is expected and he is turning routine religious and social customs on their head, all in the name of love and friendship. He preaches poverty not wealth, inclusion not exclusion, and the path of discipleship instead of religious legalism. In a word, the infancy narratives clearly describe divine power revealed in weakness, a theme that is of central importance in Jesus' ministry and especially in his death.

This same theme of power revealed in weakness is vividly exposed in the crucifixion. Martin Luther's theology of the cross developed this idea with great insight and practical import. In his Heidelberg Disputation of 1518, thesis 20, Luther wrote, "That person deserves to be called a theologian, however, who comprehends the visible and manifest things of God through suffering and the cross."[58] Gerhard Forde explains what Luther means in this way: "God refuses to be seen in any other way [than the cross] ... Theologians of the cross are therefore those whose eyes have been turned away from the quest for glory by the cross, who have eyes only for what is visible, what is actually there to been seen of God, the suffering and despised crucified Jesus."[59] In other words, "it is only *through suffering and the cross* that sinners can see and come to know God."[60]

Luther was aware that what humans typically expect and want from their gods is a show of power, something that legitimizes the strategies of human rulers and their ruthless means of getting and keeping power, a god who will reward us with favor and wealth when we are "good" and punish those who are "wicked." However, I maintain that not only in the crucifixion but also in the incarnation we are faced with a God who is very different from what we might expect. In the same way that God has "hidden" Godself in the suffering of the crucified Christ, so too has God "hidden" Godself in the face of the helpless infant fleeing for his life from Herod.

Deanna Thompson makes the following observation: "Like Moses who was allowed to see only God's back, Christians encounter God's backside in the mystery of the cross, where God's strength, power, and presence are hidden *sub contrario* in Christ's suffering and dying. It is on the cross that God 'hides' God's power by clothing it in the weakness of Christ's suffering humanity."[61] Certainly, it is this humanity that is on full display in the incarnation, where God's "weakness" is manifest to the point of utter dependency on the goodness and wisdom of Mary and Joseph.

Similarly, Jesus' adult ministry demonstrates the paradox of divine power revealed in weakness reaching mature expression: Jesus Christ is one who chooses the company of sinners over the company of the righteous, who offers forgiveness freely and without cost, who demands that his followers willingly give what they have to the poor, and who ends up dying alone and forsaken on a cross in order to be faithful to the vision of solidarity, grace, and new life that was the axis of his entire ministry. Somehow, this all seems less shocking when we remember the infancy narratives and the fact that he was born to a no-name couple, in a no-name village, in weakness and poverty.

Growing in Wisdom

A final point to note concerns the one story of Jesus' boyhood found in the canonical gospels: the story told by Luke of Jesus in the temple. Raymond Brown has pointed out that the fact that Jesus refers to God as his "Father" is very significant: "The center of the story is not the boy's intelligence but his reference to God as his Father in vs. 49. This is highly Christological, for here we have Jesus saying of himself what the heavenly voice will say at the baptism."[62] This identification is certainly important: finally there is some confirmation from Jesus himself of what was proclaimed about him by both the wise men and the angels at his birth. This is the first moment in which Jesus proclaims his own identity and steps into his promised role.

However, I maintain that of even greater significance is the very short sentence that closes this episode in Jesus' life: "And Jesus increased in wisdom and in years, and in divine and human favor" (Lk 2:52). What could it possibly mean to say that Jesus, the fully divine Son of God, "increases in wisdom"? One thing we know from the beginning: we cannot simply say that this statement refers to Jesus in his humanity, but does not refer to Jesus in his divinity. This dividing Jesus up into two separate personalities was unequivocally ruled out of bounds when Nestorianism was condemned as a heresy at both the Council of Ephesus and the Council of Chalcedon. Nestorius, who wanted to preserve the immutability of the divinity, taught that Jesus Christ had not one united nature, but two separate natures that were distinguishable and divisible. In essence, by affirming Jesus' one nature, the early church councils voided the possibility of going through scripture with a check-off sheet in two columns, putting certain actions of Jesus—weeping, getting angry, dying—on the "human side"—

and other actions of Jesus—walking on water, multiplying the loaves, causing the blind to see—on the "divine side." Instead, the Christian church holds that Jesus was always, in all his words and deeds, acting as one person, fully human and fully divine. What could be attributed to one nature could also be attributed to the other.

Yet, here is Luke's statement that in Jesus Christ God "increased in wisdom." While this might well be an unsettling idea, as the concept of an all-seeing, all-knowing God continues to dominate Christian thought, there is actually a wonderful bit of divine disclosure in this gem of a sentence. If we allow for the possibility of growth in wisdom in the Divine, a picture of God is revealed to us that is quite different from the god of common parlance today—an old man sitting on a throne far, far removed from the world, making decisions by fiat without ever getting involved in the messiness of creation.

Instead, what we have here is a God who actively engages in relationships with those around him, learns from those relationships, and even grows in those relationships. This, perhaps, is the meaning of a prior sentence in Luke: "Then [Jesus] went down with [his parents] and came to Nazareth, and was obedient to them" (Lk 2:51). It suggests that this relationship Jesus had with his parents was, at least in some ways, like most relationships between children and their parents: there are guidelines to be followed—"house rules," if you will, certain freedoms that are first prohibited and then permitted as the child grows. Like any child, Jesus received a certain amount of nurturing, education, and discipline, all of which are necessary for any child to grow into a responsible, knowledgeable adult, one who is able to function in the world at large.

This story of Jesus as a boy gives us a glimpse of a God who is fully engaged with the world, enmeshed with the world, open to the world. He is not only active in the world but is being acted upon by those with whom God comes in contact. Jesus is not only teaching but also learning, is not only making his own decisions about right and wrong but also acquiescing to the decisions of his parents. He is both exercising his own authority and accepting the authority of others.

The statement that Jesus "increased in wisdom" suggests that Jesus' infancy and boyhood are not simply God play-acting; they are not a diversion or a ruse used to disguise God's true nature until the right time. Instead, they reveal a God who is coming to know the world in a new way, as it were, from the inside out, a God who is at work doing something radically new in creation and experiencing that newness in God's own being. Jesus' "increase" here opens up the possibility of seeing a God who is not above or beyond change, a God who is willingly affected by God's relationship with creation, and—dare we say it?—a God who not only transforms us, but is transformed by and with us as well.

Conclusion

The infancy narratives, in my understanding, are pregnant, so to speak, with a great deal of soteriological significance. They give us unique insights into both the person and work of Jesus Christ as well as into the nature of God and the way in which God chooses to be in relationship with us. Far from being simple or childish stories, grist for a wealth of devotional artwork, or fantastical bits of evangelical speculation, these stories present the gospel in an inimitable, accessible form with almost inexhaustible theological richness. When examined closely, with fresh ears and an open mind, they become much more than trite stories told in endless church plays, children's books, and familiar Christmas songs. Instead, they become a pathway into thinking about God in a new way, understanding Jesus' life and ministry from a fresh perspective, and gaining a valuable lens for reading the gospel proclamation with new eyes. Raymond Brown sums up their theological significance this way:

> Whether or not the infancy narratives were historical, whether or not they were based on eye-witness testimony, whether or not they had a pre-Gospel existence, Matthew and Luke thought they were appropriate introductions to the career and significance of Jesus. To give them less value than other parts of the gospels is to misread the mind of the evangelists for whom the infancy narratives were fitting vehicles of a message they wanted to convey. Indeed, from this point of view the infancy narratives are not an embarrassment but a masterpiece. Perhaps precisely because the material had been less fixed in the course of apostolic preaching, the evangelists exercised greater freedom of composition in the infancy narratives. One is hard pressed to find elsewhere in the gospels theology so succinctly and imaginatively presented.[63]

Succinct and imaginative theology—who could ask for more than that?

The Infancy Gospel of Thomas

If the infancy narratives in the canonical gospels maintain and support the delicate balancing act of affirming both Jesus' full humanity and his full divinity with sophistication, subtlety, and grace, the Infancy Gospel of Thomas does not. In its defense, however, that does not seem to be its purpose, although it does raise the question of just what the purpose of this gospel is. Bart Ehrman describes the Infancy Gospel of Thomas as having a non-theological agenda—noting that it "does not appear to promote a theological agenda of any particular branch of Christianity." Instead, Ehrman argues, "it is probably better to think of it as a forgery...derived simply from Christian imagination, a set of entertaining episodes that explore what the miracle-working Son of God may have been like as a child growing up in the household of Joseph and Mary."[64]

On this point, however, I disagree. While Ehrman's conclusion certainly may be true from a historical perspective, I would argue that when we look at this text today we can, indeed, see a "theological agenda," one that is both controversial and astute. I see two primary insights that can shed light on a contemporary Christian understanding of who Jesus is and how he saves humankind: first, the idea of "God at play," and second, the importance of understanding Jesus as "God with emotion."

God at Play

According to a story in *The Washington Times*, most Americans still believe in God. Not surprisingly, however, when asked to describe God more concretely, a variety of opinions surface. According to one poll, only 1 percent of Americans overall think God is female. Among Protestant and born-again Christian male respondents, the number is 0 percent; among women and Catholics it is 1 percent. By contrast, more than a third—36 percent—say God is male. Overall, 37 percent say God is neither male nor female. Ten percent say God is both male and female, while 17 percent are not entirely sure what they believe.[65]

Relevant in this context, first, is the number of people who continue to believe that God is male. I am sure this comes as no surprise to anyone who works in public ministry, particularly in mainline Protestant and evangelical Christian denominations. Second, however, and in some ways more important here, is what the survey reveals about how people think about God's appearance: "Does God look like Michelangelo's vision on the ceiling of the Sistine Chapel? Maybe. The survey showed that 9 percent said God appeared 'like a human with a face, body, arms, legs, eyes,' though the percentage was slightly higher—13 percent—among Protestants."[66]

Overall, of course, this is a small number—roughly 10 percent, give or take—but nonetheless, these survey results offer a window into a much more widespread, commonplace reality. Christians, when they do envision God anthropomorphically, overwhelmingly still envision God as an older man. This data points to the fact that the most common visual depiction of God still continues to be that which has dominated Christian thinking for millennia: an older white man, usually with a beard, usually on a throne, usually with a stern countenance.

While much can and should be said about the theological and pastoral problems that come with such a narrow view of God, I want to highlight one specific facet of this view—God's "countenance," the typical facial expression that accompanies such a picture of God. We usually take it for granted that God the Father wears a severe expression. Rare are images of God where God has a twinkle in the eye, a smile playing on the lips, or anything like delight radiating out from the face. Instead, we see over and over and over again a God who is grave, a God who is burdened with the weight of sin—sometimes literally so, as in the images where God the Father is holding in his arms the crucified Christ—a God whose authority as the ruler of heaven is unquestionable. In short, a God who is all work and no play.

Most images of Jesus do nothing to mitigate this picture. The vast majority of artistic representations of Jesus either depict him in agony on the cross or serene and other-worldly in the resurrection. There are some exceptions, of course: images of Jesus surrounded by children, and images of Jesus as the good shepherd carrying the lost sheep home on his shoulders come to mind immediately. We also might think of Pantocrator images—images of a severe Jesus taking his place as Lord of the universe and judge of the living and the dead—or images from Jesus' ministry—praying in the garden of Gethsemane, changing water into wine, or stilling the waters. In all of these images, too, Jesus has the somber look of a man on a mission, often thoroughly frustrated with the inability of those around him to understand what he is saying.[67]

What is wrong with this picture? Nothing, some would argue. Such a countenance befits the king of the universe, the lord of the cosmos, the creator and judge of the world. That may all be true, but it is also true that such a picture does not tell the whole story or depict all of who God is. God is also a God who takes delight in creation, who sports with Leviathan, who is pleased by the sound of the lute and the lyre. Therefore, why should it be so difficult to imagine that such a God might periodically crack a smile at a particularly rousing hymn on a Sunday morning, or laugh at the antics of two squirrels chasing each other through the trees, or share in the joy of a newborn's first cry? Why are such images often regarded as sentimental, lacking in sophistication, and overly anthropomorphic, when the more typical images of a stern male judge or king are so sacrosanct that to deny or reject them may elicit a vociferous protest of heterodoxy? This has been a common experience of scholars, particularly feminist scholars, who have attempted to bring a wider variety of images into theological and liturgical currency.

Obviously I am speaking of God metaphorically here. I am not part of the 9 percent of Americans who think that God has a literal human face with a literal human body to go along with it. I do, however, believe in the power of visual imagery to make very compelling statements about who God is and how God is in relationship to us. Thus, I regard these images as having utmost theological importance. Such images both consciously and unconsciously mold the minds of Christians, particularly regarding their conception of God. One of the insights the Infancy Gospel of Thomas offers us is the image of a God at play, a God who is spontaneous, impulsive, and inventive—a God whose "face" bears a sly grin, clever eyes, and an ingenious appearance, testifying to a God who is very active in the day-to-day life of creation, responding to situations in creative, playful ways.

This "face" can be a helpful reminder that Jesus is not reducible to a humorless, business-only preacher and teacher, but instead possesses and displays the capacity for joy and mischief, the capacity to relax, and the capacity to recreate. In other words, the gospel message of Jesus' life and ministry also includes a capacity for creative activity that has no "purpose," except the sheer delight of creating. It includes unplanned encounters with strangers that call forth an unexpected response, and it includes tending to the needs of loved ones in inventive and resourceful ways.

This "face" of Jesus allows us to see God a new way, too, and to see the Divine as more than a serious old man—an austere judge, removed from and unmoved by creation. Instead, this face of Jesus opens up to us the frolicsome dimension of God's being, the God who creates for the simple joy of it, the God who laughs, the God who is surprising and inventive, the God who can think on her feet and respond to the unexpected with innovative new solutions.

God as Spontaneous, Impulsive and Inventive

Three brief stories suggest a very different picture of God from that typically portrayed in artistic representations of God: Jesus' creating birds from clay, his healing a man's leg, and his using his cloak to carry water for his mother. These stories, together, merit re-reading.

The first story, as told here in a slightly different translation from that in the introduction to this book, is from the second chapter of the gospel:

> When this boy, Jesus, was five years old, he was playing at the ford of a rushing stream. He was collecting the flowing water into ponds and made the water instantly pure. He did this with a single command. He then made soft clay and shaped it into twelve sparrows. He did this on the Sabbath day, and many other boys were playing with him. But when a Jew saw what Jesus was doing while playing on the Sabbath day, he immediately went off and told Joseph, Jesus' father: "See here, your boy is at the ford and has taken mud and fashioned twelve birds with it, and so has violated the Sabbath." So Joseph went there, and as soon as he spotted him he shouted, "Why are you doing what's not permitted on the Sabbath?" But Jesus simply clapped his hands and shouted to the sparrows: "Be off, fly away, and remember me, you who are now alive!" And the sparrows took off and flew away noisily. (2:1–7).

The next story, previously mentioned in chapter 4 of this book, comes from chapter 10 of the gospel:

> A few days later a young man was splitting wood in the neighborhood when his axe slipped and cut off the bottom of his foot. He was dying from the loss of blood. The crowd rushed there in an uproar, and the boy Jesus ran up, too. He forced his way through the crowd and grabbed hold of the young man's wounded foot. It was instantly healed. He said to the youth, "Get up now, split your wood, and remember me." (10:1–3)

The final story, found in chapter 11 of the gospel, immediately follows:

When [Jesus] was six years old, his mother sent him to draw water and bring it back to the house. But he lost his grip on the pitcher in the jostling of the crowd, and it fell and broke. So, Jesus spread out the cloak he was wearing and filled it with water and carried it back to his mother. His mother, once she saw the miracle that had occurred, kissed him. (11:1–4a)

What picture do these three short vignettes paint of Jesus? The first story is certainly delightful in that it offers a very different way of envisioning how God's creative activity takes place. Contrast this image of a young child, at play in the mud, spontaneously bringing to life some creatures he had made naturally and impulsively in the clay, with that of a mature adult, who with much deliberation and intentionality speaks creation into being, sequentially and logically. The wide gulf between these pictures of divine creative activity suggests two radically different understandings of how God actually creates.

Or, perhaps, compare the young child to this same mature adult, carefully forming a human being, planting a garden, and then making each animal, one by one, out of the soil. Allowing that Genesis story to be informed by this story from the Infancy Gospel helps us to see aspects of the creation story that are often overlooked: the inventiveness of God, the novel way in which God responds to Adam's situation, and the creative solution God ultimately devises. In the creation story of Genesis 2, God seems to be creating the cosmos somewhat instinctively, extemporaneously, if you will: starting with the one clay being and then going from there, according to the needs of each new situation. Perhaps God's "plan" for the world isn't quite so "planned" after all. Perhaps there is room for novelty, invention, and even surprise in God's dealings with creation.

At first glance, the second story, in which Jesus heals a man's wounded foot, seems to be consistent with many of the healings stories from Jesus' adult ministry that are found in the canonical gospels. A man is in need of healing and Jesus heals him. However, there are some key differences. First, the injured person does not ask for Jesus or come to Jesus; indeed, in the dire situation in which he finds himself, he is not even thinking about Jesus. Second, the man is not ill—he is not a leper, he does not suffer from a chronic debilitation, and his situation has nothing to do with sin. He has simply had a tragic accident, something that could happen to anyone at any time. Third, in this story, Jesus comes to the scene just like all the other "looky-loos" who run to the sound of a noise to see what has happened. No one seems to notice

Jesus and he has to push through the crowd to get to the man. Finally, Jesus heals the man with no fanfare, no mention of forgiving the man's sins, no call to repent and believe. Jesus simply sees a man who is dying, grabs his foot, and heals him. It seems to be an instinctive reaction. Once the man is healed, Jesus sends him back to his work and asks the man to "remember" him.

This account suggests a lens for viewing Jesus' ministry of healing and teaching that brings to the fore the moments in which the adult Jesus seems to act spontaneously—when his mind is changed in the course of a conversation with a mother, or when it takes him two tries to cure a blind man, or when he happens to see Zacchaeus and decides on the spot to visit his home. The Infancy Gospel of Thomas suggests to us that perhaps the course of Jesus' life was not mapped out perfectly from beginning to end, that perhaps there were modifications along the way in how Jesus presented the gospel message, and that perhaps Jesus also responded spontaneously with creativity and novelty to situations that suddenly developed around him. In this way, we can see the freedom that the divine love always enjoys to do the unexpected, the unplanned, all in service of care and healing for God's creation.

The third vignette echoes a miracle the adult Jesus performed for his mother, changing water to wine at Cana, but, again, the emphasis here is different. In that story in the Gospel of John, Jesus separates himself from his mother's authority, and the interpretation of the miracle focuses on it as the first sign of Jesus' adult ministry—not on a son fulfilling the wish of his mother. Ultimately, it is a miracle so that his disciples and others might believe in him.

By contrast, in the Infancy Gospel of Thomas, the miracle Jesus performs has no such gravitas. The young Jesus has had the same accident that every young child has had at some point: he has dropped the vessel of water he has been carrying and he risks coming home empty-handed, disappointing his mother. The text does not mention if anyone has seen Jesus or has noticed what has happened. Jesus is quite anonymous at this point and, apparently, he is focused on how to fix his predicament so his mother won't be angry. He comes up with a creative solution: opening his cloak, he fills it with water (we are not told the source of the new water) and brings it home. Mary is the only witness to this miracle and, while it clearly pleases her (she kisses her son on his return), she doesn't say anything about it to anyone else, nor, apparently, does Jesus.

Again Jesus appears as a very human little boy who has a close relationship with his mother and who is not above performing miracles out of the public eye simply for the gratification of his own family members. (A comparable example would be the story of Jesus lengthening a mismatched board for his father, who was working on an expensive bed for a wealthy client).

These miracles do not seem to serve any larger ministerial purpose; they do not bear public witness to Jesus' identity, and, indeed, they seem accidental and unprompted, simply resulting from Jesus' natural desire to please his parents. They take place in an instant and have no lasting significance. One cannot help but wonder if Jesus continued to do these sorts of miracles in his adulthood, away from the prying eyes of his chroniclers. Certainly, the four gospel writers go to great lengths to marginalize such a possibility, de-emphasizing Jesus' relationships with his family and explicitly emphasizing the necessity for Jesus' disciples to sever their own family ties.

This lowly miracle, however, suggests at the very least the possibility that there were other miracles, much more mundane, much more trivial, that occurred naturally in Jesus' private life with his family, miracles that were not planned and were not designed to reveal a larger theological purpose or meaning. Such miracles, which seem to spring from a divine openness, a divine freedom, reveal Jesus as not above playing with his divinity, if you will—using his power in unconventional ways, for unconventional ends, simply because in the moment it pleased those around him.

A New Way of Envisioning Discipleship

What might this "face" of Jesus suggest for Christians today, and what might it suggest about Christian life and Christian discipleship? I would argue that seeing Jesus as spontaneous, impulsive, and inventive creates the possibility for Christians to see themselves as Christ-like when they are at play, so that discipleship becomes a much more holistic category and can be applied much more broadly to one's own life.

Many adults, at least in the United States, have lost the ability to play. Particularly for the upper middle class, the goal of every activity is productivity: vacations are designed for learning, hobbies are practiced for proficiency, and great pride is taken in the number of hours one works each week. Technology has only fueled this trend: with one's Blackberry, iPhone, iPad, Netbook, and so on, one is never out of reach of one's employer, never unplugged. The watchwords of the day are efficiency and production. In the leisure time that we do have, we read books for our book clubs, shuttle our children from soccer practice to band camp, clean the house and do the laundry—

proud of ourselves for all we have accomplished. Often, our week-
ends are meticulously planned, rigorously scheduled so that no time
is "wasted."

Often Christians live their lives this way even more than others,
believing that it is their moral and religious duty not to squander any
of the gifts God has given and to work tirelessly to serve others. It is
not a coincidence that the phrase "Protestant work ethic" is defined as
"belief in the moral benefit and importance of work and its inherent
ability to strengthen character."[68] No matter how much Christian theology attempts to teach that humans are not saved by works, many
continue to live as though God keeps a tally sheet and we had better
have lots of gold stars if we want to be rewarded—both in this life and
the next.

What if, however, we understood playtime to be part of Christian
discipleship? What if the kind of creative spontaneity that Jesus
showed as a boy was understood to be part of what it means for us to
be followers of Christ? What if our own creative play—painting,
singing, playing music, writing—all without skill or purpose—could
be seen as mimicking the play of God who takes delight in the created world, sometimes engaging creation just for the fun of it, sometimes using God's power spontaneously, on a whim, and sometimes
exercising God's freedom not to have predetermined exactly how God
will respond to a situation until it happens? We could give ourselves
permission to simply wake up and see what the day brings us, without a plan, without a purpose, without a goal. We could take the time
to *be*, without always looking at our "to-do" list; we could act on impulse, noticing what is going on around us and reacting with our own
inventive response. In all of this, then, we would be following Christ,
who himself evidenced such impulsive, inventive behavior in his
young life. It is worth considering.

Challenging Predestination

The "face" of God we see in the boy Jesus suggests one final advantage. This view of God as impulsive and innovative directly challenges one particular Christian doctrine, and that is the doctrine of
predestination. I maintain that seeing God as playful and spontaneous is a helpful counter to an overly deterministic understanding
of the way in which God exercises God's omniscience and omnipotence. Such determinism leaves no room for chance, human error or
initiative, genetic mutation, or the movement of geological plates in
one's understanding of why things happen one way and not another.

This sort of theological explication leads to the kind of horrific theology that either blames the victim—God punished Haiti with an earthquake—or it leads to a passive fatalism in which bad events are relentlessly chalked up to "God's will"—the death of your young child was part of God's plan. None of this is either faithful or helpful. It paints a picture of a ruthless God who micromanages every single event in creation, determining from the beginning of time every detail of your life and mine, allowing neither innovation nor modification. Who could worship such a god?

Simply put, predestination is the belief that God has foreordained the ultimate destiny of every individual—and, to a greater or lesser degree, all related events that occur in creation. In further defining what predestination means and the ramifications it has in our understanding of God, I turn to the theology of John Calvin, given that it has been very influential in Protestant thought and that it is such an important part of his entire theological vision. According to Calvin: "By predestination we mean the eternal decree of God, by which he determined with himself whatever he wished to happen with regard to every man [sic]. All are not created on equal terms, but some are preordained to eternal life, others to eternal damnation."[69]

It must be noted that, in his view, Calvin's doctrine of predestination had entirely positive connotations, as its whole purpose was to secure our confidence in our own election. Calvin realized that the uncertainty of knowing whether one is damned or saved is a terrible burden for the individual conscience. Therefore, for Calvin, the knowledge that God has predestined some from the beginning of time to election, and that those elect cannot fall away—another way to say this is to say that God's grace is irresistible—is a source of great comfort. Of course, the consequences for the damned are equally sure, which to many twenty-first century ears is a cause for alarm. However, Calvin is not concerned with the damned—if God is not concerned with them, why should he be?

Instead, Calvin's concern is always for the elect alone, as they are the only ones who matter in the sight of God. Therefore, he wants them to be reassured at all costs and writes that "we shall never feel persuaded as we ought that our salvation flows from the free mercy of God as its fountain, until we are made acquainted with his eternal election, the grace of God being illustrated by the contrast—viz. that he does not adopt promiscuously to the hope of salvation, but gives to some what he denies to others."[70]

What is operative here is the very image of God discussed above: the severe, omnipotent ruler of the world who controls and oversees every aspect of creation. God is in charge of the amount of rain that falls, the amount of freedom the devil has to tempt humanity, and, of course, the living and dying of every human being. In Calvin's eagerness to make very clear that nothing we do can either earn for us or lose for us our salvation, Calvin insists that God has decreed everything from the beginning of time; therefore, the destiny of Christians is sure. No Christian need fear that God will take away God's mercy after a time, or that at some point in her life she will displease God and incur God's wrath. No, it is all decided. For the elect, salvation is beyond questioning.

However, Calvin does begin with warning that God's mystery and inscrutable will must be protected. He admonishes,

> First, then, when they inquire into predestination, let them remember that they are penetrating into the recesses of the divine wisdom, where he who rushes forward securely and confidently instead of satisfying his curiosity will enter an inextricable labyrinth. For it is not right that a man should with impunity pry into things which the Lord has been pleased to conceal within himself, and scan that sublime eternal wisdom which it is his pleasure that we should not apprehend but adore.[71]

In other words, we cannot question God's eternal election, we can only worship God and trust God's wisdom. In this, Calvin echoes Augustine: there is no appeal to anything higher than God's will. If God willed creation to be a certain way, God's judgment cannot be challenged, especially by human beings, who are wretched sinners and have no right whatsoever to question what God has ordained. Nonetheless, insofar as he is able, Calvin attempts to show the way in which God's predestination operates in the world.

It is also important to recall that Calvin's doctrine of predestination is clearly double predestination. By that I mean that Calvin asserts both that God has elected some to salvation and "elected" (it hardly seems an appropriate word) others to damnation. Some argue that this doctrine comes up only in later Calvinism, and it is certainly true that in the first edition of the *Institutes*, the discussion of predestination is much abbreviated. However, there is no escape from Calvin's own language here; its intent is unmistakable:

> We say, then, that Scripture clearly proves this much, that God by his eternal and immutable counsel determined once for all

those whom it was his pleasure one day to admit to salvation, and those whom, on the other hand, it was his pleasure to doom to destruction... Those whom he dooms to destruction are excluded from access to life by a just and blameless, but at the same time incomprehensible judgment.[72]

Those, therefore, whom he has created for dishonor during life and destruction at death, that they may be vessels of wrath and examples of severity, in bringing to their doom, he at one time deprives of the means of hearing his word, at another by the preaching of it blinds and stupefies them the more.[73]

Calvin was clear: by God's own choice and will, there were the elected, and there were the damned.

Calvin allowed for no "chance" in God's great master plan for the universe, which is another line of reasoning that led him to the same conclusion regarding predestination. Calvin thought a doctrine of single predestination—that is, the belief that God has foreordained the saved only, but left open who will and will not be damned—was absurd and illogical. How could one think that God would leave to chance such a critical decision regarding a human life? Who could imagine that God would take such responsibility for one group of people and leave the rest to fend for themselves and make their own way? No, Calvin says, this would dishonor the almighty power of God who alone controls our destiny. In his words: "There could be no election without its opposite reprobation."[74]

What was his answer, then, to those who would counter and say that such a decree makes God a tyrant? Calvin retorted that nothing is higher than God's will: "The will of God is the supreme rule of righteousness, so that everything which he wills must be held to be righteous by the mere fact of his willing it."[75] We might not like the sound of it—and it might terrify us—but even so, we have no standard by which we could judge God unfavorably, no ground on which to stand from which we might justly accuse God.

A final point should be mentioned here, for it is one of the most important reasons Calvin gave for supporting his doctrine of double predestination. Calvin, along with Augustine, argued that we have no reason to complain of God's election, because in and of ourselves every single human being deserves damnation. If God deigns to rescue a few of us poor, unworthy sinners out of the mouth of hell, we should be grateful. Even were God to save only one or two, the grace therein would be more than we deserve. Calvin wrote, "The Lord therefore may show favour to whom he will, because he is merciful; not show it to all, because he is a just judge. In giving to some what they do not merit, he shows his free favour; in not giving to all, he declares what all deserve."[76] When all are justly condemned, who can challenge God's gracious mercy to some?

Many Christians today believe that this is simply not a credible way to think about God acting in the world or being in relationship to us. In no small part this is because it seems to bifurcate both God and humanity, with God being entirely and consistently merciful to some, and entirely and consistently condemnatory of the rest. To continue with the metaphor of countenances, Calvin depicts a God with a Janus face: loving to those on God's right, terrifying to those on God's left. The picture of a playful, spontaneous God is a helpful counter to this picture, reminding us that even as we confess God's greatness, there is still room for God to do a new thing, to be surprised by the actions of humanity, to wonder at the awesomeness of God's creation, and to allow the laws of nature to unfold in their own way, in their own time.

A God with Emotion

This picture of the young Jesus painted in the Infancy Gospel of Thomas provides one last insight and that concerns the place and role of emotions in our understanding of the Divine. I maintain that the Jesus depicted by the author of this apocryphal gospel reveals the Divine to be a God of strong emotions—and complex emotions at that. Even more, this picture reveals a God who retains the capacity for strong anger, even in the incarnation.

Anger is one emotion that is particularly multifaceted in light of its historical position as one of the seven deadly sins and also because it is often associated with irrational behavior and uncontrollable feelings. However, there is no avoiding the fact that in the Old Testament God clearly gets angry—really angry—yet God's anger is always on behalf of the most vulnerable of God's people and therefore seems entirely appropriate to the Divine. It is not quite so simple, then, as to say that all anger is bad and should be avoided. However, what might be gained from seeing genuine, powerful anger coming from Jesus himself, the turn-the-other-cheek peacemaker *par excellence* in scripture?

Such an argument is naturally controversial for the simple reason that many who read this gospel would surely shudder at the idea that the mature Jesus still possesses the capacity to act out in anger as capriciously as he seems to do here as a young boy. For this reason alone, many people find nothing of value in this infancy gospel. For example, one author writes,

> The Childhood Gospel of Thomas creates the picture of the precocious boy Jesus with his downright impertinent and dangerous use of his omnipotence. Jesus as a moral figure is abandoned in favour of demonstrating this omnipotence. "The acts of the apocryphal Jesus are destructive and, indeed, morally reprehensible. He places his power at the service of his greed for revenge and his impiousness, and if he feels slighted, spares neither health nor life."[77]

And such criticism is not necessarily an exaggeration. In the course of eight very short chapters, Jesus curses one boy and then withers him completely; he causes another boy to fall down and die instantly merely for bumping into him as he is running by; he talks back to Joseph repeatedly; he mocks his teacher Zacchaeus and humiliates him; and he blinds an entire group of people for admonishing him. What can we possibly take from these episodes?

While such stories would certainly not be held up as the brightest or best model for understanding how God expresses anger, they can serve as a helpful reminder to those who wish to relegate God's anger exclusively to the Old Testament, believing that once God became incarnate in Jesus Christ, God revealed Godself singularly as a God of love, mercy, kindness, patience, and so on. This is, of course, a problem, as it is nothing more than an updated version of the Marcionite heresy discussed earlier. Thus, the stories in this gospel save us from seeing Jesus as a mild milquetoast, only slightly piqued at the money-changers in the temple, and only a touch disappointed by the treatment of the poor and outcasts by the Pharisees and religious leaders. Remembering that Jesus, too, gets angry reminds us that anger has an important place in God's relationship with the world: it vividly demonstrates God's rejection of sin and evil, of injustice and exploitation.

An Angry God[78]

As noted earlier, scripture irrefutably testifies to an "angry God." Almost any prophetic book in the Bible includes expressions of God's anger and the divine violence that accompanies it. This is troubling to many, to say the least, which is why some version of the Marcionite heresy is alive and well among many Christians today. Terence Fretheim writes that "the most basic theological problem with the Bible's violence is that it is often associated with the activity of God; with remarkable frequency, God is the subject of violent verbs."[79] In fact, when examined numerically, the evidence is both stark and overwhelming: of the 714 occurrences of both verbs and nouns designating anger in biblical Hebrew, 518 usages have a divine subject and express divine anger.[80]

However, in order to interpret this anger and violence properly it is important to consider the *why* of divine wrath. God's anger is never simply aimed at destruction, but instead is always in the service of preservation and salvation. Not only does God express anger in order to save God's people—the terrible plagues against Egypt, as well as the drowning of Pharaoh's army in the Red Sea—but even more, God expresses anger at those who would exploit and oppress the poor—widows, children, the weak, and the infirm. While this may seem to Christians like something that needs to be explained away, a problem for Christian theology, Fretheim makes a different point, arguing that such emotion and action are perfectly in line with God's divine nature and the relationship God has with God's people. He writes: "The exploitation of the poor is to us a misdemeanor; to God, it is a disaster. Our reaction is disapproval; God's reaction is something no language can convey. Is it a sign of cruelty that God's anger is aroused when the rights of the poor are violated, when widows and orphans are oppressed?"[81]

While certainly such anger terrifies us, that is just the point: God's anger points to a rejection of sin and evil in the world and it rouses Christians to stand up with God against all forms of abuse and oppression that victimize God's children: "This is one of the meanings of the anger of God: the end of indifference."[82] God's anger calls Christians to get angry, giving Christians an ethical mandate to seek justice in the world. Seen in this light, God's anger is an irreplaceable impetus for Christian action in the world: "Human anger at injustice will carry less weight and seriousness if divine anger at injustice in the service of life is not given its proper place. If our God is not angry, why should we be?"[83] Thus, Fretheim concludes that "God chooses to become involved in violence so that evil will not have the last word. In everything, including violence, God seeks to accomplish loving purposes."[84] This is clear in God's word through the prophets, in the testimony of the psalmist, and even in Jesus' own death and resurrection.

I would argue that the Infancy Gospel of Thomas includes a similar dynamic, albeit with a different "spin." For example, several stories in which Jesus responds in anger clearly serve a larger purpose of making known the truth of who he is so that he might be rightly acknowledged and praised. He uses severe methods, to be sure, but in the end it is for the people's ultimate salvation, as is recorded in chapter 8. After confounding the teacher Zacchaeus, Jesus

> laughed loudly and said . . . "I've come from above so that I might save those who are below and summon them to higher things, just as the one who sent me to you commanded me." When [Jesus] stopped speaking, all those who had fallen under the curse were instantly saved. And from then on no one dared to anger him for fear of being cursed and maimed for life. (8:2–3)

The group that was healed apparently included the boy Jesus "withered" in chapter 3, the boy who fell down and died in chapter 4, and Jesus' accusers, whom he had blinded—that is, everyone whom Jesus had punished up to that point.

Later on, the gospel presents a contrast between two different teachers of Jesus, each with a different attitude toward him. In chapter 14, one teacher, having grown exasperated with Jesus when he is unresponsive and talks back, hits Jesus. Jesus responds by cursing him, causing him to lose consciousness. Incidentally, this is the last person Jesus interacts with negatively in the gospel. In chapter 15, "a short time later," another teacher wants to attempt to instruct Jesus. Even though Joseph is reluctant, having previously warned Mary, "Don't let him go outside, because those who annoy him end up dead" (14:5), Joseph sends Jesus to the new teacher. This time the teacher responds positively to Jesus' wisdom and says, "I accepted this child as a student, but already he's full of grace and wisdom" (15:6). The story then continues: "When the child [Jesus] heard this, he immediately smiled at [the teacher] and said, 'Because you have spoken and testified rightly, that other teacher who was struck down will be healed.' And right away he was" (15:7). Even though the Infancy Gospel of Thomas includes several examples of Jesus causing both injury and death to individuals, all are restored by the end of the gospel and readers are left with his healing miracles. This is small comfort perhaps, but it is still a reminder that anger and violence, even in the life and ministry of Jesus, are for the larger purpose of reconciling people to God and to each other.

Conclusion

Both the canonical infancy narratives as well the Infancy Gospel of Thomas, in my opinion, provide important insights into understanding who Jesus is and how he saves, and also into how Christians are to live as faithful disciples. Several aspects of Jesus' person and work are uniquely present in these infancy narratives. They convey important insights not easily found in the rest of the gospel story, insights that might otherwise not be accessible at all.

First, the canonical infancy narratives remind us that Jesus' humanity is real. Second, they emphasize that true humanity cannot simply be reduced to rationality, maturity, language capabilities, or a specific age of discernment. Third, they emphasize Jesus' full divinity from the moment of his conception. Fourth, they make a strong statement about how God chooses to exercise God's power in weakness. Finally, in the one story of Jesus' youth in Luke, we see how Jesus grew, developed, and matured, which in turn opens up the possibility of understanding God as changing, growing, and being transformed by God's relationship to creation.

In addition, I maintain that the Infancy Gospel of Thomas paints a "face" of Jesus—and therefore also of God—different from what we typically imagine. It is the face of a spontaneous God at play. Finally, this apocryphal gospel opens us to a new understanding of Jesus as "God with emotion," emphasizing that Jesus, too, showed anger and that anger has a role to play in the relationship God has with creation and in the relationships we have with each other. Chapter 6 that follows examines how these insights are developed and deepened in certain paradigmatic stories of Jesus' ministry.

To conclude, describing Matthew's version of the infancy narrative, Raymond Brown calls it "the Gospel and its destiny in miniature."[85] Yes, "the Gospel in miniature" is a fitting description of the infancy narratives as a whole as they encapsulate in a very short period of time in Jesus' life many of the key themes that come to dominate his adult life, his death, and his resurrection. Much theological richness and depth hides within the crèche we take out of storage every December.

PART III

Beyond Infancy to Today

6

All Grown Up

KRISHNA AND JESUS AS ADULTS

The young Krishna and Jesus mature into adulthood, and some of the insights we gained by examining their infancy/youth narratives are deepened when we look at stories of them as adults, especially when we consider their roles as "savior." Particularly significant is Krishna's role in the *Mahabharata*, and more specifically in the *Bhagavad Gita*, and in his final sermon, the *Uddhava Gita*. Similarly, several exemplary accounts of Jesus' ministry in the Gospel of Luke, concluding with the story of Jesus' crucifixion, are rich with meaning. An exploration of these stories should reveal both what is distinctive and unique about the infancy narratives and what general soteriological themes they reinforce, albeit in different ways.

Krishna

First, let us recall some conclusions that were drawn about the soteriological import of the various stories of Krishna's youth. Examining the significance of Krishna's *lila*, the playfulness that characterizes so much of his childhood, indicates that Krishna's playfulness creates a bond with his devotees, calling them into a relationship with him. In more general terms, Krishna's play breaks down the barriers that keep individuals from coming to be in relationship with God.

Second, the kind of relationship Krishna facilitates with those who worship him suggests that the young Krishna does not desire to be worshiped in awe, nor does he desire to be feared. Instead, Krishna desires that his devotees enter into an intimate relationship of pure love and devotion with him, modeled on the relationship a mother has with her child or a woman with her lover. Such intimacy moves his devotees to love him wholeheartedly and to devote themselves to him completely. Again, in more general terms, it is this relationship that allows individuals to give their lives over to God.

Finally, the ultimate goal of this loving relationship provides an insight into the true nature of reality. In the course of his loving relationship with his devotees, Krishna reveals to individuals the true nature of existence, teaching them to focus their hearts and minds on what really matters, the supreme one who will finally release them from suffering.

The following examination of several key stories from Krishna's adult life pose the question of how these three aspects of Krishna's early life—his playfulness, the deep relationship of love with his devotees, and the revelation of the true nature of reality—fit into the larger soteriological picture of his life as a whole and how they connect to his functions as savior as an adult. The starting point must be the *Mahabharata*, one of the two great literary epics of Hinduism, and one of the longest pieces of sacred scripture in the world. Because the *Bhagavad Gita* is set in the context of the story of the *Mahabharata*, the larger story of the *Mahabharata* first needs to be told.

The Mahabharata: The Context of the Bhagavad Gita

The *Mahabharata*, which has been in existence in one form or another for at least over two millennia, originated in legendary events dating back to a thousand years before Christ.[1] The text itself is said to have been composed somewhere in the time between 400 BCE and 400 CE, and it existed as a definitive written text by 500 CE.[2] As noted above, it is one of two great Hindu epics, the other being the *Ramayana*. The *Mahabharata* is by far the longer of the two; in fact, it is the longest epic poem in the world. The longest version of the text is roughly four times longer than the Bible and seven times longer than the *Iliad* and the *Odyssey* combined. While most scholars today recognize that the story as it has come down to us is the result of the work of many hands, a wonderful legend tells of its composition.

In the first section of the text, the reader is told that it was the god Ganesh, the elephant-headed son of Shiva, who recorded the epic on paper at the request of the sage Vyasa. Ganesh is said to have agreed to Vyasa's request, but only on condition that Vyasa never pause in his recitation. Vyasa then agreed to Ganesh's stipulation with a counter-request of his own: that Ganesh first promise to understand whatever Vyasa recited before committing the verse to paper. In this way Vyasa afforded himself the possibility of a respite from continuously speaking by reciting a verse that was difficult to understand.

This narrative also provides a popular explanation of how Ganesh's right tusk was broken, a standard part of traditional Ganesh imagery. In this account of the recording of the *Mahabharata*, it is said that in the rush of trying to keep up with Vyasa's recitation, Ganesh's pen failed and he snapped off his tusk as a replacement in order that his transcription not be interrupted.

The title of the epic, *Mahabharata*, literally means "the great Bharata," with Bharata referring to a great king of India and his descendants, who are considered to be the shapers of India's history and destiny. There is a main plot, which will be summarized below, but first it is important to emphasize that the text as a whole contains voluminous information that goes far beyond the primary narrative. In addition to the central plot, long discussions of philosophy, ethics, and political analysis are woven into the text, along with many other short stories that are only marginally connected to the core of the main story.[3]

Krishna appears at various points in the epic and not only in the section known as the *Bhagavad Gita*. Here, of course, Krishna is an adult and so he acts very differently than the lively, mischievous youth of the *Bhagavata Purana*. However, there is not a complete break between the young Krishna and his adult self; his early playfulness comes through in different places, such as in the flirtatious, frisky relationships he has with his many queens and in his willingness to use deception to further a desired outcome. This is both a different Krishna and also the former Krishna, only now mature and acting on a very different stage.

The primary narrative concerns two groups of cousins, the five Pandavas who are sons of Pandu, and the Kauravas, whose name is taken from their forefather, Kuru.[4] On the Kaurava side, the main characters are Dhritarashtra and his sons. Dhritarashtra is the oldest son in the royal family and rightfully should have become the king upon the death of his father. However, Dhritarashtra is blind, and as a result the throne has gone to his younger brother, Pandu.

When Pandu dies young, after fathering five sons with the help of five gods, Dhritarashtra assumes the role of regent and takes Pandu's young sons into his home, raising them with his own sons. Pandu's sons are named Yudhishthira, Bhima, Arjuna, Nakula, and Sahadeva. They become the heroes of the epic. Yudhishthira, the oldest, is the rightful heir of the throne, but Dhritarashtra wants his own eldest son, Duryodhana, to become king—an aim Duryodhana desperately shares. The boys are reared together and, as members of the *Kshatriya* caste, they are all trained as warriors. Nonetheless, they develop very different characteristics. The Kauravas (Dhritarashtra's sons) become deceitful and vengeful, while the five Pandava brothers become wise and virtuous. Duryodhana in particular is repeatedly described as "wicked-minded."[5]

As they grow into adulthood, these characteristics become even more pronounced:

> The Kauravas use their military might for selfish reasons, while the Pandavas are spiritual-minded political leaders, and thus greatly loved. Still, Dhritarashtra naturally favors his own boys, even though it is becoming more and more clear that the Pandavas are better suited to rule the kingdom; and he successfully plots to enthrone his eldest son, Duryodhana.[6]

This sets the stage for the rivalry between the sets of brothers, and the disputed kingship becomes the impetus for the warfare that breaks out between them. The war has great metaphorical significance, providing "a context in which to examine the subtler truths of life and death, liberation and bondage. The battlefield represents life in the world, with all its perils, temptations and vicissitudes. Each day we have new battles to fight, the greatest of all being the battle against our own lower natures, the struggle for spiritual emancipation."[7]

Many events lead up to the climax of the story, which is an eighteen-day-long battle fought on the field of Kurukshetra. Events include a rigged game of dice, designed to entice Yudhishthira to gamble away the kingdom; the infamous disrobing of Draupadi, the common wife of all five Pandava brothers—a public shaming that only Krishna's miraculous intervention prevents; and, perhaps most important, the years of regency by Duryodhana and his brothers marked by terrible injustice, oppression, and malice.

During this time, the Pandavas endure a forced twelve-year period of exile and one final year in which they have to live incognito. Yudhishthira serves as a companion to King Virata; Bhima, an expert in gaming, is the cook; Arjuna, in the guise of a eunuch, teaches the ladies of the court dancing and singing (this is, of course, hilarious, as Arjuna is the greatest warrior of them all); Nakula becomes a horse trainer, and Sahadeva a cowherd. This is all in accordance with the wager lost by Yudhishthira in the aforementioned game of dice with Sakuni, Duryodhana's evil advisor.

After these thirteen years, the Pandavas return to Hastinapura, Dhritarashtra's capital city, and ask for a share of the kingdom. The text is clear that the Pandavas do not want war and will be content with a portion they can rule. However, even this is denied them.

Indeed, against all the wise words of his counselors and his father, Duryodhana says, "I shall not surrender to the sons of Pandu as much land as can be pierced by the point of a sharp needle."[8] Even after this outrageous statement, Krishna attempts to broker peace between the cousins but, still wrathful, Duryodhana rebuffs him. In a final act of defiance and disrespect, Duryodhana "got up from his seat hissing like a huge serpent... that shameless and wicked prince walked out of the court."[9]

When all avenues for making peace have been exhausted, when all attempts to reform the Kauravas have failed, and when it is clear that the evil perpetrated by them will be stopped only by warfare, the stage for the battle is set. The only thing left is to amass the armies.

At this point in the story Krishna's unique role in the battle begins to take shape, indicating why Krishna has been called "the pivot around whom the whole story revolves."[10] Before these events unfolded, Krishna had been living in Dvaraka, where he, too, had an army. When Duryodhana and Arjuna both ask for his help in the impending battle, he offers each the same choice: they can either choose Krishna himself or his vast, invincible army, but they cannot have both. In addition, the side that chooses Krishna himself will have to be content to have him as an advisor. He will not fight, but only serve as a charioteer. Faced with such a choice, not surprisingly, the wicked Duryodhana chooses the army, preferring military might to the presence of the Divine. Arjuna, wise and virtuous, chooses Krishna, "confident that God's grace is more significant than all material facility."[11] It is a choice the Pandavas will not regret.

The armies then assemble on the Kurukshetra and prepare for battle, laying out the specific rules of warfare and agreeing who is and who is not fair game in the fighting. It is at this point in the epic where the *Bhagavad Gita*, described in the next section, begins.

The terrible battle rages for eighteen days, in which carnage and death occur on a mammoth scale. The Pandavas win, but ascend to the throne of a kingdom that has been decimated. After several decades of rule, the Pandavas decide to end their reign and retire to the Himalayas to die. They undertake the great journey and, one by one, each of the Pandava brothers, as well as their wife Draupadi, dies. Yudhishthira is the only one left, along with his final companion, a dog.

The god Indra himself appears and invites Yudhishthira to ascend to heaven with him, but insists that the dog must be cast aside. Yudhishthira, proving his great virtue, refuses to abandon so faithful a companion. When Yudhishthira finally does arrive in heaven, he sees that his brothers and Draupadi are not there and he refuses to stay, choosing to suffer hell with his brothers instead of enjoying heaven without them. However, his vision of hell lasts only a moment. Then the truth is revealed to him that all the cousins, including the entire family, have been reunited in heaven with all malice and anger forgotten.

Many different and important themes are treated in this story, which makes it difficult to generalize about the text as a whole. Nonetheless, one theme that does continually come to the fore is the right understanding and performance of *dharma*—that is, the duty each individual is required to perform according to his or her station in life. One of the central teachings of Hinduism is that the proper practice of one's specific *dharma* leads not only to peace and happiness, but to spiritual liberation as well.

This teaching of *dharma* relates directly to Krishna's place in the text as a whole. In the *Mahabharata*, and more particularly in the *Bhagavad Gita*, one of Krishna's primary roles is to offer guidance regarding the proper performance of one's *dharma* in order to achieve liberation and salvation—both in this life and the next. This role most vividly comes through in the events recounted in the *Bhagavad Gita*.

The Bhagavad Gita

The *Bhagavad Gita* is believed to have been written around 150 BCE[12] by a devotee of Krishna. Note that this date precedes the composition of the *Bhagavata Purana* by at least five hundred years or so. Thus, it is no surprise that the well-developed, thorough presentation of *bhakti* does not exist here. Indeed, the deep relationship of passionate love between the individual and Krishna that characterizes book 10 of the *Bhagavata Purana* is only hinted at, and the very word takes on a much different form with even a slightly different meaning in the *Gita*.

The original purpose of the *Bhagavad Gita* was to show that liberation comes through devotion to Krishna alone and, more specifically, by carrying out one's proper activities—that is, living life according to one's *dharma*—without being concerned about the results. Instead, one's mind should always remain fixed on Krishna. While the *Gita* was not immediately popular in India, its reputation and stature increased in the nineteenth and twentieth centuries and played an important role in the development of Indian nationalism. It became central to the very definition of Hinduism itself and contributed to the growth of what was called "Oriental Studies" in the West.[13]

Many of these later interpretations of the *Gita* downplayed the role of Krishna in favor of a more esoteric, universal truth that was not specifically connected to a loving relationship between Krishna and the individual. The text has been interpreted and construed to support a variety of causes and philosophical and religious positions. For example, Gandhi, who referred to it as his "spiritual dictionary,"[14] used it to support his teaching of ethical action in general and nonviolence in particular, tempering the overall role of Krishna in the text.

It seems clear, however, that this was not the intent of the original author, nor the way in which the *Gita* traditionally has been interpreted in the wider context of Hinduism. This example illustrates, however, the hold the *Gita* has had and continues to have on a wide variety of readers, both within Hinduism and beyond. There is a reason why it is the second most translated text in the world, after the Bible.[15]

In spite of the wide variations found in the different interpretations of the *Gita,* for a large percentage of Hindus, and even for some who identify themselves with other religious traditions, the *Gita* is a profoundly spiritual and even mystical text about the loving nature of God. For many of these individuals, "The Gita is a book of divine revelation. God reveals Godself in the existential context of the agonizing search of the human. There is a correlation between the human quest and the divine self-revelation in this process. The more acute the human quest becomes, the deeper the divine revelation that takes place; the more God self-reveals, the more ardent our human thirst for God becomes."[16] The analysis that follows focuses on this explicitly religious, devotional interpretation of the text, since it is this lens that helps reveal most specifically the connections between Krishna's adult life and the stories of his youth.

With this brief bit of overview as background, we should establish the *Gita* in its place in the larger narrative. At the critical moment in the *Mahabharata* just before the great battle between the cousins is to begin, we are told that the blind Dhritarashtra is seated in a tent on the sidelines, next to his counselor Sanjaya. Dhritarashtra asks Sanjaya if he will recount to him the events of the battle, since he is endowed with supernatural sight. The story then begins with Dhritarashtra's question, "How did they act, O Sanjaya?" Sanjaya starts a narration that will focus on Krishna and Arjuna and their debate about right action, liberation, and the relationship between the human and the Divine.

Arjuna himself prompts the debate. Standing at the threshold of this great battle, the supreme warrior of the Pandavas, along with

Krishna who is serving as his charioteer, looks out across the field and sees arrayed against him uncles, cousins, relatives, and friends, and he simply loses heart. In the face of the carnage he knows is coming, he cannot bear the thought of the destruction of so many of his kinsmen—many of whom will die at his hand. Overwhelmed by the thought of it and in utter dejection, he slumps down in his chariot and refuses to fight.

This moral despair is "the spiritual abyss into which Krishna's teaching pours,"[17] and it serves as the "dramatic moral crisis"[18] at the heart of the *Gita*. It precipitates the revelation of religious enlightenment —Krishna's famous teaching of right action carried out in devotion to the Divine. Following this compelling and persuasive teaching, Arjuna is inspired to take part in the battle, his courage renewed by the confidence he gains through Krishna's assurance that fighting is the right thing to do—as long as he possesses the proper attitude about his activity.[19]

Krishna's Salvific Teaching

As noted above, in the *Gita* as a whole, not only Krishna's teaching but also his very being has a salvific purpose: "Krishna's revelation is salvific, for he proposes it as necessary for liberation. The real object of salvific knowledge is Krishna, the personal God."[20] Nonetheless, within that general affirmation, it is no easy matter to try and summarize Krishna's teaching in the *Gita*, in no small part because so many interpreters used different passages as a primary lens through which they read the text, often with some specific purpose in mind. Perhaps the larger reason, however, is that Krishna seems to teach so many different paths to liberation. In fact, one interpreter notes that "in the model presented by the *Bhagavad Gita*, every aspect of life is in fact a way of salvation. Krishna tells Arjuna of innumerable ways to achieve peace of mind, to resolve his dilemma, and it is clear that the answers are provided not only for Arjuna but are paradigmatic for people of virtually any walk of life."[21]

The *Gita* teaches four different paths or disciplines—also called *yogas* (the word literally means "to yoke" or "to link")—by which an individual can attain liberation: the way of wisdom, *jñana-yoga*; the way of mental focus and concentration, *raja-yoga*; the way of devotional love, *bhakti-yoga*; and the way of dedicated and intentional service in action in the world, *karma-yoga*.[22] These paths are not new, as they were described and taught in a variety of Hindu philosophical and religious contexts before the *Gita* was written.

What is new and unique here, however, is that Krishna teaches that all four paths come together in him. He unites and unifies them as he himself embodies their ultimate goal. This teaching reflects a significant change in religious thinking:

> The transformative process of the *yoga* can now be understood to be, and can be in fact, energized by loving participation in the reality of God (*bhakti*), a participation which can be realized meditatively, but which can also be cultivated through song, poetry, and ritualized worship of God in images, or simply through dedicating one's whole self to God in every act one does.[23]

Authors of some analyses of the *Gita* describe not four but three different paths of religious practice—*jñana*, *bhakti*, and *karma*—but the same ultimate point is emphasized. The different yogas "are envisaged not as parallel ways but as interwoven and mutually complementary ways of an integral transformation."[24] They do not compete, nor are they mutually exclusive. Instead, the practice of one is nurtured and supported by the practice of the others and a person is free to practice the path that best suits one's personality and temperament. Ultimately, all paths serve the same purpose and lead to the same end: "In the *Gita* one encounters a transcendent God in the person of Krishna, who reveals both God's love for human beings and their love for God. To realize one's absolute state of being is not enough; one must enter into communion with God in love and surrender."[25]

Within this multi-faceted character of the *Gita* as a whole, some oft-cited themes play a central role in understanding who Krishna is and how he saves. While most of these themes can be found in multiple places in the text itself, a few chapters do illustrate the way in which Krishna presents, first, the way an individual can achieve liberation from the cycle of rebirth (encompassed in the theme of renunciation); second, the nature of the saving relationship between an individual and Krishna (encompassed in the teaching of loving devotion); and finally, the revelation of Krishna's true form, which swallows up all other questions and doubts and vividly illustrates the ultimate truth about all reality. This climactic chapter of the text contains the clearest statement of the main teachings of the *Gita*: Krishna is "the mystery at the heart of the universe, the ultimate basis of matter and of the ever-creative law of cause and effect, and at the same time...the mystery at the heart of the human person, source of the never-ceasing flow of thought and feeling."[26]

Chapter 2:
The Importance of Renunciation and the True Nature of Reality

In chapter 2 Krishna begins teaching Arjuna the truth about religious practice, reality, and the way to liberation. He speaks to Arjuna, who has just sat down in his chariot, refusing to fight. As the dialogue begins, it is clear that the problem is one of *dharma*—that is, the right code of conduct for a particular caste of person. Arjuna is a *kshatriya*, a warrior who is bound by specific rules that determine the proper behavior for someone of his caste. Arjuna cannot understand how it would be right and honorable for him to engage in this terrible battle, slaying those great heroes whom he so loves and admires, members of his own family, his best teachers and moral guides. In the face of this profound spiritual and moral crisis, Krishna begins to teach Arjuna about the true nature of reality, at the same time hinting at his own true identity, which will be unveiled gradually over the course of the succeeding chapters.

Krishna explains to Arjuna that what he thinks is true and permanent is actually only an illusion: it is the impermanent masquerading as the real. The true self is eternal, neither being born nor dying. Thus, Arjuna is not to worry about the slaying of his kinsmen—the bodies in which they exist now are only temporary shells with no ultimate significance. What is true and real is indestructible—the self is not the body and therefore the killing of the body does not touch the real self: "[The self] does not take birth, nor does it ever die. Such a being has never come into being, nor shall it ever come to be. It is unborn, eternal, everlasting, and primeval. It is not slain when the body is slain" (chap. 2, verse 20, hereafter 2:20).[27]

Krishna continues, describing the way in which one should live—the way an enlightened person who knows the truth about reality should conduct himself. The heart of this description can be found in verses 55 to 72, which have been described as a "mini-*Gita*, delineating incredibly succinctly the basic theory and method of spiritual practice, which can be summed up in one word: renunciation."[28] This teaching is repeated throughout the whole book.

It is important at the outset to understand the meaning of renunciation. Renunciation does not refer to a complete relinquishment of one's active life in the world, a situation in which a person would abandon her life altogether, entirely refusing to engage in the world around her. In the *Gita*, renunciation does not signify turning away from all activity and action, but rather renouncing the fruits of one's activity in the world. What that means specifically is detaching one's mental state from the results of one's actions and not allowing one's happiness to be based on the pleasing or displeasing character of life's circumstances and events.

Thus, Krishna teaches, "One who, everywhere, is without sentimentality upon encountering this or that, things pleasant or unpleasant, Who neither rejoices nor despises—the profound knowledge of such a person is firmly established" (2:57). He uses the metaphor of a tortoise drawing its limbs back into its shell as a way to think about reining in one's senses from the objects of their attention. This prevents the senses from taking over. When they do take over, the senses inevitably draw the mind away from its rightful focus on the true nature of things (which, as we will come to see, is actually Krishna himself), generating anger and desire based on attachment to temporary, illusory things. Krishna says, "Abandoning all selfish desires, a person moves through life free from worldly longings, Without the sense of 'mine,' without the notion of 'I am acting'—that one attains peace" (2:71).

In this way, "Krishna teaches Arjuna the way to resolve the dilemma of renunciation and action. Freedom lies not in the renunciation of the world but in disciplined action. Put concretely, all action is to be both performed without attachment to the fruit of action and dedicated with loving devotion to Krishna."[29] This last caveat—the mental state in which activity is to be performed—will be expanded upon in later chapters.

Chapters 4 through 10:
The Yoga of Devotion—The Mind Set on Krishna

The entire section between chapters 4 and 10 can be treated as a unit. In these chapters, Krishna teaches a variety of religious paths that on the surface seem very different. However, as noted earlier, Krishna is the common thread holding them all together, and Krishna opens the possibility of pursuing a variety of paths to religious enlightenment without privileging one over another: all are valid, all are effective. However, each path must be pursued with devotion to Krishna in mind. Krishna is the key piece—Krishna himself and the relationship the devotee has to him—that makes each path efficacious. This is a unique new revelation that the *Bhagavad Gita* offers to Hinduism.

The teaching begins in chapter 4, as it is here that Krishna first reveals what we already know from our study of his infancy: He is an avatar of God. Unlike the understanding of a similar concept of incarnation in

Christianity, the understanding here contains a fundamental paradox. To review, in Hinduism, an avatar (of which there are many) only *appears* to be truly human, to be born and to die. In reality, "He is eternally changeless, infinite, untouched by material nature. He cannot be 'born' in any real sense, because He is without boundaries. It is a great mystery, an illusion cast by the power of *maya*."[30]

What is central to the being and activity of an avatar is deliverance —that is why the Divine condescends to clothe himself in corporeal form (not all avatars are human): "The *Avatara* is a sanctifying, saving power; whoever takes refuge in Him, seeks solace in Him, thinks only of Him, will be with Him (4.10–11)."[31] Thus Krishna tells Arjuna, "Indeed, whenever there is a decline of dharma, O Bharata [another name for Arjuna], And an emergence of what opposes dharma—at that time I send for my Self. For protection of the virtuous and for destruction of evil acts. For the purpose of establishing dharma, I become fully manifest age after age" (4:7–8). Once he has disclosed his true nature, Krishna continues, here and in subsequent chapters, to explain the importance of keeping him in mind at all times and meditating on his true nature, which is present everywhere, in everything.

What is of central importance, then, is the relationship of devotion and dedication that the believer has with Krishna, a relationship that can be characterized by the word *bhakti*. This term was used in chapter 3 in the analysis of the boy Krishna's relationship with both his mother and the *gopis*. Those stories come from a text written centuries after the *Gita* and so their use of *bhakti* has evolved considerably from the usage in chapter 4 of the *Gita*. In book 10 of the *Bhagavata Purana*, the word has evolved to describe a relationship of passionate, even erotic love that points to a state of deep emotion, strong attraction, and actual physical desirability. This fervent love for Krishna was seen as the highest form of worship and a direct path to salvation.

Here, however, the word lacks this emotional passion and ardor. Instead,

> The word *bhakti* means a variety of things but in the Gita it means devotion and loyalty to Krishna, the personal God, trust in Him and love of Him. It also means God's love for man [*sic*] and the original meaning of the word which is "participation" is never wholly lost. In the Great Epic the root *bhaj-* is frequently used of sexual love and this, of course,

played an important part in the Krishna cult of later days. In the Gita there is no trace of this and the past participle of the same root, *bhakti*, is best translated as "loyal, devoted, and devout," for it has all these meanings.[32]

This is why, in the *Gita*, devotion does not exclude other forms of religious practice, but instead can be combined with any of the other religious paths, undergirding the specific disciplines of each, including meditation, philosophical reflection, or right action in the world, while at the same time giving them ultimate meaning and significance.

Thus, throughout this whole section of the *Gita*, Krishna unfolds the truth of his existence to Arjuna, emphasizing the need to direct all forms of religious practice to him and justifying this need with the true nature of his being. Krishna is not merely a wise human being or a mere warrior, and he is not even an individual manifestation of the Divine. Instead, he is the highest of all reality, the greatest in all categories of being, a truth he describes in vivid detail in chapter 10 where he lists class after class of beings, describing himself as the foremost of each:

> Of luminaries, I am the radiant sun; of senses, I am the mind; of lofty mountains, I am Meru [the golden mountain at the center of the cosmos]; of bodies of water, I am the ocean; of animals, I am the king of animals; of fish, I am the shark; of flowing waters I am the Ganges; of letters, I am the letter A; indeed, I am imperishable time; I am death, which takes away everything, and the rising into being of all that will be. (10:20ff.)

For this reason, then, Krishna can say to Arjuna, "One who sees me everywhere and sees all things in me, To such a person I am never lost nor is such a person ever lost to me" (6:30). In other words, anyone who worships any deity, in any form, is actually worshiping Krishna, and Krishna accepts and rewards that worship as though it were directed explicitly at him: "Whoever, with faith, has offered love to whatever form that person desires to worship—Upon every such person, I bestow this immovable faith" (7:21).

From these persons, Krishna accepts anything they might offer, not because of the worthiness of the offering itself, but because it is offered in an attitude of devotion: "One who, with love, makes an offering to me of a leaf, a flower, fruit, or water—Such an offering, presented with love, I accept from one whose self is devoted" (9:26). In this multi-chapter section of the *Gita*, then, Krishna accentuates the fact that to all religious practitioners of all religious paths he is all in all, he is the object of all religious devotion, and he is the possessor and guarantor of salvation for all. It is both an overwhelming and compelling argument in which "Arjuna is transformed, not by a systematic argument, but by a mystical teaching in which Krishna becomes the object of Arjuna's intense devotion (*bhakti*)."[33] This teaching allows Arjuna to see that by performing his duty as a warrior, a *kshatriya*, with his heart and mind fixed on Krishna, without concern for the consequences—whether good or ill—of his actions, "he can unite with Krishna's cosmic purpose and free himself from the crippling attachments that bind mortals to eternal suffering."[34]

Chapter 11: Krishna's Universal Form

Having heard Krishna's proclamation about his real identity, Arjuna is convinced. His doubt has been dispelled and he is fully converted to the truth of Krishna's verbal self-revelation. Yet, perhaps unsurprisingly, he desires to see visual evidence of Krishna's true nature and so asks Krishna for a vision of his "supremely powerful form" (11:3). This vision, which Krishna grants to Arjuna, is the climax of the entire *Gita*. It provides dramatic and irrefutable evidence that what Krishna has said is true. Indeed, he is the source and font of all religious knowledge, practice, and liberation.

Out of affection for Arjuna and a desire for him to know the truth, Krishna agrees to Arjuna's request, bestowing upon him the "divine eyes" he will need to behold such a vision, which mortal eyes are not able to grasp: "Before you, in one place, behold now the entire universe, with every moving and nonmoving being within my body…" (11:7). The vision that the text describes is impossible to conceive: "What Arjuna witnesses is beyond the scope of the human mind to comprehend. The *Gita* can only give us a hint, an inkling. If we can imagine the entire span of the cosmos, every event that has ever taken place, is taking place, and will ever take place, every form, every being, every thing, manifested endlessly in the infinite body of the divine Person, we can begin to understand."[35] Krishna shows himself to have multiple mouths full of crushing teeth in which the worlds are destroyed; he has multiple eyes and unlimited arms; he has no end and no beginning; "multitudes of celestial beings" sing praises to him and the very cosmos trembles at his revelation. Indeed, the brilliance emanating from his being shines like the light of a thousand suns rising in the sky at once, burning the universe with his splendor.

This vision, then, is the culmination of all Krishna's teaching in the preceding chapters, and it confirms Krishna's identity as the highest and ultimate reality in the universe. From the perspective of the *Gita*, there is only the *appearance* of many gods—in reality, Krishna dwells within them all, sustaining them with his being, and possessing the power to create and destroy them all. Thus, "the dialogue between Krishna and Arjuna opens up a whole new dimension of religion in Hinduism. Krishna presents himself as the Supreme Lord, the Highest Personal God. All other gods are merely manifestations of him in accordance with their time, place, and spiritual aptitude."[36]

This revelation also reverses a traditional way of thinking about divine reality in Hinduism. The impersonal *Brahman* was typically viewed as higher and superior to all personal manifestations of that reality. In essence, it was believed that it was more accurate—or at least, more philosophically advanced—to conceive of the Divine in abstract, non-personal categories, rather than relying on personal, embodied forms. In the *Gita*, this hierarchy is reversed: "The new ontology of the *Gita* effectively replaced the other, impersonal notion of the ultimate reality as the eternal power-substance *brahman* with a personal deity... Within the new ontology, the entire world is a part of God, including the bodies and psyches of all people, and the ultimate, unchanging, eternal part of all people, the ultimate self in each, is also God."[37] And, specifically, of course, this God is Krishna.

This new way of thinking about the Divine leads to an interesting question, a question Arjuna poses at the beginning of chapter 12. If Krishna is really all in all—both the supreme formless Divine and also the beautiful, personal object of love—which form of worship is better? Is it better to worship Krishna in loving devotion to his personal form, or to worship him as the imperishable unmanifest Supreme Person? (12:1).

Krishna's answer is interesting as well—and not entirely surprising. Both types of worship work equally well to achieve the same end, but ultimately, in a move of loving grace, he recommends the path of *bhakti* simply because it is easier. "Difficulty is greater for those whose thought is attached to the unmanifest, Certainly, the goal of reaching the unmanifest is very hard to attain by the embodied"

(12:5). Instead, the highest and best way to worship Krishna and achieve freedom is through *bhakti*, loving devotion and dedication. The easiest and most effective way to link oneself to God is simply to love God.[38]

For all these reasons, then, Steven Rosen argues that the central meaning of the *Gita* is "that God is a person, Krishna, and that the goal of life is to develop love for him."[39] What this means is that a personal understanding of God is higher and more perfect than an understanding of God as an impersonal entity or an abstract force. Rosen writes, "The impersonal or monistic conception of the Supreme— wherein one envisions God as an inconceivable force, without form— is a legitimate part of what the *Bhagavad Gita* teaches. But it is only a part, and it is eclipsed by the idea of God as the Supreme Person."[40] This is the vision so compellingly displayed in chapter 11.

Having experienced this vision, Arjuna is overwhelmed. He can stand it for only so long and begs for Krishna to show himself as he was before: "Having seen what never has been seen before, I am exceedingly pleased, Yet my mind is distressed and filled with fear. O Divinity, allow me to see that very [intimate] form...I desire to see you just as before" (11:45–46). Krishna, of course, veils himself immediately, taking again the simple form of the charioteer Arjuna has come to know as friend. His presence calms Arjuna's frightened mind and returns him to his normal way of thinking.

The Uddhava Gita: *Krishna's Last Night on Earth*

Before we leave Krishna's adult life, it is important to review one more important episode from his later years, the account of his last night on earth. The *Uddhava Gita* comes from the *Bhagavata Purana*, the text discussed earlier. This *Gita* comprises book 11, which describes Krishna's adulthood. It is considered the last message of Krishna before he returned to his celestial realm, which is much less an actual abode or location than it is a state of enlightened realization. In fact, Krishna's realm is nothing less than "Himself, the indivisible Oneness of God. It is as much a state of consciousness, as a place."[41]

This *Gita* records a dialogue between Krishna and his faithful disciple Uddhava, who, once he realizes Krishna is preparing to leave the world for good, asks Krishna how one should live. In many ways, it reiterates and emphasizes the salvific teachings of Krishna in the *Bhagavad Gita*, but it focuses particularly on *bhakti* and the relationship of love and devotion between Krishna and his disciples articulated in the earlier cantos of the *Bhagavata Purana*. In this sense, it combines the best of both:

> Like the *Bhagavad-Gita*, the *Uddhava-Gita* is astonishing in the breadth of subjects it covers and the completeness of its treatment of both spiritual theory and practice. It also resembles the *Bhagavad-Gita* in that it synthesizes many divergent traditions and extracts the common core of meaning among them, while maintaining respect for their differences. It is an intense text, a dense condensation of the very best of the best.[42]

Krishna emphasizes to his disciple Uddhava that he must not give up or abandon his life altogether, but instead continue to live, only without attachment to people and things, without desire for wealth and fame. He must center his thoughts on Krishna at all times: "Shake off all attachments whether to family or friends. Roam the world as one free of all attachments, with impartial vision. To do this fix your mind on me."[43] Krishna's counsel is twofold, terse, and straightforward: "Strong in devotion and free from attachments"[44]

Living this way, one must also remember the transitory and illusory nature of the world, which is "here today and gone tomorrow."[45] Krishna describes it this way:

> Remember always the associations made with relatives, spouse, children, and friends are like the chance meetings of travelers—brief, and only for the duration of this lifetime. At the end of each life these relationships end—just as a dream ends upon awakening. Keeping such an awareness the householder can live free from entrapments in the ideas of "I" and "mine"—even while performing the required duties.[46]

Krishna is clear—one must release attachment to family, to friends, to work, to home, and even to one's body, to the individual self. It is this relinquishing of attraction and the concurrent establishing of a relationship of devotion to Krishna that brings peace and liberation. This liberation allows one to see the Divine everywhere and to worship the Divine in everyone, which opens up a radical new way of living in the world:

> With a pure heart resting in a pure mind, see only me as the immortal Self in all beings. See this Self as that which is

internal to you and external to you—as expansive as the sky
... One who gazes upon the world from this vantage point,
and sees in all living beings my presence, giving respect and
consideration to all that they encounter, who looks with an
equal eye upon both the high-born and the low-born, the
spark and the blazing sun, the tenderhearted and the cruel,
is considered by me to be a sage... Disregarding the con-
tempt and ridicule of friends and acquaintances, and casting
aside embarrassment with awareness of the body prostrate
sincerely before all: be they outcasts, dogs, asses or cows. Worship everyone in this way in thought, word and deed—and my
Presence within all will soon be revealed.[47]

In this way, the concluding chapter of the *Bhagavata Purana*
brings readers full circle—back to where we concluded the *Bhagavad
Gita*. Both *Gitas*, then, have two primary emphases: seeing Krishna
everywhere and in everything, and devoting oneself and the fruits of
one's actions always and at all times to him. Thus, what Barbara Powell concludes about the *Uddhava Gita* appears to be equally true of
the *Bhagavad Gita*: "This twofold discipline frees one from the bondage
of *karma* and gradually develops the perception of ultimate Truth, the
divine Oneness of everything."[48] Stated in one clear sentence, this is
the soteriological teaching of the adult Krishna.

Conclusion

Secondary sources that analyze the *Bhagavad Gita* often describe
it as "the New Testament" of Hindu scriptures, and it is widely considered to be "the most beloved scripture in Hinduism."[49] Certainly,
there are many different reasons for this: its popularity in the tradition as a whole, its vast readership, and the warmth with which
Krishna is almost universally regarded. One scholar, however, suggests another reason: "The reason, quite simply, is that it was among
the first of Hinduism's sacred books to offer a new paradigm in spirituality."[50] This may or may not be accurate, but without question it is
true that Krishna's teaching in the *Gita* does present a radically different way of living out one's faith and interpreting one's relationship
both to the world and to the Divine.

As a last note, it is important to turn to the question of what connections can be made to the previous exploration of Krishna's infancy
and youth. In what ways are there similarities between the infant
Krishna and his mature life? Where are the discontinuities? What

conclusions can we draw about the soteriological insights he embodies in his person and work?

One consistent theme that endures from Krishna's youth to his mature life can be found in the reason repeatedly given for his assuming human form, an explanation that is explicitly soteriological. One author puts it this way: "The crowning purpose of Krishna's avatara is to reveal his true nature as God, to manifest his love for human beings, and to demand love in return so that people may attain salvation, which is a state of union with God in perpetual and blissful love."[51] This is as true in Krishna's infancy as it is in his adult years, and this purpose drives Krishna's activity throughout his entire life.

Closely related is the fact that over the course of Krishna's life his teaching regarding the true nature of reality also remains the same. The ultimate point of Krishna's engagement with the world—both as a child and as an adult—is to lead people into a higher understanding about the world, to convey the knowledge of the right way to live in order to attain peace and happiness, and finally, to invite them to enter into an ultimate loving relationship with Krishna in order to attain union with the Divine.

Certainly the way in which he presented this message was different. In his adult life, his teaching about reality was explicit, rather than implicit, and it was much more philosophical and intellectual. By contrast, as a boy, the teaching was in some ways a byproduct of coming to know and love Krishna himself—it was almost an aftereffect, rather than the primary message. Nonetheless, the point was the same: through Krishna one can know the truth about the illusory and transitory appearance of the world and learn to devote oneself to what is constant and abiding.

However, this affirmation leads to another conclusion, one that elicits a point of difference rather than continuity. While his reason for taking human form was consistent from start to finish, the way in which he communicated his teaching and lived out his purpose in day-to-day life matured and developed from his infancy into his adult life. The playfulness that dominated his infancy and youth was not nearly as prominent in his adult life. As an adult Krishna relied much more heavily on sophisticated spiritual teachings to lead devotees to enlightenment. It should be noted, though, that Krishna does continue to exhibit signs of playfulness. Certain trickster characteristics are visible in the *Mahabharata* as a whole, and Krishna's actions sometimes surprise those around him with their cunning and somewhat subversive nature.

Perhaps this change should not surprise us. What adult does not conduct herself with more sophistication, intellectual deportment, and seriousness than she did as a child? If Krishna's human form is to have even the slightest resemblance to the authentic stages of a human life, there must be some changes in personality and behavior from his youth to his maturity. Yet, as previously noted, the playfulness of his youth is a key reason why the infant Krishna is so beloved. It is this playfulness that allows him to attract those around him so compellingly. In some ways, then, the discontinuity calls attention to the importance of the distinctive way in which the young Krishna relates to those around him as he draws them irresistibly into the loving relationship of devotion that leads to enlightenment.

This leads to a third point of comparison. It should be clear that in both stages of his life, the teaching of *bhakti* is of critical importance, but the way in which the loving relationship between Krishna and his devotees is described and the way in which Krishna facilitates that relationship are quite different in his infancy and in his adulthood. Specifically, the informality and the intimacy of the infant are lacking in Krishna's adult life. It is telling that after Arjuna receives the revelation of Krishna's true form in the *Gita*, he feels the need to apologize to Krishna for any lack of respect and honor that Arjuna might have thoughtlessly displayed to Krishna. After apologizing for calling Krishna "friend," "due to my carelessness or even out of affection," Arjuna goes on to say, "and if in sporting together you were treated disrespectfully by me, During play or rest, while sitting or dining, When alone, O Achyuta, or even before others' eyes—For that I beg your forgiveness, O Unfathomable One!" (11:42). Such an apology for "sporting together" would be unthinkable from the *gopis*, for example, where carelessness and affection seem to be the norm in many cases.

This is one place where the later text, the *Bhagavata Purana*, describes the characteristics of Krishna more subtly than in the earlier text, the *Bhagavad Gita*. The *Purana* expands upon them and emphasizes them in a new way, accentuating the warmth and familiarity that have really come to characterize Krishna. This is one place where it seems that the later centuries of development and growth of the role of Krishna in Hinduism as a whole have relied heavily on the infancy narratives in their portrayal of Krishna, using them to create a distinctive portrait of a god who enters into intimate relationships with his devotees with an almost shocking lack of decorum and dignity.

What does all this mean for our understanding and appreciation of the infancy narratives of Krishna? It seems quite clear why those stories are so beloved by Hindus and why this portrait of the baby Krishna is so cherished. The young Krishna teaches the same soteriological truth that he will teach as an adult, he embodies the same divine love, and he reveals the same ultimate nature. However, what is of critical significance is that all this religious profundity is wrapped up in an irresistible package—an enticing, affectionate, gregarious, beautiful little boy, whose love is easily accessible and who draws hearts to him like honey draws bees. Loving the infant Krishna is both easy and delightful, and in his infancy he shows us a face of the Divine that is perhaps more appealing, more attractive, and more desirable than possibly any other divine countenance found in any other religious tradition.

Jesus[52]

A similar analysis of Jesus' adult life can integrate insights gained from his infancy into the overall picture of his life and ministry. Before turning to this period of Jesus' life, a brief review of the conclusions drawn from Jesus' infancy and youth is in order, particularly as they relate to the doctrine of salvation. First, the infancy narratives remind us that Jesus' humanity is real. Against all those who would spiritualize him, downplay the concrete tangibility of his physical body, and emphasize the categorical differences between "him" and "us," the infancy narratives describe Jesus developing in a human womb, being birthed in an ordinary human way, and even being circumcised on the eighth day after his birth (Lk 2:21)—most definitively a vivid sign of his genuine physicality.

Second, the stories of Jesus' birth and infancy remind us that what it means to be human cannot be reduced to simple rationality, maturity, language capabilities, or a specific age of discernment. Instead, the fact that God became incarnate as an infant witnesses to the fact that every single human being, regardless of age, mental capabilities, race, or gender bears equally the image of God and is equally and fully united to the Divine by virtue of the common humanity shared with Jesus Christ.

Third, these narratives serve as a protection against adoptionism. They are the first line of defense against an attack on Jesus' full divinity in that they show us the work of the Holy Spirit present in every moment of Jesus' life. Fourth, the fact that God chose to come into creation as a helpless, vulnerable infant makes a strong statement about how God chooses to exercise divine power. Finally, the one story of Jesus' youth in Luke emphasizes that Jesus the Christ grew, developed, and matured. This in turn opens up the possibility of understanding God as changing, growing, and being transformed by God's relationship to creation, as Jesus was by his relationships to his disciples and others with whom he came in contact. Now it is time to connect these insights to Jesus' adult ministry and his crucifixion and examine the ways in which they are both consonant and dissonant.

Jesus' Ministry: His Adult Life

When describing Jesus' person and work, a sure way to annoy a New Testament scholar is to haphazardly pick and choose stories from Jesus' ministry from all four gospels, without paying attention to the specific and unique overarching circumstances and context in which each individual gospel was written. This piecemeal approach, while having the advantage of being useful for comparing and contrasting the telling of similar stories in different gospels, carries with it the danger of painting a rather schizophrenic Jesus whose attitudes and actions vacillate widely from one story to the next. To avoid this danger and also to continue with the narrative of Jesus' life begun in Luke's gospel, the focus here is on the picture of Jesus' adult years as Luke recounts it.

Like each of the gospels, Luke's gospel has a particular focus, a particular emphasis, a unique way in which Jesus is described and depicted. Two aspects of Luke's portrayal are particularly relevant. The first is Luke's stress on Jesus as the savior. Luke's is the only one of the three synoptic gospels that describes Jesus as "savior," using the verb "to save" (*sōzō*) more than any other document in the New Testament. Luke's is also the only synoptic gospel that describes Jesus' work and ministry as "salvation."[53] Luke Timothy Johnson emphasizes this point, saying that "in Jesus is the dawn of salvation...The understanding of Jesus as one who brings salvation is a specifically Lukan emphasis."[54]

Second, Luke has a target audience of outsiders in mind for this salvific work: "the despised and outcast in society, the non-Jews, the small fry, the underdogs."[55] Indeed, throughout the gospel, Luke emphasizes the connection Jesus makes to these marginalized groups and the care and concern Jesus manifests for the last and the least. This is true in Luke in a way it is not in the other three gospels: "More than any other Gospel, [Luke] shows a concern for the underprivileged members of society."[56] Jesus proclaims that it is these people who will inherit the kingdom of God, these people who find particular favor with Jesus, these people whom God will lift up and bless: "those considered outcast and excluded from the 'consolation' of full membership in God's people are accepted by God."[57] This is a radical message. Keeping these two particulars in mind, we now turn to the narrative itself.

The Public Announcement of Jesus' Ministry

The twin emphases (Jesus as savior and as savior of outcasts) take center stage at the public announcement of the start of Jesus' ministry. At the very beginning of Jesus' adult work and life, Luke sets the tone for the rest of the gospel, preparing the reader for the kind of proclamation Jesus is going to embody in his words and deeds.

After his baptism, Jesus returns to Galilee to teach and preach in the local synagogues. In the course of his itinerant preaching, he arrives in Nazareth and enters the synagogue to teach on the Sabbath. When he stands up to preach, he opens the scroll of Isaiah and reads the following text: "The Spirit of the Lord is upon me; because he has anointed me to bring good news to the poor. He has sent me to proclaim release to the captives and recovery of sight to the blind, to let the oppressed go free, to proclaim the year of the Lord's favor" (Lk 4:18–19). Jesus then says something that heralds the radical nature of his ministry, one of Luke's key commitments regarding who Jesus is and how he saves: "Today this scripture has been fulfilled in your hearing" (4:21). Justo González notes that "this passage plays an important role in the Gospel of Luke. It sets the tone for the entire book."[58]

Luke is not only concerned about salvation in the afterlife, in the then-and-there. Luke is also, and perhaps even primarily, concerned with the salvation that occurs today, in the here-and-now. Most important, Luke announces that Jesus himself is that salvation: "Today in the presence of Jesus himself salvation has arrived. The newness of the messianic hope has taken on concrete form in the presence of this young man from Galilee."[59] And salvation too takes a very concrete form, with very specific proofs of its realization. The promises that God has made regarding deliverance, redemption, rescue, and restoration are happening right now in Jesus' ministry as broken bodies are healed, community is restored, the oppressed are liberated, and new life abounds for all.

Not all are eager to see God's promise realized in such a way, that is, in a way that is unexpected, unusual, and reverses the proper order of things. The people in Jesus' hometown of Nazareth are the first of many who take offense. At first they are pleased with his words and proud that is he so well-spoken—he represents them well. However, all that changes when he announces that "no prophet is accepted in the prophet's hometown" and reminds them that the prophet Elijah was not sent to the Israelites (that is, the insiders), but to a widow of Sidon, a double-outsider. At these words they become so enraged that they drive him out of town and nearly kill him. "Thus Luke depicts the public ministry of Jesus as beginning with one of the many reversals that will appear throughout his Gospel."[60]

A Reversal of Power Dynamics: Aligning Himself with the Outsider

This motif of "reversal" is expressed in several different ways throughout the whole of Luke's gospel. One of the most important is the reversal of status and power as it relates to wealth. This is no surprise, given that the topic of money—specifically those who have too much and those who have too little—is prominent throughout Luke's gospel.[61] Rick Carlson describes this economic reversal as twofold: "the complete rejection of first century economic and power structures presented in Luke as well as the alternative, topsy-turvy, divine reality which is being inaugurated by the advent of Jesus."[62] In other words, the reality that Mary foretold in the Magnificat has finally come to fruition in Jesus' ministry, and those in power aren't at all happy that the long-awaited Messiah is inaugurating such an uncomfortable, disruptive vision of the kingdom of God.

One particular way in which Jesus demonstrates this reversal is by aligning himself with the outsiders: those who are mocked, derided, and scorned; those who are ostracized and cast out; those who are excluded from the community. Again and again, Jesus stands in solidarity with those on the margins against those in positions of power, particularly the Pharisees. Of the many possible examples that are available, one of the most well-known Lukan parables, that of the woman and the jar of perfumed oil, strongly makes this point.

> One of the Pharisees asked Jesus to eat with him, and he went into the Pharisee's house and took his place at the table. And a woman in the city, who was a sinner, having learned that he was eating in the Pharisee's house, brought an alabaster jar of ointment. She stood behind him at his feet, weeping, and began to bathe his feet with her tears and to dry them with her hair. Then she continued kissing his feet and anointing

them with the ointment. Now when the Pharisee who had invited him saw it, he said to himself, "If this man were a prophet, he would have known who and what kind of woman this is who is touching him—that she is a sinner." Jesus spoke up and said to him, "Simon, I have something to say to you." "Teacher," he replied, "speak." "A certain creditor had two debtors; one owed five hundred denarii, and the other fifty. When they could not pay, he cancelled the debts for both of them. Now which of them will love him more?" Simon answered, "I suppose the one for whom he cancelled the greater debt." And Jesus said to him, "You have judged rightly." Then turning towards the woman, he said to Simon, "Do you see this woman? I entered your house; you gave me no water for my feet, but she has bathed my feet with her tears and dried them with her hair. You gave me no kiss, but from the time I came in she has not stopped kissing my feet. You did not anoint my head with oil, but she has anointed my feet with ointment. Therefore, I tell you, her sins, which were many, have been forgiven; hence she has shown great love. But the one to whom little is forgiven, loves little." Then he said to her, "Your sins are forgiven." But those who were at the table with him began to say among themselves, "Who is this who even forgives sins?" And he said to the woman, "Your faith has saved you; go in peace." (Lk 7:36–50)

This is a perfect example of the radical nature of Jesus' ministry. After having received a coveted invitation to the home of a Pharisee, one of the most respected Jewish groups in the community, Jesus flouts every possible social convention. First, he welcomes a party-crasher; second, he allows himself to be touched by a woman deemed sinful; third, he rebukes his host in front of the other guests; and fourth, he claims the power to forgive sins, a power of God alone. Is it any wonder that the Pharisees are no friends of Jesus and repeatedly criticize and condemn him? Clearly, Jesus is not according them their proper place of honor in God's kingdom.

The fact that this encounter takes place at the dinner table is not incidental to the point of the story. Justo González points out that

The dinner table is one of the places where we most clearly manifest our values as well as our social conventions and prejudices ... Those whom no one likes, those who are most in need of it, seldom receive a dinner invitation ... Luke leads us to consider that perhaps our "good manners" at the table—both in our homes and in the larger home that is the world—need to be corrected by the manners of Jesus.[63]

In this particular story the "correction" comes in the form of reversing the traditional understanding of who is in right relationship to God. Instead of confirming the Pharisee's assumption that his piety makes him holier and more righteous than the "sinful woman," Jesus demonstrates that her radical act of love and passionate reception of God's grace is a more faithful way of honoring and celebrating who God is and what God has done for God's people. Jesus is not teaching about how to be a "better" religious person, but instead "about a God whose acceptance of sinners the religious find jarring" and "sinners who rejoice at the great forgiveness they have received."[64]

This is paradigmatic of the nature of Jesus' table fellowship, which he uses to "embody the truth of the inbreaking kingdom of God . . . His table companions are not carefully chosen to maintain and broadcast his status in the wider world; rather, he eats with toll collectors and sinners. In all these ways, Jesus communicates the presence of divine salvation for those who dwell on the peripheries of acceptable society."[65] Over and over again, we see how Jesus takes every opportunity to side with and lift up the outsider, even when such action clearly endangers not only his ministry but his very life.

A Different Kind of Messiah

Jesus' persistent and, to the Pharisees, very annoying habit of disparaging their company in favor of a motley assortment of outcasts points to another way in which Jesus himself embodies the whole concept of reversal. He talks about his own identity as Messiah and, indeed, lives out that identity in unexpected ways. Here is one example:

Once when Jesus was praying alone, with only the disciples near him, he asked them, "Who do the crowds say that I am?" They answered, "John the Baptist; but others, Elijah; and still others, that one of the ancient prophets has arisen." He said to them, "But who do you say that I am?" Peter answered, "The Messiah of God." He sternly ordered and commanded them not to tell anyone, saying, "The Son of Man must undergo great suffering, and be rejected by the elders, chief priests, and scribes, and be killed, and on the third day be raised." Then he said to them all, "If any want to become my followers, let them deny themselves and take up their cross daily and follow me. For those who want to save their life will lose it, and those who lose their life for my sake will save it. What does it profit them if they gain the whole world, but lose or forfeit themselves?" (Luke 9:18–25)

Needless to say, these two pieces of information must have come as quite a shock to the disciples. First, after Jesus finally concedes that he is, indeed, the long-awaited Messiah, he follows up what had to have been a thrilling revelation to the disciples—a confirmation that they had made the right choice in following Jesus and a sure indication of the great things that would await them in the future—with a command of secrecy, and a terrible prophecy of what lies in store not only for himself but for them as well. He will suffer and die, and they will die, too. So much for the disciples' visions of grandeur and glory!

This is just one of many indications that Jesus' life is not going to unfold in the way the disciples have imagined. Clearly, one of the primary themes of his ministry is that God incarnate does not always look and act the way humans might expect. In Luke's gospel, the disciples' "views of God and the world remain conventional throughout most of the Gospel, with the result that they are unable to correlate Jesus' status as God's Messiah with the prospect and experience of his heinous suffering."[66]

The Neighbor, Broadly Conceived

It is well known that Jesus lived in a society that operated with very strict rules regarding insider and outsider groups. Such rules were one of the basic organizing principles of early Mediterranean society. "In groups" consisted of one's household, one's extended family, and one's friends and neighbors. "Out groups" were everyone else— outsiders by virtue of geography, occupation, or ethnicity. The expectations of hospitality, courtesy, and obligation were for in groups, but not for those beyond. "Ingroup members are expected to be loyal to each other and to go to great lengths to help each other. They are shown the greatest consideration and courtesy; such behavior is rarely, if ever, extended to members of outgroups."[67]

While the boundary between in group and out group could be fluid at times, this categorization had more than social and cultural ramifications in terms of what those categories meant for one's honor, one's religious identity, and one's place in the larger community. The

categories also had important economic ramifications. One had economic responsibilities only for those in one's in group, and those in
out groups were often considered to be irrelevant and marginal. "Economic sharing was embedded in social relations. To share with someone without expectation of return was to treat them as kin, as family.
Conversely, to refuse to share with others was tantamount to relating
to them as though they were outside one's community."[68]

Over and over again in Luke, however, Jesus subverts these categories of insider and outsider, insisting that God does not recognize
such distinctions and that God actually demonstrates a particular
care and concern for the last and the least. In this way Jesus' own
words and deeds "run roughshod over important social conventions
related to one's honor and status in the community and one's religious identity."[69] This subversion is most vividly evident in Jesus' exchange with a lawyer, which can be categorized as a "challenge-ri-
poste" scenario, a game Jesus gets drawn into repeatedly, not only in
the Gospel of Luke, but in all the gospels. In a context in which
people are always competing for honor, "the game of challenge-ri-
poste is a central phenomenon and is always played in public. It consists of a challenge...that seeks to undermine the honor of another
person and a response that answers in equal measure or ups the ante
and thereby challenges in return."[70] In this particular exchange, Jesus
"ups the ante" with one of the most famous parables in the Bible, the
story of the Good Samaritan.

> Just then a lawyer stood up to test Jesus. "Teacher," he said,
> "what must I do to inherit eternal life?" He said to him,
> "What is written in the law? What do you read there?" He an-
> swered, "You shall love the Lord your God with all your heart,
> and with all your soul, and with all your strength, and with all
> your mind; and your neighbor as yourself." And he said to
> him, "You have given the right answer; do this, and you will
> live." But wanting to justify himself, he asked Jesus, "And
> who is my neighbor?" Jesus replied, "A man was going down
> from Jerusalem to Jericho, and fell into the hands of robbers,
> who stripped him, beat him, and went away, leaving him half
> dead. Now by chance a priest was going down that road; and
> when he saw him, he passed by on the other side. So likewise
> a Levite, when he came to the place and saw him, passed by
> on the other side. But a Samaritan while travelling came near
> him; and when he saw him, he was moved with pity. He went

to him and bandaged his wounds, having poured oil and wine on them. Then he put him on his own animal, brought him to an inn, and took care of him. The next day he took out two denarii, gave them to the innkeeper, and said, "Take care of him; and when I come back, I will repay you whatever more you spend." Which of these three, do you think, was a neighbor to the man who fell into the hands of the robbers?" He said, "The one who showed him mercy." Jesus said to him, "Go and do likewise." (Lk 10:25–37)

Justo González insightfully observes that the lawyer "uses theological debate as a means to avoid obedience"[71]—he isn't concerned with learning more about divine teachings; instead, he wants to "justify himself" and reassure himself that he has done enough and covered all his bases. In other words, he wants to confirm his honorable place in society, he wants to confirm his understanding of scripture, and, perhaps most important, he wants to confirm his religious identity, his righteousness. However, Jesus categorically refuses to allow this.

A key point to note about this parable is that "the exclusion of the Samaritan is not only racial or ethnic, it is also religious. From the point of view of the Jewish doctor of the law, the Samaritan was a heretic...Now it is the Samaritan heretic who is the obedient servant of God. Thus the parable has much to say about recognizing the action of God in those whose theology we may find faulty—in itself a very valuable lesson in these times of theological and political polarization."[72] This parable, then, is another good example of the kinds of reversals Jesus pronounces throughout his ministry: those who are sure they are in are shown to be out, and those who are sure they are right are shown to be wrong. All who were hoping that the Messiah would come and sanction the traditional religious and cultural norms of their society must have been gravely disappointed.

The story of the Good Samaritan, then, illustrates one of the key themes of Jesus' entire ministry: "It is not just a matter of loving and serving those who are near us (which is what 'neighbor' means) but also of drawing near to those who for whatever reason—racial, ethnic, theological, political—may seem to be alien to us."[73] The story confirms what already has been learned about God in the incarnation. In Jesus, God bends low and comes near to those who hover on the fringes of society, standing with them and revealing Godself to them.

No One Left Behind: The Three "Lost" Parables

According to Luke, all of these events in Jesus' ministry empha-size one of the key ways in which Jesus demonstrates himself to be a "savior," the way in which he continually shows his persistence at seeking out those whom it would be easy to overlook and forget. As noted earlier, Luke is adamant that salvation in Jesus Christ is first and foremost for the outsider. The three "lost" parables that Jesus tells in quick succession in Luke 15 make this point explicit.

Justo González comments that while these parables are often used to evangelize "the lost," in reality, they are addressed to the "never lost"—the Pharisees and the scribes—who are grumbling about Jesus' welcome of sinners and tax collectors.[74] Thus, while typ-ical Christian interpretation of these parables invites one to see one-self in the character of the "lost," which is being sought with such vigor, in actuality, these stories push Christians to rethink God's rela-tionship to those whom they typically relegate to a place beyond God's loving compassion.

The last of the three—the parable of the prodigal son—is perhaps the most well-known. However, for illustrative purposes here, only the first two are recounted: the parable of the lost sheep and the para-ble of the lost coin.

> Now all the tax-collectors and sinners were coming near to listen to him. And the Pharisees and the scribes were grum-bling and saying, "This fellow welcomes sinners and eats with them." So he told them this parable: "Which one of you, having a hundred sheep and losing one of them, does not leave the ninety-nine in the wilderness and go after the one that is lost until he finds it? When he has found it, he lays it on his shoulders and rejoices. And when he comes home, he calls together his friends and neighbors, saying to them, 'Re-joice with me, for I have found my sheep that was lost.' Just so, I tell you, there will be more joy in heaven over one sin-ner who repents than over ninety-nine righteous people who need no repentance. Or what woman having ten silver coins, if she loses one of them, does not light a lamp, sweep the house, and search carefully until she finds it? When she has found it, she calls together her friends and neighbors, saying, 'Rejoice with me, for I have found the coin that I had lost.' Just so, I tell you, there is joy in the presence of the angels of God over one sinner who repents." (Lk 15:1–10)

The first parable is a paradigmatic account of bad shepherding: "According to the parable, the shepherd is willing to abandon the faithful ninety-nine sheep in the desert while seeking for the lost one."[75] What shepherd worth her crook would do that? The Pharisees could hardly have missed the point: they, of course, are the sheep abandoned in favor of the wandering miscreant. However, in case it has gone over their heads, Jesus' states plainly the reversal of their religious assumptions: "There will be more joy in heaven over one sinner who repents than over ninety-nine righteous people who need no repentance." The important point here is that "Jesus is speaking to the supposedly never lost about God's preferential attention to the lost!"[76] In case we miss the significance of Jesus' message in today's context, González sharpens the question for us: "Are we being warned about our own supposedly superior piety and behavior, about our reluctance to see others whom we consider unworthy be given as least as much importance as we have—and perhaps even more?"[77]

While the first story puts the focus on the lost, that is, the sheep, the parable of the woman seeking her coin—an extremely underused and ignored female image for a loving, seeking God—brings attention back to the God who is the actor in both stories. In some ways, it is astounding that Jesus would use such a humble metaphor for imaging God and God's work in the world. It is no wonder that this story is not regularly cited as an image of God: a simple woman, so poor that not only does the loss of one coin necessitate her turning her house upside down to find it, but finding it warrants a big party with her neighbors. Isn't it somehow scandalous to view God in such meager form? Yet, scandal or not, this is exactly how Jesus describes God—a God "at work actively in changing history"[78] in consistently surprising and unexpected ways.

One of the Lost

It is an easy transition from these "lost" paradigmatic parables to the concrete encounter that Jesus has with a person who epitomizes the "lost" category—Zacchaeus. This story is an ideal example of how Jesus embodies in his person the widow looking for the lost coin. Jesus seeks out and finds this tax collector who, by virtue of his physical stature and also his occupation, stands on the margins. Zacchaeus's role in society is that of an outsider: "Tax collectors in general were despised as collaborators with the Roman regime, as exploiters of the powerless, and often contaminated by ritual uncleanness... That Zacchaeus was rich implies that he was not just one of many tax collectors but an important one. A sinner among sinners!"[79] In other words, a ram among sheep.

> [Jesus] entered Jericho and was passing through it. A man was there named Zacchaeus; he was a chief tax-collector and was rich. He was trying to see who Jesus was, but on account of the crowd he could not, because he was short in stature. So he ran ahead and climbed a sycamore tree to see him, because he was going to pass that way. When Jesus came to the place, he looked up and said to him, "Zacchaeus, hurry and come down; for I must stay at your house today." So he hurried down and was happy to welcome him. All who saw it began to grumble and said, "He has gone to be the guest of one who is a sinner." Zacchaeus stood there and said to the Lord, "Look, half of my possessions, Lord, I will give to the poor; and if I have defrauded anyone of anything, I will pay back four times as much." Then Jesus said to him, "Today salvation has come to this house, because he too is a son of Abraham. For the Son of Man came to seek out and to save the lost." (Lk 19:1–10)

This is one of the few places in Luke where the word "salvation" is used, and it is the only place where Jesus himself uses it. Significantly, in this passage Jesus claims that he himself personifies salvation and that through his encounter with Zacchaeus, Zacchaeus has been saved—right now, today. There is no mention of that Zacchaeus believes in Jesus, no mention even of the forgiveness of his sins: all Zacchaeus does is acquiesce to Jesus' request to stay in his home and welcome him. This seems a surprisingly low bar for salvation.

Yet, this simple welcome does not quite tell the whole story, for Zacchaeus goes on to offer an extraordinarily generous financial donation, both as a gift to the poor and also to pay back any ill-gotten gains he might have received in the course of his work. Here, then, is another example that emphasizes the negative role that wealth and money, and, by extension, status and privilege,[80] play in Luke's gospel.

For Luke, wealth was the chief obstacle that kept someone from being in right relationship with God and right relationship with the neighbor: "Within the Gospel, the primary competitor for this focus is wealth—not so much money itself, but the rule of money, expressed in the drive for social praise and in the forms of life divorced from the least and the lost."[81] Thus, when Zacchaeus's response to

Jesus is an immediate divesting of half of all that he owes, it is a clear sign that he truly understands who Jesus is and that he is prepared to do what is needed to follow Jesus. It is a lesson the Pharisees and religious leaders never quite seem to learn.

The Crucifixion

From its inception, Jesus' life and ministry put him on the road to Jerusalem and to Golgotha. In that sense, one can say that Jesus' whole life was lived in anticipation of his death, under the shadow of the cross. Certainly in the whole of both the New Testament and Christian tradition, Jesus' death on the cross is interpreted as the defining moment of his ministry and the one event in the gospels that traditionally has been given the most theological significance. This is particularly true when it is seen and interpreted in conjunction with the resurrection.

The story of Jesus' crucifixion is told in all four gospels, of course, but the way it is told—the information that is included, the portrait of how Jesus acts and what he says—varies dramatically from Matthew to John. Here, then, for the sake of congruity, we turn to Luke's account, highlighting several unique aspects of Luke's presentation of the story.

Before looking at the text itself, however, it is worth noting that, as so often in the case of the incarnation, Christians often take the crucifixion for granted. They have heard about it and been taught about it for so long that it often no longer registers as anything particularly surprising or scandalous. However, in reality, the affirmation of the literal and concrete death of the Divine, occurring in the person of Jesus Christ, is a shocking claim. Taking a step back and examining this fact with a critical eye, we must be struck by the fact that the death of the Divine on the cross is an impossible reality, an astounding proclamation of a God that is almost startlingly incomprehensible to us, God acting in ways we can scarcely begin to fathom.

If the incarnation is a vivid reminder of Jesus' true humanity at the beginning of his life, the crucifixion is an even more dramatic reminder of his humanity at the end of his life. It is no surprise that Paul talked about the crucifixion as being a "stumbling block." Consider several of the events that preceded the actual event itself. Jesus was abandoned in the garden, betrayed by Judas, denied by Peter, left in the lurch by Pilate, mocked, stripped, scourged. Do any of these verbs make any sense when used with God as their object? Yet, all four gospels are clear that Jesus did suffer and that he was killed; it was not an illusion or a divine deception.

Although a detailed examination of the entire passion narrative lies outside the scope of this book, several specific episodes highlight events in Luke's larger crucifixion narrative. The first is the account of Jesus praying on the Mount of Olives, the second is Jesus' exchange with the two thieves between whom he is crucified, the third is Jesus' actual death on the cross, and finally, there is his post-resurrection appearance.

Jesus Prays on the Mount of Olives

In Luke's gospel, Jesus enters into Jerusalem to great acclaim and begins teaching every day in the temple after having driven out the merchants who had been engaging in their business there. Almost immediately, the authorities start to plot ways to have him killed, and the text makes clear that things will be coming to a head sooner rather than later. The pattern Jesus establishes is that every day he teaches in the temple, and every night he goes up to the Mount of Olives. After sharing the Passover meal with his disciples, he again goes up to the Mount of Olives to pray.

> [Jesus] came out and went, as was his custom, to the Mount of Olives; and the disciples followed him. When he reached the place, he said to them, "Pray that you may not come into the time of trial." Then he withdrew from them about a stone's throw, knelt down, and prayed, "Father, if you are willing, remove this cup from me; yet, not my will but yours be done." Then an angel from heaven appeared to him and gave him strength. In his anguish he prayed more earnestly, and his sweat became like great drops of blood falling down on the ground. When he got up from prayer, he came to the disciples and found them sleeping because of grief, and he said to them, "Why are you sleeping? Get up and pray that you may not come into the time of trial." (Lk 22:39–46)

This is one of the times when Jesus' true humanity comes to the fore. It seems incredible that someone who is himself divine could both need and want permission to avoid what was the culmination of his entire life's work, the logical end to which his preaching and teaching have been leading him. Several aspects of this short account are significant. First, Jesus' prayer that his Father's will be done rather than his own emphasizes Jesus' complete obedience to God the Father, even to the point of willingly accepting his own death. Second, his disciples' own inability to wait with, pray with, and support Jesus is surely a symbolic abandonment. These pieces of the story create a portrait of a very human Jesus, alone, afraid, and anxious, full of foreboding of what lies ahead yet determined to fulfill the will of God the Father.

At the same time, it is clear that Jesus is more than a mere human, and something more is being conveyed here than simply the account of a pious person in prayer who faces a great trial. Rick Carlson notes that there are hints of a cosmic struggle between Jesus' divine power of good and the demonic power of evil. This divine struggle was first suggested in Jesus' own temptation by Satan in Luke 4, and is further emphasized here by Jesus warning his disciples not to fall into temptation. The divine struggle is further highlighted when Jesus states baldly at his arrest that this is the hour of "the power of darkness" (Lk 22:53).[82]

It is reasonable to ask what this portion of the entire passion narrative reveals about Jesus, both specifically and distinctively. By way of response, I would suggest that it is Jesus' sinlessness that sets him apart from the rest of humanity; this is demonstrated by his perfect obedience to God, even as his suffering and sorrow link him to the rest of humanity.

The Christian church has consistently and universally held that the specific attribute of Jesus' sinlessness distinguishes him from humanity in general, even though he shares humanity's true nature in every other way. Further, it is precisely this sinlessness that allows Jesus to perfectly obey God and follow unwaveringly the will of his Father—neither of which any other human being is able to do on his or her own. On the Mount of Olives Jesus is the perfect human being, free from sin and in perfect communion with God, not without grief and not without fear—for neither of these emotions are in and of themselves sinful or imperfect—but fully willing and able to follow the path his Father has set before him.

Crucified with Two Thieves

Immediately after the preceding story, the events of the crucifixion itself are set in motion. Jesus is confronted by a crowd of people led by Judas, who by prearranged sign kisses Jesus to identify him to the authorities. A brief scuffle ensues that Jesus quickly quells and he is led away to the house of the high priest. Peter denies Jesus, just as Jesus predicted, and Jesus is mocked and beaten all night. In the morning, he is placed before his accusers and the antagonistic mob that supports them. Then he is taken before Pilate, a seemingly reluctant participant in Jesus' trial, who famously capitulates to the will of the people, granting them what they desire. Pilate hands Jesus over to be crucified.

> Two others also, who were criminals, were led away to be put to death with him. When they came to the place that is called The Skull, they crucified Jesus there with the criminals, one on his right and one on his left. Then Jesus said, "Father, forgive them; for they do not know what they are doing." And they cast lots to divide his clothing. And the people stood by, watching; but the leaders scoffed at him, saying, "He saved others; let him save himself if he is the Messiah of God, his chosen one!" The soldiers also mocked him, coming up and offering him sour wine, and saying, "If you are the King of the Jews, save yourself!" There was also an inscription over him, "This is the King of the Jews." One of the criminals who were hanged there kept deriding him and saying, "Are you not the Messiah? Save yourself and us!" But the other rebuked him, saying, "Do you not fear God, since you are under the same sentence of condemnation? And we indeed have been condemned justly, for we are getting what we deserve for our deeds, but this man has done nothing wrong." Then he said, "Jesus, remember me when you come into your kingdom." He replied, "Truly I tell you, today you will be with me in Paradise." (Lk 23:32–46)

Positioning Jesus on the cross between two thieves emphasizes his ignominious death and the incongruity between the circumstances of his death and his identity as the Son of God. The entire scenario is one of humiliation and defeat. As Jesus hangs on the cross in agony, his clothing is being divided among the guards. Meanwhile, the religious leaders deride him, sure that they have been right about him all along as he clearly does not even have enough power to save himself from his own death—let alone save others, as he had alleged throughout his ministry. Even one of his condemned compatriots mocks him, demanding a show of power that is not going to come.

Yet Jesus goes to his death demonstrating his power over salvation, showing himself to be "savior" with what is almost his last breath. In a manner consistent with the rest of Luke's gospel, this display of saving power is unexpected and surprising. It is power manifested in weakness and not a show of power that the world typically presumes or desires. As Jesus is dying, he turns to the condemned man on his other side, a man who acknowledges the justness of his own death sentence yet dares to ask Jesus for mercy. Jesus promises him salvation. This act is congruent with the gospel message as a whole. Even on the cross Jesus demonstrates his desire to seek out and save the lost. It is no mere coincidence or accident that the very last person to whom Jesus proclaims salvation is a condemned criminal.

The Death of Jesus

The tone of the account of Jesus' death in Luke falls somewhere between that in the account in the Gospel of Matthew with Jesus' agonizing and reproachful cries of abandonment to God and that in the account in the Gospel of John in which Jesus makes a masterful, controlled pronouncement of his own death. According to Luke, "It was now about noon, and darkness came over the whole land until three in the afternoon, while the sun's light failed; and the curtain of the temple was torn in two. Then Jesus, crying with a loud voice, said, 'Father, into your hands I commend my spirit.' Having said this, he breathed his last" (Lk 23:44–46).

Here again is a combined emphasis on Jesus' perfect humanity and his divinity, as was in evidence on the Mount of Olives. Jesus' humanity is shown both by his quoting of Psalm 31:5, by which he shows himself to be a pious Jew who trusts God up to the very end, and through his mien in death, which can only be described as composed, self-assured, and dignified. In this way, Jesus resembles a Socrates—a great man, superior to others by virtue of his extraordinary courage and wisdom:

> Luke does not deny the scandal of the cross, but he shades the image of Jesus to more closely resemble the *sophos* (wise man/sage) of Hellenistic moral ideals, whose self-control, freedom from fear, and courage are a model for his followers... Jesus is thus portrayed as confronting death with a courage, resoluteness, and dignity befitting the great individuals of the ancient world.[83]

However, Jesus' divinity is also manifested through the cosmic witness that something dramatic has happened here: the sun darkens and the temple curtain rips seemingly of its own accord. It is as if the whole of creation grieves the death of the Son of God, and the ramifications of what has just happened are felt by the world as a whole. The loss of the light of the sun, signifying the world slipping into darkness at the death of the Divine on the cross, seems particularly significant. These types of cosmic portents are common in both Buddhism and Hinduism as well, signifying some supernatural event involving either a superhuman being or, as is often the case in Hinduism, a god.

Before leaving the crucifixion proper, it is helpful to note one more nuance to this account that is not quite as easy to interpret, that is, exactly how the death of Jesus relates to his identity as savior. González describes the problem as follows:

> There is no doubt that in the story of the crucifixion the theme of Jesus as savior appears repeatedly. Yet the text does not answer the question, How is it that Jesus saves? . . . Clearly [Luke's] readers would know that Jesus was their Savior, and would see in Luke's writing the narrative of how this came about. But Luke would not tell them exactly how they ought to understand it.[84]

Given all that readers have seen and heard in Jesus in his life and ministry, particularly the way in which salvation has been interpreted as a here-and-now encounter with Jesus, Luke does not make entirely clear *how* the death of Jesus itself is salvific. Obviously there are no remnants of Pauline theology whereby Jesus suffers the death humanity deserves, paying the penalty we owe for our sinfulness, reconciling us to God by this great sacrifice of himself. Indeed, the argument can be made that for Luke, Jesus' death is not the central component of his salvific work and instead represents the forces of evil that reject Jesus' embodiment of God and his proclamation of God's kingdom. Jesus' resurrection, then, reveals the validity of his ministry and the conquering of those evil powers, but not some sort of divine acceptance of Jesus' sacrifice.

A Post-Resurrection Appearance

Luke and John are the only two gospels that describe Jesus' post-resurrection appearances with any detail or emphasis. Matthew includes only a few verses in which Jesus gives a brief final sermon to his disciples; and Mark's gospel includes only the bald fact that Jesus commissioned his disciples, with no particulars and a short account along the lines of Matthew, depending on which ending of Mark is used. Luke's narrative of the resurrection is unique in the way he accentuates Jesus' physicality—that is, Jesus' resurrection in the body.

> While they were talking about this, Jesus himself stood among them and said to them, "Peace be with you." They were startled and terrified, and thought that they were seeing a ghost. He said to them, "Why are you frightened, and why do doubts arise in your hearts? Look at my hands and my feet; see that it is I myself. Touch me and see; for a ghost does not have flesh and bones as you see that I have." And when he had said this, he showed them his hands and his feet. While in their joy they were disbelieving and still wondering, he said to them, "Have you anything here to eat?" They gave him a piece of broiled fish, and he took it and ate in their presence. (Lk 24:36–43)

Certainly John's gospel shares some commonalities with Luke's account. In John's gospel, Thomas demands physical proof of Jesus' resurrection, and Jesus also appears to have a meal with the disciples, although in John's gospel nothing is said about Jesus actually eating, nor does Jesus actually speak about his "flesh and bones" as he does in Luke. Clearly, Luke is highlighting the physicality of Jesus in the resurrection, the fact that although he has been resurrected, he still has the same earthly and physical human body: "The theological emphasis of this passage lies on the true, physical resurrection of Jesus ... The Jesus who repeatedly ate with his disciples, with sinners, with publicans, and with Pharisees now eats his last meal before leaving his disciples in the ascension. He does this in order to prove that he is not just a vision or a ghost, that he really conquered death."[85]

Again, this seems consistent with what has come before in Luke's account of Jesus' life and ministry. Over and over again in Luke, Jesus saves in the flesh. He saves by touching, by healing, by redeeming those who are corrupted and polluted in the flesh. In fact, it is the personal, physical encounter with Jesus and Jesus' body that has proved over and over to be saving in Luke's gospel.

Bodies matter to Jesus, both in his life and now, too, in the resurrection. Particularly in seeing him eat with his disciples, the reader is reminded of the many meals he ate with sinners and outcasts. Once again, a meal becomes a source of revelation and transformation, just as it did on the road to Emmaus a few verses before. The stress on Jesus' body in the resurrection reminds us that his humanity has not

188 ALL GROWN UP

dissolved, it has not been obliterated, and it has not simply vanished, as though it were simply an illusion. Even in the resurrection, Jesus retains the human body with which he was born, in which he realized his identity as savior.

Yet, all is not so simple. While Jesus remains the embodied Jesus the disciples have known, followed and loved, he has also been transformed beyond recognition. At points in the story, his disciples see him and don't know him; they can't identify him. It seems obvious that what Luke is describing is more than just a restoration to Jesus' previous mode of existence, a "resuscitation," or "re-inspiration." Instead, the resurrected Jesus is somehow thinly veiled in the unknown, his true likeness hidden from the disciples who do not have the mind to grasp the true nature of his identity. They can see and know him only in fits and starts, only for a moment and then he is gone.

In this way, "Luke's appearance accounts combine matter-of-factness with mystery. On one side, the reality of Jesus' bodily resurrection is stressed, above all in 24:39. This is one of the functions of his eating and drinking with the disciples (24:30, 41–43; Acts 1:4; 10:41) . . . On the other side, although the one who appears to the disciples is the same Jesus—It is I myself—he is difficult to recognize."[86] This seems to suggest the mystery of Jesus' divinity, which can never be fully understood, described, or explained. In the end, Luke is clear: Jesus is not only human, he is also God.

Conclusion

The end of Luke's gospel suggests the same question asked about Krishna: What connections can be made between Luke's account of Jesus' adult life, death, and resurrection and the prior exploration of his infancy and youth? In what ways are there similarities between the infant Jesus and his life as an adult? Where are there discontinuities and what conclusions can be drawn about the soteriological insights he embodies in his person and work?

This comparison elicits several important insights. First, certainly both the story of Jesus' incarnation and the whole character of Jesus' adult ministry point to a very different kind of God than we might have imagined. After reading the last part of Luke's gospel and then re-reading his account of Jesus' birth, nothing should be a surprise. Of course, God chooses a lowly, ordinary woman as Jesus' mother; of course, Mary should announce her pregnancy using the metaphor of reversal and a shake-up of the social order; of course Jesus should be born away from home, in a barn with shepherds and animals as the first witnesses to his birth. This is how God chooses to come into the world, surprising everyone, and Jesus' divine ministry will be no different.

This leads to the second, related insight, which is the very different understanding of what constitutes worthiness and favor before God as it relates to human beings. Again, where a reader might have expected Jesus to be born into the family of an upstanding religious leader and to be honored by the Jewish authorities of his time, instead, those who purportedly have the greatest understanding of God consistently and repeatedly reject Jesus and Jesus rejects them as well. In his adult life, Jesus stresses that one's outward piety and holiness—as evidenced by fasting, prayer, and keeping the law—do nothing to raise one's standing in the sight of God. In fact, they can actually alienate one from God, as happens repeatedly to the Pharisees in their encounters with Jesus.

Yet, at the same time, the religious community itself shows favorable signs of welcome and honor, both at Mary's pregnancy and Jesus' birth. Elizabeth (wife of the priest Zechariah) is filled with the Holy Spirit when coming into Jesus' presence for the first time, though he is still in Mary's womb. Later come the consecutive proclamations of the righteous Simeon and the prophet Anna, which occur around Jesus' circumcision. These early signs of acceptance and welcome are not carried through into his adult ministry, however.

Third, both the incarnation and the crucifixion emphasize Jesus' true humanity, a point that has been emphasized throughout this chapter. Jesus is born in a real human birth, to a real human mother, with a real human body, and he dies a real human death, with real human suffering and grief. There can be no question at all that Luke's Jesus is a real human being—he is not merely God in a human suit—and his true humanity persists all the way through his death into the resurrection and therefore through and into eternity as well.

This stress on Jesus' humanity is connected to another Lucan theme that is consistently emphasized from Jesus' birth to his death and that is the importance of Jesus' physical body and, by extension, the physical bodies of others and even the physical world itself. Because both Jesus' incarnation and resurrection are real, "not a merely spiritual matter," the disciples then and Jesus' disciples today are reminded that "they cannot limit their service to purely spiritual matters. The Lord who showed his resurrection to his disciples by eating with them invites his followers to show his resurrection to the world by feeding the hungry. The Lord who broke the bonds of death calls his followers to break the bonds of injustice and oppression."[87]

Yet, both the incarnation and the crucifixion also emphasize Jesus' true divinity. Miraculous signs announced Jesus' birth: the first and most obvious was the manner of his conception, but also included were the appearance to the shepherds of an angel of the Lord and a sky filled with the "heavenly host" praising God. Miraculous signs at his death included the darkening of the sun and the tearing of the temple curtain. It seems clear that Luke is concerned throughout to hold together in tension Jesus' true humanity and true divinity. We see evidence of this at the very beginning of Jesus' life and also at the very end of it. Thus, it is fair to say that Jesus saves not by being only divine, and certainly not by being only human, but rather by being fully both.

Looking Ahead

A brief word about what lies ahead may be helpful at this point. The following chapter brings together all the threads that have been discussed thus far, reiterating and restating what has been learned through the stories of the baby Krishna and the infant Christ, and how that information sheds new light on a Christian understanding of who Jesus is and how he saves. Then we will return to the themes of chapter 1, noting the importance of comparative theology, and suggesting possibilities for further study and research.

7

Rethinking the Incarnation

THE SOTERIOLOGICAL EFFICACY OF JESUS' LIFE

This concluding chapter summarizes insights from the preceding chapters and applies them directly to a Christian context. It examines specifically how the comparison between Krishna and Jesus and the study of Jesus' infancy narratives helpfully inform how Christians think about salvation today and how we can better understand Jesus' particular identity as savior. Later in the chapter we return to a larger discussion of comparative theology, again emphasizing the importance of this kind of interreligious study for understanding who Jesus is and how he saves, as well as what it means to be a disciple of Jesus.

Learning from Baby Krishna

Before delving specifically into what Christians might learn about God from the stories told about Krishna's infancy and youth, it is important to note that very important distinctions between the divine revelation as described in the lives of Krishna and Jesus preclude any simple transfer of information from one to the other. As already noted, one of the key theological claims of Krishna's human existence is that he is not "truly human" as you and I are human, but rather only takes the form or appearance of a human in order to reveal the truth of existence to humankind and to facilitate a loving relationship of devotion with his devotees.

Thus, in what follows, I am not arguing that Krishna and Jesus are somehow "the same" or even that the god Hindus worship is "the same" god that Christians worship. Others may want to make that argument but, to be honest, I do not find such statements all that helpful or constructive. Frankly, it seems beyond the capacity of humans to know such a thing, as it implies a "God's-eye view" of the totality of divine revelation and human existence, which is far beyond finite human abilities. Thus, making such equivocal statements is neither the goal of comparative theologians in general nor the purpose of this book. Instead, the theological assertion proposed here is that examining the stories of Krishna's infancy and youth can help Christians return to their own texts and traditions with new eyes, seeing God in a new way and with fresh insights. These insights then have positive ramifications for how we understand Jesus' person and work and the relationship Jesus has with his disciples.

It is important to note that the standard for determining whether or not a characteristic or attribute of God can be utilized with integrity is first and foremost Jesus Christ himself. Closely tied to that is the robust picture of God disclosed to Christians in both the Hebrew Scriptures and the New Testament. For example, a religion in which a central experience of the Divine came as a malicious sprite who delighted in tormenting believers with leg tremors or heart palpitations while they slept could not justifiably be used as a lens in a Christian context because it directly contradicts what God has revealed about Godself in scripture in general and in Jesus Christ in particular. Thus, when suggesting a divine attribute of Krishna's that might be applied to God in a Christian context, the assumption is that it does not contradict who God already has revealed Godself to be; nonetheless, it certainly can reveal something new, something that complements, augments, and deepens God's self-revelation in scripture and the tradition. I maintain that two significant attributes are Krishna's disposition of love and his playfulness.

Chapter 3 highlighted specific conclusions about the young Krishna, specifically how Krishna embodies divine love. First and perhaps most important is the *erotic* character of Krishna's loving relationships, particularly with his mother and with the *gopis*. Second, and related to this first point, is the positive role the body in general and physical desire in particular play in the loving relationships Krishna cultivates. Third is the joy that characterizes these relationships.

Re-envisioning Divine Love

Chapter 3 makes it quite clear that one of the most important attributes of the young Krishna is that he is a god of love. In addition, Krishna's embodiment of love is not to be understood in the traditional Christian sense of a soul friendship, or of neighbor love, or of intellectual or spiritual affection. Instead, Krishna is a passionate, erotic lover: a lover of bodies, a lover of beauty, a flirtatious, teasing lover who makes young women blush and maternal women coo. Is there a way in which Christians can use this image of the Divine to shed light on their own understanding of "God as love"?

Certainly, as has been discussed, the idea of God as lover is well-attested to in both scripture and the Christian tradition. One need only read the Song of Solomon for an allegorical account of God's love for humanity written in language that some might be embarrassed to read aloud in church. How, then, can this very specific picture of Krishna as lover positively inform a Christian understanding of how God loves and how Christians are called to love? I suggest the following three insights: first, God loves all of who we are and encourages Christians to love in, with, and through the body as well; second, God is passionate, not neutral or impartial; and third, human erotic loves also reflects divine love.

God Who Loves Humanity in Toto

Often when Christians talk about God's love for them, they think about that love in a rather disembodied, abstract way—either in the context of God loving the whole world such that the particularities of any one individual are lost in the whole, or in the context of God loving sinners, such that one's individual characteristics are subsumed under the larger umbrella of being loved unconditionally in spite of one's unworthiness. Neither of these concepts of God's love is inherently problematic in and of itself, but both seem incomplete in isolation. Neither of them speaks to the unique gifts of a particular individual: someone's beautiful singing voice or skill in the kitchen, another person's infectious laugh or quilting abilities. In the former way of thinking, the particular is lost in the general, and in the latter way of thinking, what could be celebrated in the person herself is heavily downplayed in favor of what is celebrated about God. All this can leave Christians in the position of being able to talk at length about a God who loves humanity, who loves the world, and who loves sinners—who even loves me, personally, as a sinner—but leaves us unable to think about or be in relationship to a God who loves me for my love of chocolate or my runner's calves.

A concrete example may be helpful. One of the more challenging aspects of Reformation thought is an emphasis on the radical nature of God's saving grace and humankind's inability to either cooperate with that saving grace or merit such grace. In Lutheran theology in particular, this emphasis manifested itself in what can be called its "low anthropology." Over and over, Luther emphasized the utter lack of positive capabilities in the human being in relationship to God and the need to be fully convicted of one's deep abiding sinfulness (one's helplessness in one's sinful condition) before being able to fully receive Jesus Christ. For example, in the Heidelberg Disputation, Luther wrote: "It is certain that man [sic] must utterly despair of his own ability before he is prepared to receive the grace of Christ."[1] For many, then, this emphasis leads either to downplaying one's own particular gifts and characteristics or deeming them unimportant or irrelevant to God. What matters, it seems, in the sight of God, is our sinfulness and our ability to recognize that sin and then to go before God in a posture of humility and repentance. There is nothing theologically problematic in realizing the depth of human sin or in knowing that there is nothing Christians can do to save themselves. A problem arises, however, when that is all that is said about an individual, as if sin constituted the entirety of human nature, the whole of a human being. Even Lutheran theology rejected that view in the intra-Lutheran controversies of the late sixteenth century.[2]

But Christians often do not think about the qualities that characterize them as individuals pleasing to God in and of themselves, especially when it comes to physical attributes or other qualities that don't serve any purpose per se other than simply expressing someone's individuality. Does God love the beautiful coffee hue of someone's skin, or someone else's dark brown eyes, or someone else's thick blond hair? Does God love the care with which someone bakes cookies or mows the lawn? Does God love the joyful abandon with which someone dances or someone else paints? Normally, it seems that Christianity emphasizes the equality with which God loves everyone and everything, thus minimizing any discussion about this person's gifts or talents or that person's physical attributes, unless attention is being called to the way in which those gifts or attributes are being used in service of the neighbor. In other words, Christians usually think it is appropriate to lift up and celebrate the skill of a surgeon's hands, but not a model's long, slender fingers. What's more, Christians tend to assume that God also thinks that way.

Certainly, I am not arguing that God is unmoved or displeased by those who use their gifts—physical or otherwise—in service to others; nor do I argue that God has the same tastes in beauty that present American society evidences. However, I do suggest that reading about the delight Krishna takes in the individual, particular physical presence and attributes of those around him recommends to Christians a different lens for understanding God's love for them. I maintain that God does not simply love people in general, or humanity as a whole, but rather that God loves specific individuals concretely and physically, appreciating them in their own uniqueness—not just for what they can do for others, but for who they are in and of themselves. God loves the grace and strength of the athletic body of a sumo wrestler and a jockey; the happy glow of a bride, whether blushing at eighteen or slightly shaky at seventy; the guy with the infectious, snorting laugh; and the girl with the two dimples in her smile. God notices these things, God cares about these things, and God celebrates these things. Who each person is as an individual not only matters to God but God takes delight in each person, just for who he or she is. Plainly speaking, God loves individuals not in spite of and not independent of who they are, but for who they are, for their unique qualities—their bodies, their passions, their quirks, and their habits.

God then loves each individual where and how she exists in the world, in the physical context in which she lives, with a love that embraces the whole of her life. God loves the woman who walks a mile to get water every morning, as well as the woman who takes a few minutes for herself in the morning to read a novel before her children wake up, as well as the woman who starts her day by swimming a mile in the local high school pool. God loves the child who falls asleep to the sound of his cat purring next to him in bed, as well as the child who curls up to sleep in an inner city homeless shelter, as well as the child who can't sleep because he is worried about tomorrow's math test. God doesn't love these women or these children "the same," just as parents don't love their children "the same," as though they were identical or interchangeable. Instead, God loves each individual as an individual, and cares about them with the special love appropriate to them and to their circumstances.

A Passionate God

This leads naturally to the next insight that stories of the young Krishna suggest to Christians, which is that God is neither impartial nor impassive. Instead, I argue that God cares passionately about each individual, and not just about saving him or her from sin, and not just with the passionate love a parent has for a child. Instead, God is emotional, God is fervent, and God's love is erotic, full of desire for humanity—and indeed, for creation as a whole.

On one hand, this idea of a passionate God is nothing new. The very word "passionate" comes from the Latin *passio*, which means to suffer, and the suffering of God in Jesus Christ has been a central Christian theme for centuries. At the same time, however, this "passion" of God has been very strictly interpreted, and sometimes in ways that are not entirely helpful. First, there is the theological thread that associates God's passion almost exclusively with suffering, so that the only emotion God displays with any gusto is anguish; any other sentiment is off-limits, viewed as somehow unworthy of the Divine. Other emotions that might potentially be attributed to the Divine—love, grief, frustration—are interpreted through a spiritual lens and thus seen as incorporeal and ethereal, more an idea of an emotion than an actual emotion.

This lends credence to the second theological thread that interprets God's love for humanity as a very "dispassionate," otherworldly, angelic kind of love—pure *agape*, no *eros*—a love that exists on a higher plane, untouched by the corruptibility of human bodies, the fluctuations of human experiences, and the caprices of circumstance and chance. Christians who interpret God's love in this vein are the ones who can say things such as "It is all part of God's plan" at the funeral of a young child who dies of leukemia, or "God must have known that this was for the best" to a woman who has just miscarried. These examples demonstrate how we Christians often interpret God's love as functioning in a way that is radically dissimilar to human love. Such an interpretation gives God's love an entirely different nature than human love, a love that is impossible for humans to understand or explain. Christians, then, are in the unenviable position of having nothing else to say about God's love beyond the stubborn assertion, even in the midst of terrible human tragedy, that "God loves you and someday you will understand it."

Finally, a third theological thread continues to emphasize God's immutability, God's unchangeable nature, and God's lack of anything remotely resembling human emotions. In this stream of Christianity, attributing any type of "feeling" to God weakens God's omnipotence and omniscience. After all, what would be the cause of feeling anything negatively or positively if every event in the universe is at all times and in all places under your full control and occurring with your full knowledge and support? This is particular true when God is seen as entirely removed from creation, existing apart from it and untouched by its vagaries, basically allowing it to operate on its own principles and laws.

Counter to all these ideas, I suggest that God's love is not nearly as neat and tidy as Christians often assume and that Christians would be well-served by a more "earthy" interpretation of God as a "lover." This is not a new idea: Sallie McFague has argued for such an understanding in her book *Models of God: Theology for an Ecological, Nuclear Age*, in which she writes extensively about the model of God as "lover," noting that the Christian tradition has been very particular in its treatment of God's love: "Not only should God's love contain no need or interest, it should also contain no desire. It should, in other words, be totally gratuitous, disinterested, and passionless."[3] Instead, McFague suggests a vision of God as love in which God not only "relates to all that is, not distantly and bloodlessly but intimately and passionately,"[4] but even "needs the world," as lovers need each other.[5]

These insights are deepened and enhanced by connecting them with the infancy narratives about Krishna's young life. Reading about Krishna's passionate attachment to the world—again, particularly in his relationship to his mother and the young *gopis*—helps Christians see an image of a God who loves creation and humanity with great desire, personal investment, and emotional attachment. This God loves each individual enough to weep over her when she turns from God and pursue him with great ardor when he runs from God. This God rejoices in the pleasant company of the beloved and is pleased by the attentions of the one God loves.

In this way, these stories of Krishna and his relationship to his devotees offer a helpful expansion of traditional Christian ways of envisioning God as a "lover," suggesting new metaphors that might be used to envision God's relationship with humanity: a man fretting over a cool and distant lover, a woman happily distracted by thoughts of a new suitor, a young teenager in love for the first time, and a widower grieving the loss of his wife of fifty years. Seeing God through this new lens provides a new way of understanding God's love as personal, intimate, impassioned, and all-encompassing. It also gives Christians a new lens for understanding their own ways of loving.

Human Erotic Love Reflects Divine Love

I maintain that there is a validity in seeing human *eros* and desire as reflections of divine love. In December 2010 an article was published in the religion section of The Huffington Post website in which Fr. James Martin posted an Advent reflection on "Desire and the Spiritual Life." He wrote that while desire has a "disreputable reputation" for many Christians today, the word should be rehabilitated, since "desire is a key way that God can communicate with us."[6] Martin argued that what he called "holy desires" (rather than the desire for a new car or a new computer) "help us know God's desires for us, and how much God desires to be with us."[7]

Martin described how human desires can reflect God's desires for us in that it is those desires that "lead us to become who we are," that is, both who God has created us to be and who God is calling us to be. Martin wrote, "Desire is a primary way that God leads people to discover who they are and what they are meant to do. On the most obvious level, a man and a woman feel sexual, emotional and spiritual desire for one another and in this way discover their vocations to be married."[8] This statement is bold and provocative, no less so because it is true. Fr. Martin is arguing that our deepest human longings—the emotional longing for relationship, as well as the physical longing for partnership, and even our sexual, erotic longings—can reflect God's own desires for us, and in those experiences of erotic love we can also experience God's love.

Let me be clear: I said that our sexual love *can* reflect God's love. Our erotic love, like all human experiences of love, is marred by sin. It hardly needs to be said that distorted and selfish expressions of sexual love can be extraordinarily damaging to those involved. Sexual love is no more and no less tainted by sin than any expression of human love, and we do well to remember that caveat in any conversation about human love.

Nevertheless, this insight of Fr. Martin, which certainly echoes what is described in the narratives about young Krishna as well, opens up wonderful possibilities for expanding the ways in which Christians think about their experiences of the Divine here on earth. In thinking particularly about the incarnation and the way in which Christ is present to and among Christians here on earth, some clear affirmations can be made. Certainly Christ comes to Christians in word and sacrament, and certainly God is present with Christians in the gathered Christian community as Christ promises, "Where two or three are gathered in my name, I am there among them" (Mt 18:20). In addition, Christians certainly experience Christ in the face of the neighbor, and certainly in their own hearts, mouths, and hands they bear Christ to the neighbor. Further, because the creation continues to be enlivened and connected to the Creator, even creation itself makes God known to us and we experience God in our relationship to nature.

Yet, here Christians are offered the possibility of adding to all this, not taking away from any of it, but enhancing and deepening what is known of God in our relationships with one another and our relationship with creation. As Fr. Martin's argument suggests, Christians might consider the possibility that God's love might be known and experienced in the rapid heartbeat and sweaty palms that the sight of our beloved simulates in us; God's love might be known in the husband who races home at lunch to meet his wife at just the right time as they try to conceive; God's love might be known in a first kiss or in the thousandth kiss; and God's love might be known in the unrequited love one has for a secret crush. In other words, the very human experience of physical desire, erotic arousal, and sexual

fulfillment are all possible channels for experiencing divine love—
and all reflect facets of God's own love for humanity.

Fr. Martin concludes his article by saying that "desire is a key part
of Christian spirituality because desire is a key way that God's voice is
heard in our lives."[9] Similarly, the stories of the young Krishna give
Christians a way in which they might see physical, erotic desire as a
part of their Christian spirituality.

Learning about a Playful God

Earlier, I argued that Krishna's playfulness reveals three related attributes. First, Krishna's playfulness demonstrates divine freedom, revealing a god who is not bound by the past, who is inherently unconditioned, and whose own actions are self-justifying. Second, the
divine freedom Krishna lives out in his young life reveals a god who
reveals himself in action, a god who is inherently dynamic, inherently
active, and constantly on the move in creation. Third, Krishna's playfulness is one facet of his physical beauty, another characteristic of
Krishna that points to the "non-utilitarian" nature of Krishna's existence in which he reveals himself to be a god who overflows necessity
and also takes delight in the simple fact of existence without an ulterior motive or purpose. Finally, bringing these threads together, I
noted how Krishna's playfulness serves to erase the distance between
the Divine and the human, bringing children, women, and men into
deeply personal, intimate relationships with himself.

Chapter 3 also noted that "playful" is hardly a common adjective
used to describe God in the Christian tradition. Yet, this concept of
"playfulness" applied specifically to the Christian understanding of
God might affect the traditional picture of God painted in scripture
and the tradition.

One characteristic attribute of play is its inherently novel and creative nature; one might even argue that this is what separates "play"
from a "sport" or "game." While the latter may have an element of
"play" associated with them, by definition both sports and games are
governed by strict rules. A baseball game in Colorado will be played
the same way as a baseball game in Taiwan; a chess match in Russia
will be played according to the same procedures as a chess match in
South Africa; and the only reason the Olympic Games can be international is that the 100-meter hurdles are raced with the same guidelines in Germany as in Brazil. Play, however, is different. "Tag" can be
played with an almost infinite variety of rules, and new ones can be
made up each time, according to how many people are playing, what

the boundaries are, the age and athletic ability of those involved, and so on. Sometimes making up rules is part of the fun.

A good example comes from the old "Calvin and Hobbes" cartoon strip, in which a regularly occurring event was the game of "Calvinball"—Calvin's rebellion against all forms of organized sports. Calvinball had only one permanent rule: the game could never be played the same way twice. Here is the theme song:

> Other kids' games are all such a bore!
> They've gotta have rules and they gotta keep score!
> Calvinball is better by far!
> It's never the same! It's always bizarre!
> You don't need a team or a referee!
> You know that it's great, 'cause it's named after me![10]

This intrinsic originality, this "never the same way twice," is appealing in thinking metaphorically about God's creative activity. For many Christians, it seems the whole concept of a "divine plan" has been overused such that God's very nature has been excessively constricted and regulated. When all of God's activity in creation is viewed through the lens of a divine plan, one begins to think that God never acts without forethought, without a reason, and without a larger purpose. All of God's activity seems to follow a divine order, a system, a rule, leaving no room for improvisation, a change of mind or direction, or ad-libbing. This God is predictable, changeless, and, frankly, more than a little boring.

Instead, borrowing from the infant Krishna and using the concept of play as a lens for viewing the Divine helps Christians envision a playful God, a God who always and ever maintains the freedom to do something new and unexpected, something fully original. This is the God with whom Abraham can bargain, who gives humanity multiple chances to get things right, who parades a variety of creatures before Adam, trying them out until finally deciding upon a course of action that will result in Eve, his helpmate and companion. This also is a God who plays with the Leviathan (Job 41:5) and is attentive to the roaming and leaping of the wild ass and the horse, a God who even "plays" with Satan with the life of unlucky Job as the playground. These stories warrant more attention, I think, because they suggest to Christians a God who is fully and thoroughly dynamic, open to being influenced by creation itself and humanity in particular, open to doing something different, open even to changing God's mind. This playful God exhibits a sense of humor, flexibility, originality, and imagination—wonderful qualities that greatly contribute to a full and rich picture of the Divine.

Christians Honor a Playful God through Their Own Play

When Christians begin to see God as a God of play, they are also open to seeing their own play as a way of reflecting the divine nature and even honoring God's playful, creative nature. As previously discussed in some detail, Christians have no problem seeing themselves honoring God through their work. The way in which Christians are encouraged to see their professional occupation as a "vocation" (a "calling") testifies to this. Similarly, Christians place importance on service to one's neighbor, often living this out in congregations all over the United States through "service projects" that perform some type of work on behalf of and for the sake of the neighbor: a building project, working in a soup kitchen, or providing care for children. Indeed, the belief that "without works, faith is dead" is an important part of Christian life. Many Christians believe that those who do not show forth their faith in some form of "holy work" in the world are not worthy of being called Christian.

Play, on the other hand, gets no respect in the Christian tradition. The assumption is that for adults at least—and even children, to some degree—play is selfish, serving no good purpose in the world, something that should be undertaken only in moderation. Too much play distracts from one's proper purpose in the world and can hinder one in serving the neighbor. Play is at cross purposes with work, and the former is often seen as a threat to the latter. No one has ever been canonized by excelling at play!

However, our reading of Krishna suggests another way of thinking about play, particularly if, taking a page from our Hindu brothers and sisters, Christians were to use an understanding of God's "play" in the world to re-think their own attitude toward play. I suggest that just as God exhibits God's playful nature in dealings with the world, so too can Christians honor and serve God by their own play in the world. In many ways, this is a small step to take. Who would argue, for example, that a parent is not honoring God when he whiles away the afternoon playing Legos with his son, or that two girls are not honoring God when they play with their dolls, or spend the morning swinging on swings at the playground? The step becomes a little bigger, however, when we turn to adults and their play: riding mountain bikes, doodling, or playing with a dog on the beach—in short, doing nothing—or at least nothing that has a purpose, serves a final goal, or helps anyone in particular. Is it possible to think about these activities as serving and honoring God?

I maintain that it is in fact quite possible, insofar as it is also a part of human nature to be inventive, to be creative, and to enjoy life itself by taking delight in the feel of the wind in our face, relishing making something new and original, and reveling in the pure joy of those around us. Christians do honor the God who created them when they loiter in God's creation, appreciating the smells and the sights of the forest, the field, or the mountain. Christians do praise God when they tell jokes just to hear others laugh, when they fill a sketch book that no one will ever see, and when they read a great book, delighting in the author's prose.

Human inventive, inspired activity recalls God's inventive, inspired activity. It is not coincidental that one synonym for play is "recreation"—that is "re-creation": the activity of creating anew, celebrating both God's creative activity and the creative gifts of others in our own unplanned and spontaneous inventive behavior. Play, as well as work, honors God. Not every human activity has to have a utilitarian function or a practical application for it to be considered "holy" or reflective of the Divine.

Rethinking Heaven

Finally, let us briefly look at how the preceding reflections on the nature of God—in light of what we learned about the Divine through the narratives of the young Krishna—might offer a fresh perspective on the picture Christians have of heaven. Fully recognizing that this is an area outside the realm of human experience and human control, I acknowledge that these reflections are merely speculative, but they do follow logically from the conclusions just suggested regarding God's nature.

Krishna's young life and its soteriological efficacy is that his whole being, and every encounter with his devotees, is bound up with his teaching about the true nature of reality. I noted that *bhaktis*—those Hindus whose religious path involves deep devotion to one god, such as Krishna—believe that their love and worship of their god can intervene in their particular karmic cycle and liberate them from the endless round of birth and death. *Bhaktis*, then, regard their god as their redeemer and their savior, and their whole-hearted devotion and submission to their god is the focus of their soteriological path. As demonstrated earlier, devotion to Krishna according to the *Bhagavata Purana* is an unquestionably soteriological action—one that, by all ac-

counts, is richly rewarding to all who undertake it. It provides the
faithful with a means of liberation from the mundane world in this life
and also guarantees that the individual will be able to continue his or
her devotion after death. For Krishna's devotees, then, the "salvation"
that is envisioned, desired, and achieved through loving devotion to
Krishna is not perfect absorption into some impersonal Ultimate, but
rather a kind of eternal non-dualistic union with Krishna, which is
often envisioned as the everlasting joy of delighting in Krishna's presence and worshiping him in his heavenly abode for eternity.

In light of this soteriological vision promoted in Krishna's young
life, it seems reasonable then to suggest that Christians also might re-
think heaven not merely as a spiritual paradise but also as a paradise
for bodies, for beauty, for joyous, loving erotic relationships, and for
an eternal life of playful engagement with God. If Christians confess a
belief in "the resurrection of the body," why, then, should heaven be
thought of as a place where disembodied phantoms float around in a
nebulous, otherworldly ether? Why should heaven not be envisioned
as having its own form of "physical" existence in which concrete, particular, and unique resurrected bodies live?

Christians confess that God loves them, and that they love God.
Why shouldn't that loving, joyous, discrete, and individual relationship between lover and beloved continue eternally rather than having
everyone subsumed into some sort of universal, undifferentiated, de-
personalized spirit of love? Finally, if play can be seen as a key attribute of God and a central part of God's creation, why not think
about humanity having a "playful" existence in heaven? Why would-
n't one's relationship with God continue to be marked by a spirit of
lively, spontaneous, energetic engagement? While such reflections
need not cover all that heaven is or could be, they can help give substance to a fuzzy picture of the afterlife that is all too often devoid of
tangible, tactile existence, bereft of palpable passion, and lacking a
concrete image of the individual's enduring relationship with God.

Learning from the Canonical Infancy Narratives

Chapter 4 suggested that using the infancy narratives as a lens for
interpreting who Jesus is and how he saves can yield several key and
unique insights for Christians. First, of course, the infancy narratives
in Matthew and Luke emphasize Jesus' true humanity. The statement
in Luke that Jesus was circumcised on the eighth day after his birth is
one very concrete example. Second, God's incarnation as an infant

points to the inherent value given to all human beings, regardless of intellectual capabilities, age, or any other standard—including race and gender—that might be used to rank one human being as "closer" to God than another.

Third, the infancy narratives also support Jesus' full divinity, rejecting the idea that Jesus became divine only at his baptism. By virtue of the Holy Spirit's role in Jesus' conception, he was fully divine from the first moment of his existence. Fourth, the fact that God chooses to become incarnate as a helpless infant in a lowly family makes a strong statement about how God chooses to exercise power and be in relationship with the world. Finally, the one story in Luke of Jesus' boyhood offers Christians a tantalizing picture of a God who is open to change and growth.

It is time to look at the whole of who Jesus is and how he saves in light of these narratives. With that more overarching picture, I argue that several aspects of Jesus' soteriological efficacy come to the fore: the realization that, when it comes to salvation, Christians should expect the unexpected; the emphasis on the salvific import of Jesus' life; the importance of relationships in the overarching view of salvation; and the positive roles bodies play in a Christian understanding of salvation.

Expecting the Unexpected

In the entirety of Luke's gospel, one of the key themes in Jesus' adult life and ministry is how Jesus consistently and deliberately reverses expectations around what it means to be a faithful follower of the law and who are the insiders and outsiders. If Christians learn only one thing from Luke's gospel, it should be that when it comes to Jesus they should expect the unexpected. Here, however, I want to look specifically at how one can and should draw that conclusion from the infancy narratives.

As noted earlier, all of the circumstances surrounding Jesus' conception and birth are entirely unexpected and somewhat shocking. For example, God does not become incarnate in a prominent, powerful Jewish family, instead choosing a young, insignificant, unwed woman to be the mother of God. After Jesus has been conceived, she comes dangerously close to being sent away by her future husband. In some ways, however, what is most unexpected and shocking of all is that God chooses to come into the world not merely in the form of a baby, but as a truly human baby boy with no special powers, no extraordinary strength, and entirely reliant on the protection and care of his parents for his survival.

One can hardly imagine a more vulnerable, weaker image than that of a baby. Babies are small, they cannot verbalize their pain or their desires, they cannot move on their own, and they are fully dependent on others to fulfill their most basic needs. When it comes to the human condition, a baby is the ultimate example of powerlessness, and a baby born to a poor family, with no social status or influence, is doubly powerless. A more helpless, vulnerable incarnation would be hard to imagine. Yet, this is how God chooses to come into the world, how God chooses to embody divine power and wisdom, how God chooses to position Godself in relationship to humanity and the whole of creation. This is indeed the unexpected!

The particulars of the incarnation set the stage for the whole of Jesus' salvific life and ministry, clearly indicating that with regard to salvation, things are not going to go according to human expectations. Mary's proclamation in the Magnificat is exactly what Jesus embodies throughout his life: the powerful are not the first in line and the pious do not have a privileged place; instead, both will be judged and brought low by Jesus. Jesus puts a premium on reaching out to the marginalized and the outsider and proclaims God's preference for them. He doesn't spend his time rewarding the healthy, wealthy, and wise, but instead he spends most of his time seeking the lost and aligning himself with the lowly.

The surprising, unexpected nature of the incarnation serves to remind Christians that they should be very wary of their own certainty regarding who is in and who is out when it comes to salvation. God rarely works according to human expectations and, as scripture often reminds us, God's ways are not human ways. Thus, the standards by which humans might judge whether someone is saved, whether someone is a "good" Christian or a "faithful" follower of Christ, simply are not the standards God uses when arbitrating salvation.

As much as we might wish it were so, salvation does not come like a strong emperor of the most powerful nation in the world, riding in on a white horse to save the day. Instead, salvation comes in the dead of night, behind an out-of-the-way inn, to the small, motley assortment of the working poor who don't have the luxury of going to bed at a decent hour. Salvation doesn't come with a trumpet blast, but with a newborn's cry; it doesn't come as a reward for good behavior to the blessed, but as a "get-out-of-jail-free" card to the condemned. Salvation doesn't come how and when we look for it. It comes on its own terms and it demands that we reorganize our way of thinking and accept it for what it is, just like the baby Jesus.

The Life of Jesus Is Salvific

Sometimes called "substitutionary atonement" or the "penal sub-stitution theory," one of the most popular and enduring theologies of atonement comes from Anselm of Canterbury. In his book, *Cur Deus Homo*, Anselm attempts a rational explanation for the incarnation in the form of a conversation with Boso, an abbot who serves as his foil. According to Anselm, the central problem that needs both explication and resolution is that humanity, in its sinfulness, has disrupted the cosmic order and violated God's justice. However, humanity by itself cannot pay restitution for this violation against God, because nothing of human origin can possibly compensate for a stain on the divine honor. In other words, human sin is an infinite offense against God and humanity owes an infinite debt to God, yet only "God" can com-pensate "God."

This formulation of the fundamental problem that sin creates be-tween God and humanity leads to the ultimate answer to the ques-tion Anselm asks in the title of his book: "Why did God become Human?" The reason is that in no other way could God have received "satisfaction" for the offense of human sinfulness and restored the right relationship between God and humanity. Only a "God-human" could provide the necessary satisfaction, offering up a divine sacrifice on behalf of humanity. In Anselm's view, if God had simply forgiven humanity without proper recompense, the offense would have re-mained against God's justice, and the rent in the cosmic order would not have been repaired. On the other hand, if God had simply chosen to punish humanity for eternity, God's grace and mercy would have been thwarted along with God's ultimate plan for humans. Therefore, the incarnation was essential.

There is much to commend this theory, of course, and the Chris-tian church, particularly the Western Christian Church, has found it compelling for centuries. In some denominations it is the primary lens through which Jesus' life, death, and resurrection are interpreted. At the same time, however, it should be clear even from this brief overview that one of the main problems with such an interpretation is that it makes Jesus' entire life nothing more than a footnote to his death—a means to an end, as it were, and it gives credence to the idea that Jesus was simply "born to die." In such a view, "salvation" doesn't happen until the cross. Everything leading up the cross is a prelude to salvation, but is not salvific in and of itself.

However, as we have seen, a strong counter-argument could be made that salvation comes in the incarnation itself—not at the end of

Jesus' life, but at its beginning. Indeed, all the auguries of Jesus' birth indicate that the relationship between God and humanity is fundamentally, irrevocably changed and even restored when God becomes human in the incarnation and not simply when Jesus dies on the cross. The advantage of this theological shift is that moving the focus of salvation back to the incarnation allows us to see all the ways in which the salvation that is not only promised in the future but exists now is made known to people in their present-day encounters with Jesus in the flesh. In other words, Jesus' life is not primarily a precursor to, a movement toward some far-off salvation in the future, but rather an unfolding of the salvation that has happened in the incarnation and continues to happen every time Jesus meets someone in faith, as will happen at his resurrection.

It is not just Jesus' dying that is salvific, but also his living. It is not just the end of Jesus' life that brings salvation to creation, but also the beginning of that life. God did not become incarnate in order to die, but also to live, and to bring this new life into human relationships. The incarnation shows humanity how we are to live in love with God, with one another, and with the whole creation. In this way, we are inspired to see the connection between our own lives and the life of Jesus. We are to be open to the experience of salvation in the present time and not simply wait passively for it after death. Seeing salvation in the incarnation reminds Christians that Jesus' life is not incidental to God's salvific plan for creation. Instead, Jesus' life reveals concretely what salvation means and looks like under the conditions of human existence, not only two thousand years ago, but also today.

Relationships Matter for Salvation

Another important insight regarding the soteriological efficacy of Jesus' life is closely connected: this is the importance of relationships in the experience of salvation. Seeing salvation through the lens of the infancy narratives reminds us that salvation is fundamentally relational. It is always experienced in the larger context of one's relationships with family and friends, rather than in some exclusive, isolated connection between God and an individual.

Looking exclusively at the cross to define salvation can falsely further the idea that the salvation that Jesus brings has nothing to do with anyone but himself. If only the death of Jesus is salvific, we are forced to conclude that, in general, those closest to Jesus play only a negative role in his death. His disciples fall asleep, Judas betrays him,

Peter denies him, and his friends abandon him at the end. Only his mother and his female companions seem to stay faithful, along with John, his "beloved disciple," who also remains at the foot of the cross.

To be clear, I do not intend to imply that Jesus needs a "co-savior" or that Jesus in and of himself is not "saving enough." Instead, I challenge the idea that the profound relationships Jesus had with his mother and Joseph, with his disciples, and with those he healed and touched are somehow irrelevant to Jesus' saving activity. By contrast, particularly when we look at his birth and early life, we see how critically important Jesus' relationships were to his very existence, how he was nurtured and sustained by those relationships, and how those relationships exemplified and furthered his message of salvation.

Certainly, his relationship to his mother—and even the relationship that developed between Mary and Elizabeth through their pregnancies—is a central component in the picture of salvation. Mary's experience of salvation in her son is in many ways the paradigmatic experience for all humanity of what it means to come to know Jesus as "savior." Similarly, the relationship Jesus had to Joseph, in which Jesus depended on Joseph for protection and safety in the early years of his life, emphasizes how deeply Jesus embedded himself in his human family, putting his own life and safety in the hands of his earthly father. In their own ways, then, both Mary and Joseph played a critical role in supporting the divine work of salvation, in saying "yes" to who Jesus was and in taking responsibility for him in his incarnation and infancy. Jesus could not have been who he was without them.

This rooting of Jesus' life and the experience of salvation in the human relationships he had from his infancy on lends significance to our own relationships today and also serves as an important reminder that salvation is not an exclusively vertical relationship between God and an individual. Instead, salvation is always known, experienced, and responded to in the larger network of relationships in which one lives. In his book, *Caminemos con Jesús*, Roberto Goizueta gives a concrete example of the importance of relationships in the lives of Latino/a Catholics:

> In popular Catholicism, theological truth is encountered not in clear and distinct ideas but in relationships; not in universal, abstract concepts but in particular, concrete sacraments, or symbols; not through observation but through participation, by kissing the statues, or walking with Jesus, or kneeling alongside Mary, or singing to Mary... If lived human experience is inher-

ently relational, embodied, and affective, then we cannot understand that lived experience through concepts alone.[11]

I would argue that, in fact, this is true for most Christians. They come to understand the love of God through the love of a parent, a partner, a child, or a friend. Most Christians come to appreciate God's steadfast, abiding presence in the neighbor who sits with them in the hospital waiting room or who comes in the middle of the night when tragedy strikes. Most Christians learn of their deliverance in the experience of baptism, the Eucharist, or the preaching of the word. Few people have a direct, unmediated experience of God; instead, most of us see God in the faces of our loved ones, touch God in the hands of our neighbors, and taste God in the bread and wine given to us as we are gathered together as the body of Christ. Salvation comes to "us" —not exclusively or even primarily to "me." This is why the news of Jesus' birth was "good news of great joy for *all people.*" Jesus' incarnation is a communal event of salvation, and the experience of salvation continues to be a communal event today.

Salvation Happens "in the Flesh"

In early October 2010 an interesting story circulated through the news media: Albert Mohler, president of the Southern Baptist Theological Seminary in Louisville, Kentucky, made headlines by calling for Christians to avoid yoga, arguing that the practice is not a Christian pathway to God. Specifically, Mohler had said that he objected to "the idea that the body is a vehicle for reaching consciousness with the divine." "That's just not Christianity," Mohler said."[12]

Because I am someone who comes from a strong sacramental Christian tradition, this statement seemed ludicrous to me. Of course "the body" is a vehicle for connecting with the Divine. In the Lutheran Church, my tradition, we profess every Sunday that when we celebrate the Eucharist we receive Jesus Christ himself in the flesh—his body and blood in, with, and under the elements of bread and wine. I was rather stunned to think that any Christian—whether or not he comes from a strong sacramental tradition—would make such a statement, given that the core confession of the Christian Church is that in Jesus Christ God became fully human, taking on the physical body of a human being—bones, muscle, and sinew included—in order that the whole of humanity could be redeemed.

Yet, Mohler's view, which reflects a rather low opinion of the body, as well as a spirit/body dichotomy, is not uncommon within the

Christian tradition. There are many Christians who continue to think that the body is less important than the spirit, that there is some "soul," which is detachable from the body and is the object of salvation rather than the whole person. The body, then, is the locus of sin. In other words, the body is the problem. For many Christians, the body does not play a positive role in salvation, and is either irrelevant to the relationship Christians have with God or even detrimental to it.

However, when Christians use the incarnation as a lens for viewing salvation, such a position becomes untenable. When Christians take the incarnation seriously, they cannot avoid the genuine fleshliness of Jesus' existence—his true physical body, which, as noted earlier, even was circumcised in accordance with the Jewish customs of the time. As was noted above, Jesus was a real, human baby, who nursed, pooped, and slept, just like every newborn baby. His infancy wasn't an illusion, a game, or a ploy. His humanity was real.

This is by no means insignificant. This emphasis on Jesus' physical humanity is linked to an emphasis on his physical ministry in which the physical bodies of the people around him are on center stage: the diseased bodies he healed, the possessed bodies he freed, and the polluted bodies he purified. Without a doubt, bodies mattered to Jesus, who came to bring salvation to them in the flesh, in their bodies. Jesus did not simply proclaim a spiritualized, disembodied message about salvation. He didn't just talk about salvation—he embodied salvation in his own flesh and blood. Jesus brought salvation to people in their bodies by breaking bread with them, staying in their houses, walking with them, and laying his hands on them.

This means that today Christians are also obligated to teach and preach salvation in the flesh, a vision of salvation that is not only after-death, that is not merely about one's spirit or soul, or that disparages the concrete bodies Christians have in the here-and-now. The fact of Jesus' own bodily existence—and the fact that those around him experienced his salvation in their own bodies—serves as an important caution to warn Christians away from any vision of salvation that does not take into account the present condition of people's bodies in the here-and-now.

Learning from the Infancy Gospel of Thomas

I have argued that, in a manner similar to what was seen in the young life of Krishna, the Infancy Gospel of Thomas also describes Jesus at play, particularly in the stories where he creates live birds from clay, heals a man's leg on impulse, and uses his cloak to carry water for his mother. After examining these stories, I suggested that perhaps Christians rely too heavily on God's "plan" and the idea of divine predestination and should instead reflect more on the ways in which God acts spontaneously, innovatively, and inventively in dealing with creation. Finally, this particular gospel describes in the young Jesus a God who has strong emotions—not all of them positive—and, in particular, in this young Jesus we see a God who gets angry.

Salvation in the Mundane

In addition to all this, these particular stories of the young Jesus also suggest to Christians that salvation happens in the most ordinary of moments, in the most ordinary of encounters with Jesus, in the very midst of our mundane, everyday lives. For example, the simple miracle of bringing clay birds to life right in the middle of typical boyish play serves as a helpful reminder that most of the time salvation is experienced not in dramatic mountaintop epiphanies but in the sudden in-breaking of the miraculous. One moment, it is business as usual, and the next moment, someone says something or does something, or we see something or hear something, and we are reminded of God's saving presence with us. Then that moment is gone.

Too often, when Christians go looking for a miracle or for proof of God's existence or God's love, they think big: a sign in the sky, a voice from the heavens, a burning bush by the side of the road. Certainly God can work those academy-award types of miracles, the kinds of miracles we find in the adult life of Jesus: the multiplication of the loaves and fishes, the walking on water, the driving out of demons. More often than not, however, God comes in the still, small voice, in the brief encounter with a stranger or in a quick exchange around the dinner table. In other words, not every saving encounter with Jesus ends in a healing, and not every encounter results in a radical change of heart. Sometimes a saving encounter with Jesus is much less earth-shaking, and only those directly involved even notice that anything has happened at all.

Two more examples emphasize this point. First is the miracle of Jesus fixing a carpentry problem for Joseph, previously recounted in chapter 4. Briefly, the text describes a time when Joseph was at work on a bed that a rich man had ordered. As Joseph was putting the bed together, he discovered that one crossbeam was shorter than the other—a serious problem. As he sat wondering what he should do,

Jesus told him to put the two boards next to each other, lining them up at one end. Joseph did as Jesus asked, and then watched as Jesus stretched the shorter board, making it the same length as the longer one. In the grand scheme of things, this was not much, but in that brief moment, Jesus showed himself to Joseph as one who cared about his welfare, who understood the importance of what he was doing, and who provided just what was needed for Joseph to continue with his work. Jesus didn't do the work for him and he didn't alleviate the need for Joseph to work altogether. He simply met Joseph where he was and facilitated the good work Joseph was already doing. This encounter with Jesus was a glimpse of salvation for Joseph, just a brief glimpse, and no more.

The second story, mentioned previously in chapter 5, concerns Jesus' trip to fetch water for his mother. It is a provocative idea in and of itself, is it not, that the Divine could actually have an accident or make a mistake? When Jesus was six years old, Mary sent him to a nearby spring to fetch water—a common occurrence all over the world still today. As he was making his way to the spring, he accidentally broke the pitcher and thus had nothing in which to hold the water. He continued on to the spring, however, spread out his cloak, filled it with water, and brought the water back to his mother. Mary, it is said, kept this to herself, and did not share it with anyone—but she recognized it as a miracle, in line with the other miracles she had seen Jesus perform. This event, then, had no lasting significance. It did not serve as a tool for evangelism: apparently no one else at the time found out about it, nor did it give Mary any new insight or new information about who Jesus was. Instead, it was a small moment of encouragement, of confirmation that Mary correctly understood who her son was. This brief episode reaffirmed both Jesus' love and care for Mary and Mary's delight in the abilities of her little boy. Such stories suggest that Christians should pay more attention to trivial events and be on the lookout for brief glimpses of salvation in the little corners of our lives where God continues to be at work.

What Is the Proper Response to Jesus?

A typical Christian proper response to Jesus' saving activity would likely include a fairly narrow range of closely related verbs: praise, worship, bow down, and so on. One verb that would be unexpected is "laugh." Laughter might well be seen as disrespectful, informal, and unworthy of the great thing God has done. Yet, the Infancy Gospel of Thomas recounts a story in which laughter is the response to a saving encounter with Jesus Christ. What might be learned from this?

The story, also mentioned in chapter 4, which takes place when Jesus is eight years old, concerns an infant in Jesus' neighborhood who dies. When Jesus hears the wailing from the household, he runs to see what has happened. He finds the child dead, but he touches the baby on the chest and says, "I say to you, infant, don't die but live, and be with your mother." Immediately upon hearing these words, "the infant looked up and laughed." Jesus gives the child back to the mother, and returns to play with the other children.

In this context, clearly the infant's laughter is genuine and spontaneous, an expression of the pure delight of one who has been dead but now finds oneself restored, renewed, and alive. Of course the baby doesn't offer an eloquent soliloquy. However, when we reflect upon it, we realize that words would fail anyone in such a situation. Indeed, "Thank you" would hardly do. Even adults might have something to learn from this simple, impulsive outburst of joy from the infant in the experience of being touched and brought back to life by Jesus.

In their relationship to Jesus, Christians often get caught up in their prayer life with making sure they have the most articulate, most stirring, most original prayers. How can I say "thank you" to God most eloquently? How can I find the perfect words to express to God what I am feeling? While it is not wrong to desire a beautiful, meaningful prayer, like so many other things in life, prayer is not first and foremost about the individual. Prayer is about God and what God is doing, about the relationship God has with the individual and the way God is at work in his or her life. An excessive concern about the right word or the perfect phrase can itself be a form of idolatry that gets in the way of genuine and heartfelt response to God. Such a response is sometimes expressed most faithfully, most honestly, in music, in song, and even in laughter. Communication with God doesn't have to be contained in only words, and sometimes a whole-hearted, joyous laugh says more than words ever could.

Anger Also Has a Place in Salvation

One last point, although perhaps the most controversial, cannot be avoided. As noted earlier, one of the main problems many Christians have with the Infancy Gospel of Thomas—besides its non-canonical status—is that it presents a very capricious Jesus with a hair-trigger temper, a Jesus who is not afraid to punish those who question or challenge him, and sometimes with what seems like an excess of violence. Recall the withering of the son of Annas, the slaying of the young child who bumped Jesus' shoulder while running through the village, and the blinding of those who were speaking against him. What possibly could be taken from such stories?

What these contentious stories do suggest to Christians is that God does feel things—emotion is not inimical to God. Jesus' salvific work is not a dry, analytical business; it, too, includes strong emotions. Jesus cares about how others respond to him—whether or not they support him or reject him—and he gets angry when he is mocked, trivialized, or criticized. He gives his teachers trouble when they patronize him and treat him as an ignorant boy, and he talks back to Joseph when Joseph seems to side with the villagers against him.

It actually matters to Jesus whether or not the world receives and understands him. It matters that people come to believe in him, and it matters that they see him for who he really is. God is not indifferent to the way in which people receive God in the incarnation. Thus, these stories reveal a God who is passionately interested and involved in the welfare of God's people to the degree that God is strongly moved and even thoroughly disgusted by those who react negatively, rejecting Jesus and the salvation he offers. The relationship God has with God's people in Jesus is not merely a one-way street, nor is God a serene, unemotional, detached deity. God cares about God's people—deeply, fundamentally, and passionately. If it is true that the opposite of love is not hate but indifference, then these stories of the boy Jesus reveal a God who could never be characterized as indifferent, a God who instead freely expresses displeasure, frustration, and disapproval, for the sake of gaining a right understanding of who he is and a right relationship with him. After reading these stories, Christians may wish that Jesus had used different methods, but certainly they could not argue that Jesus did not care.

Comparative Theology Revisited

Sometimes when I am introducing the topic of comparative theology to seminary students or to adult study groups in local churches, someone will ask, "Isn't the Bible enough?" What they are asking, of course, is why Christians should have to take the trouble of learning about another religious tradition—or even consider the possibility that they might learn something of God through it—when there is more than enough about God in the Bible to last a lifetime.

The answer is yes and no. Of course, Bible contains enough texts for study in any one lifetime.

Sacred texts—classics, to use David Tracy's language—are by definition overflowing with meaning: they are living and they compel us to believe "that something else might be the case."[13] This surplus of meaning demands that we continually revisit them, continually mine them for new and undiscovered riches. For Christians, of course, the Bible is the classic text *par excellence*, with the continual inspiration of the Holy Spirit providing a never-ending spring of insight around who God is, how God is in relationship to the world, and what it means to be faithful to this God.

Yet, at the same time, it seems there is more to be said. After all, the world has other religious classics; they too have their truths to share with us, they too make a claim upon us, and they too have insights to offer about God and God's relationship with the world. Why must this be an "either/or" situation? Why can't Christians carve out for themselves a comfortable and even potentially exciting position of "both/and" if their reading of Christian scripture is deepened and challenged by their reading of sacred Hindu texts, or Buddhist sutras, or the Qur'an; or if those other sacred texts offer new pathways into the Bible, helping Christians learn more about the Bible than they would have otherwise?

Whether or not Christian are persuaded by such an argument, the fact remains that we live today in a profoundly pluralistic world. As a result, at least to some degree, our very lives are interreligious. The walls are down, the doors are open, and there is no going back. When Christians talk, others listen; and when others talk, Christians listen—sometimes eagerly and sympathetically, and sometimes with hostility and mistrust. Simply put, we *live* in the midst of an interreligious conversation, no matter how hard we try to pretend otherwise. As Francis Clooney has observed,

> A community may intend simply to speak to itself, but once it ventures to think and speak its theology out loud, it will find itself in conversation with others who are listening, including people of other faith and theological traditions. They will join the community's internal conversation, sometimes to agree and sometimes to disagree, and will offer competing claims about what is reasonable and worth believing.[14]

The more we know—about our own religious tradition as well as about the religious tradition of others—the more we can engage

constructively and intelligently in the conversation. Correspondingly, the more open we are to the knowledge of the other, the more
we can learn, the more we can grow, the more we can speak and listen with integrity, sensitivity, and nuance. Such dialogue is never
easy. It is risky, challenging, and, at times, frustrating: learning new
words, new concepts, and new ways of thinking. Yet, the rewards are
great, both for ourselves as individuals and for the faith communities for whom and with whom we speak. The rewards are also great
for the other, whom we come to know as a sister or brother, rather
than as an enemy. Interreligious dialogue isn't about agreement, it's
about transformation, and that transformation can happen only
through dialogue and conversation.

Conclusion

Serendipitously, as I finish writing right in the middle of Advent,
the baby Jesus is everywhere. The songs that resound throughout
Christians churches at this time emphasize many of the same points I
have made regarding who Jesus is and how he saves. "Awake! Awake,
and Greet the New Morn" recounts how "the child of our longing"
comes "as a baby weak and poor," whose "humble song is quiet and
near." "Creator of the Stars of Night" reminds us that "you came; but
not in splendor bright, not as a monarch, but the child of Mary." "Unexpected and Mysterious" tells us that "unexpected and mysterious is
the gentle word of grace."[15]

Yet, the Christmas season is bracingly brief and all too soon the
crèches will be stored away and churches will take down the greens
and begin to prepare their sanctuaries for Lent. Unlike Advent, a season of repentance and preparation, Lent is a very long season,
roughly one and a half times the length of Advent; and the Easter season that follows is almost four times as long as the Christmas season.
Practically, this means that the incarnation will all too soon give way
to the crucifixion, and the life of Jesus will all too soon yield its place
on the stage to his death and then his resurrection.

Perhaps this book will provide a bit more of a stop between Advent and Lent, creating both the space and the possibility for fresh reflection on how the infancy narratives of Jesus might give Christians
new insight into what it means to call him savior. There is deep, profound soteriological meaning in the incarnation, and if Christians either ignore or marginalize Jesus' birth and young life, we lose a rich
resource for gaining insight into both Jesus' person and work and for

understanding more about the loving God who was pleased to dwell in human form and take on human nature for the sake of the salvation of the world.

Further, I maintain that doing theology interreligiously is not merely an academic luxury but a necessity in the twenty-first century world in which we live. Learning about Krishna and what his birth and young life mean to Hindus, especially regarding salvation, and how that knowledge shapes the relationship Hindus have with the Divine creates the possibility for a new way of seeing Jesus and his saving activity, and a new way of being in relationship to him.

In W. H. Auden's poem, "For the Time Being: A Christmas Oratorio," the character of Simeon reflects on the birth of Jesus Christ, saying, "And because of [Christ's] visitation, we may no longer desire God as if He were lacking: our redemption is no longer a question of pursuit but of surrender to Him who is always and everywhere present. Therefore at every moment we pray that, following Him, we may depart from our anxiety into His peace."[16] God is with us—that is the promise of the incarnation. Sure of that promise, then, Christians are invited to go out in both confidence and joy, seeking God where God may be found—even in the most unexpected of places, even in the forests and hills of Vraj.

Notes

Introduction

1. *Krishna: The Beautiful Legend of God*, trans. Edwin F. Bryant (London: Penguin Books, 2003), 39.

2. Ibid., xxiii.

3. Bart Ehrman, *Lost Scriptures: Books That Did Not Make It into the New Testament* (New York: Oxford University Press, 2003), 58.

1. Comparative Theology and Learning about Jesus

1. James Fredericks, "A Universal Religious Experience? Comparative Theology as an Alternative to a Theology of Religions," *Horizons* 22, 1 (1995): 68.

2. Ibid., 72.

3. George Lindbeck, *The Nature of Doctrine: Religion and Theology in a Postliberal Age* (Louisville: Westminster John Knox Press, 1984).

4. Fredericks, "A Universal Religious Experience?" 79.

5. Ibid.

6. Ibid., 81.

7. Ibid., 83.

8. As quoted in James Fredericks, "A Universal Religious Experience?" 84.

9. Ibid., 86.

10. Ibid., 87; my emphasis.

11. Francis Clooney, SJ, *Theology after Vedanta: An Experiment in Comparative Theology* (Albany: State University of New York Press, 1993), 8.

12. John Thatamanil, *The Immanent Divine* (Minneapolis: Fortress Press, 2006), xi.

13. Luther's Small Catechism, in *The Book of Concord*, ed. Robert Kolb and Timothy Wengert (Minneapolis: Fortress Press, 2000), 353.

14. Luther's Large Catechism, *The Book of Concord*, 412; my emphasis.

15. *Guidelines on Dialogue with People of Living Faiths and Ideologies*. (Geneva: World Council of Churches, 1979), nos. 17–18.

16. "Declaration on the Relation of the Church to Non-Christian Religions," in *The Documents of Vatican Council II: The Basic Edition*, ed. Austin Flannery (Collegeville, MN: The Liturgical Press, 1987), no. 2.

17. "Dogmatic Constitution on the Church," in *The Documents of Vatican Council II: The Basic Edition*, ed. Austin Flannery (Collegeville, MN: The Liturgical Press, 1987), no. 16.

18. Ibid.

19. Karl Rahner, *Foundations of Christian Faith*, trans. William Dych (New York: Seabury Press, 1978), 53.

20. Rahner writes that "In this Spirit of [Jesus Christ's] he is present and operative in all faith" (ibid., 318).

21. John B. Cobb, "The Religions," in *Christian Theology*, ed. Peter Hodgson and Robert King (Minneapolis, MN: Fortress Press, 1994), 357.

22. Francis X. Clooney, SJ, *Hindu Wisdom for All God's Children* (Maryknoll, NY: Orbis Books, 1998), xii.

2. A Savior in Disguise—The Stories

1. As cited in Edwin Scott Gaustan and Philip L. Barlow, *New Historical Atlas of Religion in America* (New York: Oxford University Press, 2000), 272. See http://pluralism.org/resources/statistics/tradition.php#Hinduism (accessed June 20, 2009).

2. Ibid.

3. Steven Rosen, *Essential Hinduism* (Lanham, MD: Rowman & Littlefield Publishers, Inc., 2006), 17.

4. Steven Rosen notes that the very concept of "Hinduism" as a world religion developed only with the British colonization of India in the nineteenth century (*Essential Hinduism*, 23).

5. Quoted in Axel Michaels, *Hinduism: Past and Present* (Princeton: Princeton University Press, 2003), 12.

6. James B. Robinson, *Hinduism* (Philadelphia: Chelsea House Publishers, 2004), 3.

7. Rosen, *Essential Hinduism*, 18.

8. *World Religions*, ed. Thomas Robinson and Hillary Rodrigues (Peabody, MA: Hendrickson Publishers, 2006), 175.

9. Robinson, *Hinduism*, 11.

10. For an accessible introduction to the *Rig Veda*, see the Penguin Classics edition (September 2005), trans. Wendy Doniger, which contains 108 of the over 1,000 hymns that make up the collection.

11. Here I recommend the Oxford World's Classics edition (June 2008), trans. Patrick Olivelle, which contains twelve principal Upanishads.

12. A good introduction to the *Mahabharata* is R. K. Narayan's *The Mahabharata: A Shortened Modern Prose Version of the Indian Epic* (Chicago: University of Chicago Press, 2000).

13. Jonah Blank, *The Arrow of the Blue-skinned God: Retracing the Ramayana through India* (Boston: Houghton Mifflin Co., 1992), ix.

14. The Penguin Classics edition (August 2006) as told by R. K. Narayan is a good first introduction to the text.

15. This is, of course, problematic for women, as Sita's primary role is that of submissive wife, and feminists critique many aspects of her role. See, for example, R. P. Goldman and S. J. Sutherland Goldman, "Ramayana," in *The Hindu World*, ed. Sushil Mittal and Gene Thursby (London: Routledge, 2004); and Jacqueline Suthren Hirst and Lynn Thomas, eds., *Playing for Real: Hindu Role Models, Religion, and Gender* (Oxford: Oxford University Press, 2004).

16. Freda Matchett, "The Puranas," in *The Blackwell Companion to Hinduism*, ed. Gavin Flood (Oxford: Blackwell Publishing, 2003), 132. However, Edwin Bryant argues for an earlier date, suggesting that most of the material in the Puranas was compiled in the Gupta period, around the fourth to the sixth century CE. See his own essay on the *Bhagavata Purana* in *Krishna: A Sourcebook*, ed. Edwin F. Bryant (Oxford: Oxford University Press, 2007), 113.

17. Ibid.

18. Ibid., 129.

19. Rosen, *Essential Hinduism*, 143.

20. John Esposito et al., *World Religions Today* (Oxford: Oxford University Press, 2008), 303–4.

21. Rosen, *Essential Hinduism*, 27–28.

22. Ibid., 25.

23. Ibid., xv; my italics.

24. Ibid., xvii.

25. Edwin Bryant notes that "the Krishnaite theologies that emerged in the sixteenth century, initiated by influential teachers such as Vallabha and Chaitanya, find grounds to hold that it is not Krishna who is an incarnation of Vishnu but Vishnu who is a partial manifestation of Krishna. These sects extol Krishna as the supreme Absolute Truth from whom all other deities, including Vishnu, evolve, and the *Bhagavata Purana* is presented as the epistemological authority in this regard" ("Krishna in the Tenth Book of the *Bhagavata Purana*," in *Krishna: A Source Book*, ed. Edwin F. Bryant (Oxford: Oxford University Press, 2007), 112).

26. This devotional song is transcribed by Tracy Pintchman in her chapter, "The Month of Kārtik and Women's Ritual Devotions to Krishna in Benares," in *The Blackwell Companion to Hinduism*, ed. Gavin Flood (Oxford: Blackwell Publishing, 2003), 334.

27. Barbara Powell, *Windows into the Infinite: A Guide to the Hindu Scriptures* (Fremont, CA: Asian Humanities Press, 1996), 35.

28. Rosen, *Essential Hinduism*, 122.

29. See, for example, *Krishna: The Beautiful Legend of God*, trans. Edwin Bryant (London: Penguin Books, 2003).

30. See, for example, *Krishna: Myths, Rites, and Attitudes*, ed. Milton Singer (Honolulu: East-West Center Press, 1966), xiv.

31. Powell, *Windows into the Infinite*, 253.

32. Ibid., 254.

33. Ibid., 304.

34. *Krishna: The Beautiful Legend of God*, 10.

35. Ibid., xxi.

36. Sister Nivedita, *Cradle Tales of Hinduism* (Kolkata: Advaita Ashrama, 2008), 141.

37. *Krishna: The Beautiful Legend of God*, 36.

38. Ibid., 39.

39. Ibid., 46.

40. Ibid., 76.

41. Ibid., 55.

42. Sister Nivedita, *Cradle Tales of Hinduism*, 156.

43. *Krishna: The Beautiful Legend of God*, 64.

44. Ibid., 72.

45. Sister Nivedita, *Cradle Tales of Hinduism*, 1166.

46. *Krishna: The Beautiful Legend of God*, 89.

47. Ibid., 61.

48. Ibid., 105.

49. See, for example, the description of Akrura's first meeting with Krishna, where he is described as made "anxious by love," with "eyes overflowing with tears of ecstasy," simply by seeing Krishna for the first time. He is so overcome with longing he is not even able to announce his own name (*Krishna: The Beautiful Legend of God*, 160).

50. David Kinsley, *The Sword and the Flute* (Berkeley: University of California Press, 1975), 75.

51. Ibid., 23.

52. *Krishna: The Beautiful Legend of God*, 180.

53. Ibid., 325.

54. Ibid., 298.

55. Ibid., 396.

56. Ibid., 404.

57. Ibid., 417.

58. Ibid.

59. Diana Eck, *Encountering God: A Spiritual Journey from Bozeman to Banaras* (Boston: Beacon Press, 2003), 104.

60. *Krishna: The Beautiful Legend of God*, 43–44.

61. Eck, *Encountering God*, 46–47.

62. Rosen, *Essential Hinduism*, 134.

63. Sister Nivedita, *Cradle Tales of Hinduism*, 158.

64. *Krishna: The Beautiful Legend of God*, 139–41.

65. Ibid., 143.

3. Krishna and His Followers—How He Saves

1. From a poem composed in the sixteenth century by the poet Surdas, quoted in John Stratton Hawley, "Braj: Fishing in Sur's Ocean," in *Krishna: A Source Book*, ed. Edwin F. Bryant (Oxford: Oxford University Press, 2007), 231.

2. That is, it is written from the perspective of those Hindus who worship Vishnu as the highest embodiment of the one supreme god.

3. David Kinsley, *The Sword and the Flute* (Berkeley: University of California Press, 1975), 11.

4. David Kinsley has an interesting discussion of the whole theme of "combat as play" in his book *The Divine Player: A Study of Krishna Lila* (Delhi: Motilal Banarsidass, 1979). He notes examples from Krishna's young life, as well as examples involving other gods and goddesses, concluding, "One gets the impression that the gods are really never in trouble at all, that they condescend to battle the demons simply because it is all part of some cosmic script or because they enjoy it... The combat-as-*lila* theme suggests in a straightforward way that the gods are so powerful, so removed from the finite limitations of the human sphere, that for them the most monumental struggle is resolved effortlessly" (49, 55).

5. Kinsley, *The Divine Player*, 56.

6. *Krishna: The Beautiful Legend of God*, trans. Edwin Bryant (London: Penguin Books, 2003), xxiii.

7. Ibid., xxii.

8. Ibid., xxv.

9. Kinsley, *The Divine Player*, xi.

10. Ibid.

11. David Kinsley, *The Sword and the Flute*, 73.

12. Kinsley, *The Divine Player*, 112.

13. Kinsley, *The Sword and the Flute*, 15.

14. McKim Marriott describes his first encounter with Holi while doing field research in the village of Kishan Garhi, near Vraj. When he asked his barber, "What is it all going to be about this afternoon?" the barber replied, "Holi is the Festival of Love." When Marriott pressed his neighbors further, they said, "All greet each other with affection and feeling. Lord Krishna taught us the way of love, and so we celebrate Holi in this manner" ("The Feast of Love," in *Krishna: Myths, Rites, and Attitudes*, ed. Milton Singer (Honolulu: East-West Center Press, 1966), 203, 205.

15. Holi is by no means the only or even the most important Hindu festival relating to Krishna. Krishna's birth, for example, Krishna Janmashtami, is also a festival of great importance. In her study, "The Month of Kārtik and Women's Ritual Devotions to Krishna in Benares," Tracy Pintchman notes that "several informants associated the month of Kārtik with the sum total of Krishna's life as a cowherd in Braj, from his birth until his eventual departure

for Dvaraka, even insisting that all the major events of this period of his life took place during the month of Kārtik" (*The Blackwell Companion to Hinduism*, ed. Gavin Flood [Oxford: Blackwell Publishing, 2003], 332).

16. One of the interesting ways in which this has played out, both in the Krishna iconography and in the descriptions of Krishna, is that his beauty is often illustrated with what are typically feminine attributes—jewelry, make-up, soft curvaceousness, etc. On this topic see Graham Schweig's chapter, "The Divine Feminine in the Theology of Krishna," in *Krishna: A Source Book*, ed. Edwin F. Bryant (Oxford: Oxford University Press, 2007).

17. Kinsley, *The Divine Player*, 74.

18. One extended example of multi-volume, well-developed theological aesthetics is Hans Urs von Balthasar, *The Glory of the Lord: A Theological Aesthetics* (San Francisco: Ignatius Press).

19. Steven Hopkins, "Sanskrit from Tamil Nadu: At Play in the Forests of the Lord: The *Gopalavimshati* of Vedantadeshika," in *Krishna*, ed. Edwin F. Bryant (Oxford: Oxford University Press, 2007), 299–300.

20. David Kinsley, *The Sword and the Flute*, 77.

21. Barbara Powell, *Windows into the Infinite* (Fremont, CA: Asian Humanities Press, 1996), 307.

22. Kinsley, *The Sword and the Flute*, 18.

23. Rosen, *Essential Hinduism*, 132.

24. Ibid.

25. Francis X. Clooney, SJ, *Hindu Wisdom for all God's Children* (Maryknoll, NY: Orbis Books, 1998), 69.

26. Francis X. Clooney, "Ramanuja and the Meaning of Krishna's Descent and Embodiment on This Earth," in *Krishna: The Source Book*, ed. Edwin F. Bryant (Oxford: Oxford University Press, 2007), 331.

27. Diana Eck, *Encountering God* (Boston: Beacon Press, 2003), 104.

28. John L. Esposito, Darrell J. Fasching, and Todd Lewis, *World Religions Today*, 3rd ed. (New York: Oxford University Press, 2008).

29. Axel Michaels, *Hinduism Past and Present*, trans. Barbara Harshav (Princeton: Princeton University Press, 2004), 24. Sometimes this list is described as various "yogas"—that is, disciplines—and it often includes a fourth: *raja-yoga*, the way of mental focus and concentration. This is how the *Bhagavad Gita* describes the various paths of salvation—see chapter 6 for more on this point.

30. For more information and examples of some of this poetry, see Vasudha Narayanan, "Tamil Nadu: Weaving Garlands in Tamil: The Poetry of the *Alvars*," in *Krishna: The Source Book*, ed. Edwin F. Bryant (Oxford: Oxford University Press, 2007).

31. Thomas J. Hopkins, "The Social Teaching of the *Bhagavata Purana*," in *Krishna: Myths, Rites, and Attitudes*, ed. Milton Singer (Honolulu: East-West Center Press, 1966), 7.

32. For more information on the *bhakti* movement, see the excellent chapter in Wendy Doniger, *The Hindus* (New York: The Penguin Press, 2009).

33. Ibid., 252.

34. Thomas J. Hopkins, "The Social Teaching of the *Bhagavata Purana*," 17. Hopkins also notes that "the most desirable characteristics are those compatible with devotion, and these are independent of class."

35. Ibid., 257–58.

36. Edward C. Dimock, "Doctrine and Practice among Vaishnavas of Bengal," in *Krishna: Myths, Rites, and Attitudes*, ed. Milton Singer (Honolulu: East-West Center Press, 1966), 47.

37. As quoted in Rosen, *Essential Hinduism*, 159.

38. Rosen, *Essential Hinduism*, 124.

39. Andres Nygren's work, *Eros and Agape,* is particularly significant in this regard (Chicago, IL: University of Chicago Press, 1982), translated by Philip S. Watson.

40. *Krishna: The Beautiful Legend of God*, xxv.

41. Kinsley, *The Sword and the Flute*, 55.

42. Steven J. Rosen, *Krishna's Song: A New Look at the Bhagavad Gita,* (Westport, CT: Praeger Publishers, 2007), 77.

43. Ibid., 81.

44. Edwin Bryant, "Krishna in the Tenth Book of the *Bhagavata Purana*," in *Krishna: A Source Book*, ed. Edwin F. Bryant (Oxford: Oxford University Press, 2007), 115.

45. Kinsley, *The Divine Player*, 203.

46. Clooney, *Hindu Wisdom for all God's Children*, 53.

47. Ibid., 59.

48. The connection between the different schools of Hindu philosophy and devotion to Krishna is a very interesting topic that unfortunately lies outside the scope of this book. This connection is of particular interest in terms of soteriology, as there is a perceived divide between the forms of Hindu practice and thought that focus on non-personal or transpersonal forms of the Supreme and those that focus on a personal embodiment of the Supreme. That divide is not always as gaping as it has been described. I point the interested reader to several excellent essays in the volume *Krishna: A Source Book*, ed. Edwin F. Bryant (Oxford: Oxford University Press, 2007) that note the place of Krishna in Advaita Vedanta ("Krishna in Advaita Vedanta: The Supreme *Brahman* in Human Form," by Lance E. Nelson), Vishishtadvaita ("Ramanuja and the Meaning of Krishna's Descent and Embodiment on This Earth," by Francis X. Clooney), and Madhva Vedanta ("Madhva Vedanta and Krishna," by Deepak Sarma).

49. Graham Schweig, *Dance of Divine Love* (Princeton: Princeton University Press, 2005), 148.

50. *Krishna: The Beautiful Legend of God*, trans. Edwin Bryant (London: Penguin Books, 2003), xlviii.

51. Rosen, *Essential Hinduism*, 125.

52. W. G. Archer, *The Loves of Krishna* (New York: Grove Press, Inc., 1957), 19.

53. *Krishna: The Beautiful Legend of God*, xxvii.

54. Vasudha Narayanan, "Tamil Nadu: Weaving Garlands in Tamil: The Poetry of the *Alvars*," in *Krishna: A Source Book*, ed. Edwin F. Bryant (Oxford: Oxford University Press, 2007), 193.

55. Barbara Powell, *Windows into the Infinite* (Fremont, CA: Asian Humanities Press, 1996), 310–11.

4. Immanuel—The Stories

1. Fred Lapham, *An Introduction to the New Testament Apocrypha* (New York: T & T Clark International, 2003), 129.

2. Mark Allan Powell has a helpful description of the characteristics of ancient biographies in his book *Introducing the New Testament* (Grand Rapids, MI: Baker Academic, 2009), in which he explains that "the point of ancient biographies was to relate accounts that portrayed the essential character of the person who was the subject of the work. Indeed, the purpose of the biography was to define that person's character in a manner that would invite emulation" (84). This explains why such biographies didn't bother about physical appearance or historical data such as names, dates, and places, or even specific chronology.

3. Ibid., 82.

4. Barbara Reid, *The Gospel According to Matthew* (Collegeville, MN: Liturgical Press, 2005), 19.

5. All Bible translations are from the New Revised Standard Version.

6. For examples of such images and a short discussion of this theme in Christian art, see Neil MacGregor, *Seeing Salvation* (New Haven: Yale University Press, 2000), 11–16, and also Gabriele Finaldi, *The Image of Christ* (New Haven: Yale University Press, 2000), 44–73.

7. For more information on how the understanding of the role of the wise men developed in the subsequent Christian tradition, see Raymond Brown, *The Birth of the Messiah*, rev. ed. (New York: Doubleday, 1993), 197ff.

8. Joseph A. Fitzmyer, S.J., *The Anchor Bible: The Gospel according to Luke (I-IX)* (Garden City, NY: Doubleday & Co., 1981), 204.

9. Ibid., 222.

10. Alice Walker, *In Search of Our Mothers' Gardens* (Orlando: Harcourt Books, 1983), xi.

11. Edwin D. Freed, *The Stories of Jesus' Birth* (Sheffield: Sheffield Academic Press, 2001), 146–47.

12. Joan Acocella, "Betrayal: Should We Hate Judas Iscariot?" *The New Yorker*, August 3, 2009, 70.

13. *The Non-Canonical Gospels*, ed. Paul Foster (New York: T&T Clark, 2008), xvii.

14. Ibid., xvii–iii.

15. Paul Achtemeier, Joel B. Green, and Marianne Meye Thompson, *Introducing the New Testament* (Grand Rapids, MI: Wm. B. Eerdmans, 2001), 69.

16. Ibid., 74.

17. Ibid., 589.

18. Ibid., 598.

19. Ibid., 599.

20. *The Non-Canonical Gospels*, ed. Paul Foster (New York: T&T Clark, 2008), vii.

21. Ibid., vii.

22. Bart Ehrman suggests four criteria that were used to determine whether a particular text should or should not be admitted into the canon: "a book was to be admitted into the proto-orthodox canon of Scripture only if it was a) Ancient; b) Apostolic; c) Catholic; d) Orthodox" (Bart Ehrman, *Lost Christianities* [Oxford: Oxford University Press, 2003], 242–43).

23. Achtemeir et al., *Introducing the New Testament*, 602.

24. Ibid., 603.

25. Fred Lapham, *An Introduction to the New Testament Apocrypha*, 131.

26. Paul Foster notes the existence of others, such as the *Gospel of Pseudo-Matthew*, the *Arabic Infancy Gospel*, and the *History of Joseph the Carpenter*. However, in his view, such texts are "expansionist retellings based on" the two infancy gospels discussed in this chapter (Foster, ed., *The Non-Canonical Gospels*, x).

27. See Edgar Hennecke, *New Testament Apocrypha*, vol. 1 (Philadelphia: The Westminster Press, 1963) for some examples of stories from these two and other later infancy gospels.

28. Foster, *The Non-Canonical Gospels*, xiv.

29. Paul Foster, "The *Protoevangelium of James*," in *The Non-Canonical Gospels*, ed. Paul Foster (New York, NY: T&T Clark, 2008), 110.

30. Ronald F. Hock, *The Infancy Gospels of James and Thomas* (Santa Rosa, CA: Polebridge Press, 1996), 11.

31. All translations of both the Infancy Gospel of James and the Infancy Gospel of Thomas are taken from Hock's *The Infancy Gospels of James and Thomas*.

32. Paul Foster, "The *Protoevangelium of James*," in *The Non-Canonical Gospels*, ed. Paul Foster (New York: T&T Clark, 2008), 119–20.

33. Ibid., 124.

34. Hock, *The Infancy Gospels of James and Thomas*, 84.

35. Ibid., 85.

36. Tony Chartrand-Burke, "The *Infancy Gospel of Thomas*," in *The Non-Canonical Gospels*, ed. Paul Foster (New York: T&T Clark, 2008), 126.

37. Hock, 86.

38. Ibid., 91.

39. See both Hock (91) and Lapham, *An Introduction to the New Testament Apocrypha*, 129.

40. Hock, *The Infancy Gospels of James and Thomas*, 97.

41. Chartrand-Burke, "The *Infancy Gospel of Thomas*," 134.

42. Lapham, *An Introduction to the New Testament Apocrypha*, 130.

43. Hock, *The Infancy Gospels of James and Thomas*, 97.

44. Lapham, *An Introduction to the New Testament Apocrypha*, 130.

5. Jesus and His Disciples—How He Saves

1. Joseph F. Kelly, *The Ecumenical Councils of the Catholic Church: A History* (Collegeville, MN: Liturgical Press, 2009), 34.

2. There are many helpful introductions to and overviews of the first seven ecumenical councils of the Christian church, including, of course, the key Christological and soteriological debates on which they centered. A few bibliographic suggestions are J. N. D. Kelly, *Early Christian Doctrines*, rev. ed. (San Francisco: HarperSanFrancisco, 1973); Stephen Need, *Truly Divine and Truly Human: The Story of Christ and the Seven Ecumenical Councils* (Peabody, MA: Hendrickson Publishers, 2009); Jaroslav Pelikan, *The Christian Tradition: A History of the Development of Doctrine, Vol. 1: The Emergence of the Catholic Tradition* (Chicago: University of Chicago Press, 1971); and Margaret R. Miles, *The Word Made Flesh: A History of Christian Thought* (Malden, MA: Blackwell Publishing, 2005).

3. Of course, there have been many different attempts to positively explain the role of non-Christians in the economy of salvation, particularly in the twentieth and twenty-first centuries. In some of these explications, Jesus is depicted as *a* savior, but perhaps not the only savior. Even in such theological analysis, however, Jesus Christ almost always has a place of special consideration.

4. For example, Bart Ehrman, in *Lost Christianities: The Battles for Scripture and the Faiths We Never Knew* (New York: Oxford University Press, 2003), notes how Origen's star rose and then fell over time. See pages 154–56 in particular.

5. Ibid., 4.

6. Terence Fretheim, "God and Violence in the Old Testament," *Word & World* 24, 1 (Winter 2004): 26.

7. See, for example, Terence Fretheim, "'I was only a little angry': Divine

Violence in the Prophets," *Interpretation* (October 2004): 365–75; and Scott Ashmon, "The Wrath of God: A Biblical Overview," *Concordia* (October 2005): 348–58.

8. Jaroslav Pelilkan notes that there are some conflicting accounts about how Marcion described this God—some imply that Marcion called this God "evil," while others argue that Marcion called him just and juridical, but not evil (Pelikan, *The Christian Tradition, Vol. 1* (Chicago: University of Chicago Press, 1971), 74.

9. Ibid., 73.

10. Ibid., 75.

11. Ehrman, *Lost Christianities*, 105.

12. Ibid., 105.

13. Pelikan, *The Christian Tradition*, vol. 1, 82.

14. Ehrman, *Lost Christianities*, 125–26.

15. Ibid., 152.

16. J. N. D. Kelly, *Early Christian Doctrines*, 140.

17. Ehrman, *Lost Christianities*, 101.

18. Ibid., 250.

19. J. N. D. Kelly, *Early Christian Doctrines*, 223.

20. Need, *Truly Divine and Truly Human*, 41–42.

21. J. N. D. Kelly, *Early Christian Doctrines*, 223.

22. Ibid., 227ff.

23. Miles, *The Word Made Flesh*, 71.

24. Ehrman, *Lost Christianities*, 194.

25. Ibid., 252.

26. Need, *Truly Divine and Truly Human*, 93.

27. Ibid., 93–94.

28. As quoted in *Documents of the Christian Church*, ed. Henry Bettenson (New York: Oxford University Press, 1947), 71–72.

29. Ibid., 72–73; emphasis in the original.

30. Raymond Brown, *The Birth of the Messiah*, rev. ed. (New York: Doubleday, 1993), 26.

31. Ibid., 28.

32. Ibid., 240.

33. Ibid., 29.

34. Joseph F. Kelly, *The Ecumenical Councils of the Catholic Church*, 36.

35. Ibid., 36.

36. *The Early Christian Fathers*, edited and translated by Henry Bettenson (Oxford: Oxford University Press), 78–79.

37. Denis Minns, OP, *Irenaeus* (Washington, DC: Georgetown University Press, 1994), 91.

38. Joseph F. Kelly, *The Ecumenical Councils of the Catholic Church*, 34.

39. Adam Gopnik, "What Did Jesus Do?" *The New Yorker* (May 24, 2010), 76.

40. Margaret R. Miles, *A Complex Delight: The Secularization of the Breast, 1350–1750* (Berkeley: University of California Press, 2008), 41.

41. Ibid., 43; emphasis in the original.

42. Ibid.

43. Ibid., ix.

44. Ibid., 2.

45. See http://www.ojp.usdoj.gov/ovc/ncvrw/2005/pg5l.html (accessed August 11, 2010).

46. Ibid.

47. Vincent J. Miller, *Consuming Religion: Christian Faith and Practice in a Consumer Culture* (New York: Continuum, 2004), 16.

48. Rosemary Radford Ruether, *Many Forms of Madness* (Minneapolis: Fortress Press, 2010), 138.

49. Ibid., 139.

50. Rita Nakashima Brock and Rebecca Ann Parker, *Saving Paradise: How Christianity Traded Love of This World for Crucifixion and Empire* (Boston: Beacon Press, 2008), 170.

51. Ibid.

52. Brown, *The Birth of the Messiah*, 31.

53. Ibid., 181.

54. Ibid., 314.

55. Ibid., 357.

56. Ibid., 360.

57. Diana Eck, *Encountering God: A Spiritual Journey from Bozeman to Banaras* (Boston: Beacon Press, 2003), 103–4.

58. Gerhard Forde, *On Being a Theologian of the Cross* (Grand Rapids, MI: Eerdmans Publishing Company, 1997), 77.

59. Ibid., 79.

60. Ibid., 86.

61. Deanna Thompson, *Crossing the Divide: Luther, Feminism and the Cross* (Minneapolis: Fortress Press, 2004), 61–62.

62. Brown, *The Birth of the Messiah*, 483.

63. Ibid., 38.

64. Ehrman, *Lost Christianities*, 206. Ehrman contrasts the Infancy Gospel of Thomas with the Proto-Gospel of James, which, he argues, shows a clear theological agenda, desiring to demonstrate that Jesus Christ was the Son of God even at birth, against the claims of the Marcionite Christians and the Ebionite Christians. See pages 209ff.

65. See http://www.washingtontimes.com/news/2006/nov/12/20061112-125119-7426r (accessed September 4, 2010).

66. Ibid.

67. One notable exception is the sculpture of "Jesus the Good Shepherd" at St. Francis of Assisi Catholic Church in Ann Arbor, Michigan, where Jesus clearly is smiling. See http://www.sculpturebyghadd.com/jesusshepherd.htm (accessed November 29, 2010).

68. Definition from www.dictionary.com (accessed September 6, 2010).

69. John Calvin, *Institutes of the Christian Religion*, vol. 2, trans. Henry Beveridge (Grand Rapids, MI: Eerdmans Publishing Company, 1975), 206.

70. Ibid., 203.

71. Ibid., 204.

72. Ibid., 210.

73. Ibid., 251.

74. Ibid., 226.

75. Ibid., 227.

76. Ibid., 235.

77. Aloys Grillmeier, S.J., *Christ in Christian Tradition*, vol. 1, 2nd rev. ed., trans. John Bowden (Atlanta: John Knox Press, 1975), 67.

78. A similar version of this argument appeared as a portion of my article, "The Role of Fear in Our Love of God: A Lutheran Perspective," *Dialog* 50, 1 (Spring 2011).

79. Terence E. Fretheim, "God and Violence in the Old Testament," in *Word & World* 24, 1 (Winter 2004): 21.

80. Ellen van Wolde, "Sentiments as Culturally Constructed Emotions: Anger and Love in the Hebrew Bible," in *Biblical Interpretation* 16 (2008): 8.

81. Fretheim, "God and Violence in the Old Testament," 23.

82. Ibid., 25.

83. Ibid., 24.

84. Ibid., 28.

85. Brown, *The Birth of the Messiah*, 231–32.

6. All Grown Up—Krishna and Jesus as Adults

1. *The Bhagavad-Gita: Krishna's Counsel in Time of War*, trans. Barbara Stoler Miller (New York: Columbia University Press, 1986), 2.

2. James L. Fitzgerald, "The Great Epic of India as Religious Rhetoric: A Fresh Look at the *Mahabharata*," *Journal of the American Academy of Religion* 51, 4 (December 1983): 612.

3. For those who are looking for a condensed version of the story, I recommend Chakravarthi Narasimhan's translation: *The Mahabharata*, rev. ed. (New York: Columbia University Press, 1965, 1998).

4. Technically, both the Pandavas and the Kauravas are descended from Kuru, but in the story the name is applied specifically to the sons of Dhritarashtra.

5. Narasimhan, *The Mahabharata*, 28.

6. Steven J. Rosen, *Essential Hinduism* (Lanham, MD: Rowman & Littlefield, 2006), 87.

7. Barbara Powell, *Windows into the Infinite: A Guide to the Hindu Scriptures* (Fremont, CA: Asian Humanities Press, 1996), 38.

8. Narasimhan, *The Mahabharata*, 99.

9. Ibid., 107–8.

10. Ibid., xxvi.

11. Rosen, *Essential Hinduism*, 89.

12. Some say earlier, around 250 BCE. See John Moffitt, "The Bhagavad Gita as a Way-Shower to the Transcendental," in *Theological Studies* 38, 2 (June 1977): 316.

13. Robert N. Minor, ed., *Modern Indian Interpreters of the Bhagavadgita* (Albany: State University of New York Press, 1986), 4. This volume offers an interesting variety of influential interpretations of the *Gita* in the modern period.

14. J. T. F. Jordens, "Gandhi and the *Bhagavadgita*," in *Modern Indian Interpreters of the Bhagavadgita*, ed. Robert N. Minor (Albany: State University of New York Press, 1986), 88.

15. Minor, *Modern Indian Interpreters of the Bhagavadgita*, 5.

16. Sebastian Painadath, "The Integrated Spirituality of the Bhagavad Gita—An Insight for Christians: A Contribution to the Hindu-Christian Dialogue," in *Journal of Ecumenical Studies* 39, 3-4 (Summer-Fall 2002): 308.

17. *The Bhagavad-Gita: Krishna's Counsel in Time of War*, 6.

18. Ibid., 1.

19. I want to note here that this aspect of the text justifiably raises the question as to whether it is some sort of divine license for warfare in the Hindu tradition. While there certainly has been scholarly debate about this, it must be stated that the *Gita* is not typically interpreted this way. In fact, the *Gita* is said to advocate non-violence, with fighting justifiable only as a very last resort and only under very specific conditions. See "Fight or Flight: Violence in the Saga of the Pandavas," in *Krishna's Song: A New Look at the Bhagavad Gita*, ed. Steven J. Rosen (Westport, CT: Praeger Publishers, 2007); see also Powell, *Windows into the Infinite*, 38.

20. Vitaliano Gorospe, "Krishna Avatara in the Bhagavad Gita and Christ Incarnate in John's Gospel," *Dialogue & Alliance* 1, 2 (Summer 1987): 56.

21. Christopher Chapple, ed., *The Bhagavad Gita*, trans. Winthrop Sargeant (Albany: State University of New York Press, 1984), xix.

22. Moffitt, "The Bhagavad Gita as a Way-Shower to the Transcendental," 317.

23. Fitzgerald, "The Great Epic of India as Religious Rhetoric," 618.

24. Painadath, "The Integrated Spirituality of the Bhagavad Gita," 312.

25. Gorospe, "Krishna Avatara in the Bhagavad Gita and Christ Incarnate in John's Gospel," 56.

26. Moffitt, "The Bhagavad Gita as a Way-Shower to the Transcendental," 331.

27. All citations from the *Bhagavad Gita* are taken from the translation by Graham M. Schweig (New York: HarperCollins Publishers, 2007).

28. Powell, *Windows into the Infinite*, 40.

29. *The Bhagavad-Gita: Krishna's Counsel in Time of War*, 8.

30. Powell, *Windows into the Infinite*, 44.

31. Ibid.

32. R. C. Zaehner, *The Bhagavad-Gita*, with a commentary based on the Original Sources (Oxford: Oxford University Press, 1969), 26–27.

33. *The Bhagavad-Gita: Krishna's Counsel in Time of War*, 9.

34. Ibid., 12.

35. Powell, *Windows into the Infinite*, 63.

36. Robinson, *Hinduism*, 33.

37. Fitzgerald, "The Great Epic of India as Religious Rhetoric," 618.

38. Rosen, *Essential Hinduism*, 113.

39. Rosen, *Krishna's Song*, 73.

40. Ibid.

41. Powell, *Windows into the Infinite*, 343.

42. Ibid., 361.

43. *The Uddhava Gita,* trans. Swami Ambikananda Saraswati (Berkeley, CA: Ulysses Press, 2002), 32.

44. Ibid., 59.

45. Ibid., 87.

46. Ibid., 124–25.

47. Ibid., 237–38.

48. Powell, *Windows into the Infinite*, 361.

49. Ibid., 33.

50. Rosen, *Essential Hinduism*, 109.

51. Gorospe, "Krishna Avatara in the Bhagavad Gita and Christ Incarnate in John's Gospel," 57.

52. I want to thank Rick Carlson for his detailed reading of this section, and his very helpful comments. Any errors that remain are my responsibility alone.

53. Delbert Burkett, *An Introduction to the New Testament and the Origins of Christianity* (Cambridge: Cambridge University Press, 2002), 197.

54. Luke Timothy Johnson, *The Writings of the New Testament* (Minneapolis: Fortress Press, 2010), 200. This same point is made in *Introducing the New Testament: Its Literature and Theology* by Paul Achtemeier, Joel Green, and Marianne Meye Thompson. They write, "Luke's message is

fundamentally oriented around the theme of salvation—its derivation, scope, and embodiment" (Grand Rapids, MI: Eerdmans Publishing Company, 2001), 149.

55. Burkett, *An Introduction to the New Testament and the Origins of Christianity*, 197–98.

56. Ibid., 195.

57. Johnson, *The Writings of the New Testament*, 202.

58. Justo L. González, *Luke: Belief, a Theological Commentary on the Bible* (Louisville: Westminster John Knox Press, 2010), 64.

59. Charles Cousar, *Introduction to the New Testament: Witnesses to God's New Work* (Louisville: Westminster John Knox Press, 2006), 127–28.

60. González, *Luke*, 66.

61. Cousar, *Introduction to the New Testament*, 128.

62. Rick Carlson, "'Who Then Is the Faithful, Insightful Steward?' Consumerism and Luke's Stewarding Vision," *Dialog* 49, 4 (Winter 2010): 275.

63. González, *Luke*, 10.

64. Ibid., 102.

65. Achtemeier et al., *Introducing the New Testament*, 151.

66. Ibid., 150–51.

67. Bruce J. Malina and Richard L. Rohrbaugh, *Social-Science Commentary on the Synoptic Gospels* (Minneapolis: Fortress Press, 1992), 354.

68. Achtemeier et al., *Introducing the New Testament*, 172.

69. Ibid., 149.

70. Malina and Rohrbaugh, *Social-Science Commentary on the Synoptic Gospels*, 306–7.

71. González, *Luke*, 102.

72. Ibid., 139.

73. Ibid., 140.

74. Ibid., 184.

75. Ibid., 185.

76. Ibid., 186.

77. Ibid.

78. Cousar, *Introduction to the New Testament*, 129.

79. González, *Luke*, 221–22.

80. Achtemeier et al., *Introducing the New Testament*, 173.

81. Ibid., 151–52.

82. Private communication with Rick Carlson, November 26, 2010.

83. Johnson, *The Writings of the New Testament*, 206.

84. González, *Luke*, 253.

85. Ibid., 279.

86. Johnson, *The Writings of the New Testament*, 208.

87. González, *Luke*, 280.

7. Rethinking the Incarnation—The Soteriological Efficacy of Jesus' Life

1. "Thesis 18," in Gerhard O. Forde, *On Being a Theologian of the Cross: Reflections on Luther's Heidelberg Disputation, 1518* (Grand Rapids, MI: Eerdmans Publishing Company, 1997), 65.

2. See Articles I and II of the Formula of Concord, Epitome and Solid Declaration, *Book of Concord*, ed. Robert Kolb and Timothy J. Wengert (Minneapolis: Fortress Press, 2000).

3. Sallie McFague, *Models of God: Theology for an Ecological, Nuclear Age* (Philadelphia: Fortress Press, 1987), 126.

4. Ibid., 130.

5. Ibid., 133.

6. "Desire and the Spiritual Life: An Advent Reflection," by Rev. James Martin, S.J., http://www.huffingtonpost.com/rev-james-martin-sj/desire-and-the-spiritual-_b_790488.html (accessed December 6, 2010).

7. Ibid.

8. Ibid.

9. Ibid.

10. See http://calvinandhobbes.wikia.com/wiki/Calvinball (accessed December 14, 2010).

11. Roberto Goizueta, *Caminemos con Jesús* (Maryknoll, NY: Orbis Books, 1995), 140–41.

12. See http://www.huffingtonpost.com/2010/10/07/albert-mohler-southern-ba_n_753797.html (accessed October 20, 2010).

13. David Tracy, *The Analogical Imagination: Christian Theology and the Culture of Pluralism* (New York: Crossroad Publishing Co., 1991), 102.

14. Francis X. Clooney, SJ, *Hindu God, Christian God* (Oxford/New York: Oxford University Press, 2001), 7–8.

15. All hymns are from *Evangelical Lutheran Worship* (Minneapolis: Fortress Press, 2006).

16. W. H. Auden, "For the Time Being: A Christmas Oratorio," in *For the Time Being* (New York: Random House, 1944).

Selected Bibliography

Comparative Theology and Interreligious Dialogue

Clooney, Francis X., SJ. *Hindu Wisdom for All God's Children*. Mary-knoll, NY: Orbis Books, 1998.

———. *Theology after Vedanta: An Experiment in Comparative Theology*. SUNY Series, Toward a Comparative Philosophy of Religion. Albany: State University of New York Press, 1993.

Eck, Diana. *Encountering God: A Spiritual Journey from Banares to Boise*. Boston: Beacon Press, 2003.

Fredericks, James. "A Universal Religious Experience? Comparative Theology as an Alternative to a Theology of Religions," *Horizons* 22, no. 1 (1995): 67–87.

Locklin, Reid, and Hugh Nicholson. "The Return of Comparative Theology," *Journal of the American Academy of Religion* 78, no. 2 (June 2010): 477–514.

Thatamanil, John J. *The Immanent Divine: God, Creation, and the Human Predicament*. Minneapolis: Fortress Press, 2006.

Krishna

Bhagavad Gita. Trans. Graham M. Schweig. New York: HarperCollins Publishers, 2007.

The Blackwell Companion to Hinduism. Ed. Gavin Flood. Oxford: Blackwell Publishing, 2003.

Doniger, Wendy. *The Hindus: An Alternative History*. New York: The Penguin Press, 2009.

Krishna: The Beautiful Legend of God. Trans. Edwin Bryant. London: Penguin Books, 2003.

Krishna: A Sourcebook. Ed. Edwin F. Bryant. Oxford: Oxford University Press, 2007.

The Mahabharata: A Shortened Modern Prose Version of the Indian Epic. Trans. R. K. Narayan. Chicago: University of Chicago Press, 2000.

Powell, Barbara. *Windows into the Infinite: A Guide to the Hindu Scriptures*. Fremont, CA: Asian Humanities Press, 1996.

Rosen, Steven J. *Essential Hinduism*. Lanham, MD: Rowman & Littlefield Publishers, Inc., 2006.

———. *Krishna's Song: A New Look at the Bhagavad Gita*. Westport, CT: Praeger Publishers, 2007.

Schweig, Graham. *Dance of Divine Love: India's Classic Love Story, the Rasa Lila of Krishna*. Princeton: Princeton University Press, 2005.

The Uddhava Gita. Trans. Swami Ambikananda Saraswati. Berkeley: Ulysses Press, 2002.

Jesus: The Canonical and Non-Canonical Infancy Narratives

Brown, Raymond. *The Birth of the Messiah*. Rev. ed. New York: Doubleday, 1993.

Ehrman, Bart D. *Lost Christianities: The Battles for Scripture and the Faiths We Never Knew*. Oxford: Oxford University Press, 2003.

———. *Lost Scriptures: Books That Did Not Make It into the New Testament*. New York: Oxford University Press, 2003.

Freed, Edwin D. *The Stories of Jesus' Birth*. Sheffield, England: Sheffield Academic Press, 2001.

González, Justo L. *Luke: A Theological Commentary on the Bible*. Louisville: Westminster John Knox Press, 2010.

Hock, Ronald F. *The Infancy Gospels of James and Thomas: With Introduction, Notes, and Original Text Featuring the New Scholars Version Translation*. Scholars Bible. Santa Rosa, CA: Polebridge Press, 1996.

Lapham, Fred. *An Introduction to the New Testament Apocrypha: Understanding the Bible and Its World*. New York: T&T Clark International, 2003.

The Non-Canonical Gospels. Ed. Paul Foster. New York: T&T Clark, 2008.

Index